The Tupac Amaru and Catarista Rebellions

An Anthology of Sources

The Tupac Amaru and Catarista Rebellions

An Anthology of Sources

Edited and Translated by
WARD STAVIG and ELLA SCHMIDT

Introduction by
CHARLES F. WALKER

Hackett Publishing Company, Inc.
Indianapolis/Cambridge

13 12 11 10 09 08   1 2 3 4 5 6 7

For further information, please address
Hackett Publishing Company, Inc.
P.O. Box 44937
Indianapolis, Indiana 46244-0937

www.hackettpublishing.com

Cover design by Jean Whitman and Abigail Coyle
Interior design by Elizabeth L. Wilson
Composition by Agnew's, Inc.
Printed at Edwards Brothers, Inc.

Acknowledgments of documentary sources appear on page xvi.

Library of Congress Cataloging-in-Publication Data

The Tupac Amaru and Catarista Rebellions : an anthology of sources /
 edited and translated by Ward Stavig and Ella Schmidt ; introduction
 by Charles F. Walker.
    p. cm.
 Includes bibliographical references.
 ISBN-13: 978-0-87220-845-2 (pbk.)
 ISBN-13: 978-0-87220-846-9 (cloth)
    1. Peru—History—Insurrection of Tupac-Amaru, 1780–1781—
 Sources.   2. Indians of South America—Wars—Andes Region—
 Sources.   3. Katari María, Tomás, ca. 1740–1781—Sources.   4. Tupak
 Katari, 1750–1781—Sources.   5. Quechua Indians—Wars—Sources.
 6. Aymara Indians—Wars—Sources. I. Stavig, Ward. II. Schmidt, Ella.
 F3444.T959 2007
 985'.033—dc22

                                                                  2007042337

The paper used in this publication meets the minimum requirements of American
National Standard for Information Sciences—Permanence of Paper for Printed
Library Materials, ANSI Z39.48–1984.

CONTENTS

IV. The Breakdown of the Colonial Order

V. The Rebellion

VI. Capture, Confession, Execution, Retribution, and the Instilling of Fear

VII. The End of the Struggle: Diego and Andrés Tupac Amaru, Lessons to the Spanish, and Indigenous Afterthoughts

PART TWO
The Catari Brothers and Rebellion in Chayanta and La Plata (Bolivia)

VIII. *Kurakas, Corregidores, Repartos,* Protest, and Defiance

IX. Rebellion, Defeat, and Death

PART THREE
Tupac Catari, the Siege of La Paz, and the Struggle for the *Altiplano*

X. Tupac Catari, the Growth of Discontent, and Rebellion

XI. The Siege of La Paz and the Death of Tupac Catari

ACKNOWLEDGMENTS

We would like to express our gratitude to Sergio Serulnikov, Sinclair Thomson, Scarlett O'Phelan Godoy, and Charles F. Walker for their willingness to allow us to use their translations. We would also like to thank Duke University Press, the University of Wisconsin Press, and the University of Oklahoma Press for granting permission to use copyrighted materials. This work would not have been possible without the efforts of the compilers of the volumes *Colección documental de la independencia del Perú* and the commission that had the foresight to take on this monumental task so others could have access to disparate documents dealing with the insurgencies of the early 1780s. Very special thanks go to Carole Rennick at the University of South Florida for her help with the organizing and editing of the manuscript, and to Rick Todhunter at Hackett Publishing Company for his patience, understanding, and help in a process that took much longer than we anticipated. Liz Wilson guided us through the production process with grace and style. We would also like to thank the many people of Peru and Bolivia who, through their kindness and curiosity, further inspired us to want to make this important part of their history available to an English-speaking audience. Lastly, we wish to thank Mariana and Lucía for being so supportive and understanding of the time we had to take from being with them.

Ward Stavig and Ella Schmidt

FOREWORD

Ward Stavig

The Tupac Amaru rebellion, along with the uprisings of the Catari brothers in southern Bolivia (Alto Peru) and Tupac Catari in the region of La Paz, have been a source of great, and even revitalized, interest. People interested in colonialism, indigenous societies, rebellions, and the drama of human experience in its everyday form find themselves attracted to this topic. This has been especially true in the last two to three decades, as the 200th anniversary of the rebellions brought renewed interest in what they meant, and what they mean now for Andean society. Together, these three uprisings constituted the most serious challenge to Spanish colonial authority in South America during the long colonial period, and for this reason they continue to be the source of considerable attention. The rebel leaders and their cause have become increasingly popular, with Tupac Amaru even becoming a symbol of social justice in Peru for a few years. Other people, such as the urban residents of Sucre (La Plata), whom we observed shutting down their city upon the arrival of an indigenous march on what used to be known as Columbus Day, still fear, loathe, and hope to exploit the indigenous population just as they seemed to during the rebellion. The fear and dread have historical roots that are covered in these pages and are still alive on both sides of the racial, cultural, and economic divide. The destruction and loss of life was massive, with most estimates putting the total deaths during the insurrection at somewhere around 100,000 souls. Places such as Sucre, which was threatened by the rebellion, still live with this fear even though many residents are probably unaware of the events that created these tensions.

This book is divided into three main sections. By far, the longest part deals with Tupac Amaru and the rebellion he led in the zone stretching from Cuzco to the *altiplano* around Lake Titicaca. The second longest section deals with the upheaval that began in Chayanta and spread through the region from Sucre to Potosí and beyond, which was led by the Catari brothers. The final section focuses on Julián Apaza (Tupac Catari) and the rebellion in the vicinity of La Paz and the surrounding region. Those curious about the causes and courses of the rebellions; those interested in indigenous society or the colonial world; those curious about the difference between the way events play out on the ground and as expressed in royal ordinances; and especially those interested in the drama, heartache, suffering, dignity, courage, and sacrifice of the human experience will find much to reflect on in the pages of this book.

This collection of documentary source readings was designed to allow English speakers access to a wide range of documents that until now have been available only in Spanish, and even then often in disparate and sometimes uncataloged archives. Thus, only a relatively small group of scholars has been allowed intimate knowledge of these fascinating documents up to now. Our desire was to make these documents available to a much wider group of people, including undergraduates, graduate students, professional scholars, and, of course, the interested and curious from all walks of life who are fascinated by the human experience and whose curiosity has led them to the Andes in the eighteenth century.

To help those beginning to explore and analyze the many and varied aspects of the lives of the peoples involved in the rebellion, we have provided introductions to each document that are designed to aid readers in better understanding and orienting themselves to its contents, context, and significance. However, the main point of this collection is to bring readers into direct contact with the source readings so that they can read and think about the material in the documents—the peoples of different races, ethnicities, classes, and interests whose lives were intimately linked to the rebellion—on their own.

Putting this book together proved to be much more difficult than anticipated. The primary problem was the translation of the source readings. These documents, for the most part, are not narratives designed to tell a story or convince the reader of a point of view through a clearly presented logical argument. Most of these documents were written in the midst of a war and often during the heat of real crises. They were also intended for people who understood what was being discussed and were familiar with the historical actors. Thus, the writer often had no reason to refer to events and people by names, pronouns being just fine for their usage. For the modern reader, this presents a significant obstacle to understanding the text. These are not the well-crafted documents of Bartolomé de Las Casas or Pedro de Cieza de León, who had time to craft their writing and logic with a learned audience in mind. The producers of these documents were sharing important information with those who needed it. Grammar, logic, and readability were not necessarily their immediate concerns. Sometimes they wrote for pages without a period ever bringing a thought or statement to a close, the colon and semicolon being the preferred punctuation in most cases. At the same time, the subject of a document often changed over and over again, with the author eventually heading back to the original point—or not. Thus, the documents are convoluted and complex. It was a major task to try to render many of them readable in English, when the Spanish itself was almost incomprehensible.

Additionally, many words and terms prevalent in the colonial era are not common now, which requires that choices be made as to intent and meaning.

One is forced to make a judgment call on the intended meaning of words and phrases based on lengthy archival experience with such documents and knowledge of the context. There are also lesser difficulties, such as those related to the technical language of warfare and arcane weaponry. The same holds true for the nomenclature of religion and applies to all of the specialized clothing and paraphernalia used in various sacraments and to the meanings with which they were imbued. The language of social hierarchy and protocol presents yet another challenge. Sometimes this can be simply formulaic—what is often referred to as "boilerplate"—but other times it can be quite complex and laden with honorific significance or with derision. In some situations, it is impossible to know exactly what was meant by a word. For instance, a *pedrero* can be a mortar that fired stones or it may refer to a cannon. The difference can be significant; it might give clues about the strategies and topography of the battle zone.

We have worked hard to make the complexity, style, and meaning of the documents understandable, readable, and clear while maintaining the integrity of the work. This necessarily involved changing punctuation, tenses, and often considerable restructuring of sentences and paragraphs. In some instances, we have allowed the complexity of the document to remain fairly intact to give readers a taste of the original writing style. We have also maintained some of the older structures and ways of saying things to further engage readers by giving them a stronger sense of being in the time and place they are reading about. The sources of the documents have also been provided so that those who wish can more easily refer to the original Spanish document. We hope that the readers of these documents will not only learn a great deal about colonialism, indigenous peoples, and this very important and interesting history, but especially that they will come to have a deeper understanding and respect for the people whose lives (and deaths), sufferings, hopes, and dreams they are about to enter.

Abbreviations and Copyright Acknowledgments

CDIP   *Colección documental de la independencia del Perú.* Comisión Nacional del Sesquicentenario de la Independencia del Perú. Lima, 1971. Vol. 2. *La Rebelión de Túpac Amaru.* Vol. 2 contains books 1–4 (Tomo II, Volumen 1–4). Most of the materials are from Vol. 2, books 2–3. The references in the work are to document numbers, not page numbers.

             Vol. 2, book 2 contains numbers 1–206
             Vol.2, book 3 contains numbers 207–327.

LIR   *The Last Inca Revolt, 1780–1783.* Lillian Estelle Fisher. Norman: University of Oklahoma Press, 1966.

RR   *Rebellions and Revolts in Eighteenth Century Peru and Upper Peru.* Scarlett O'Phelan Godoy. Köln: Böhlau Verlag, 1985. Reprinted by permission of the publisher.

RTA   *La rebelión de Túpac Amaru y los orígenes de la independencia de hispanoamérica.* Boleslao Lewin. Buenos Aires: Sociedad Editora Latino Americana, 1967.

SCA   *Subverting Colonial Authority. Challenges to Spanish Rule in Eighteenth-Century Southern Andes.* Sergio Serulnikov. Durham, NC: Duke University Press, 2003. Selections from *SCA* appear on pages 170–73, 176, 179–86, 201, 205–7, 208–10, and 212–14. Reprinted by permission of the publisher.

WAWR   *We Alone Will Rule: Native Andean Politics in the Age of Insurgency.* Sinclair Thomson. © 2003. Reprinted by permission of The University of Wisconsin Press.

WOTA   *The World of Túpac Amaru: Conflict, Community and Identity in Colonial Peru.* Ward Stavig. Lincoln: University of Nebraska Press, 1999. Reprinted by permission of the University of Nebraska Press. © 1999 by the University of Nebraska Press. Selections from *WOTA* appear on pages 4–6, 8–9, 12–13, 17–20, 26–28, 30–31, and 39. Reprinted by permission of the publisher.

All translations are by Ward Stavig and Ella Schmidt unless otherwise noted.

CHRONOLOGY OF THE
TUPAC AMARU REBELLION

1719–1720	Pandemic sweeps the Andes.
1742	Juan Santos Atahualpa rebellion begins.
1750s	Revolts begin in Huarochirí.
1754	The *reparto de mercancías* is legalized, increasing economic pressure on indigenous communities.
1760s–1770s	A period of increasing minor, mainly localized, revolts in the indigenous communities.
1772	The *alcabala* (sales tax) increased from 2 percent to 4 percent.
1774	Customhouses (*aduanas*) are established in Cochabamba, Bolivia.
	On August 2, there is a revolt against the *aduana* in Cochabamba. *Alcabala* is imposed on grain.
1776	José Antonio de Areche is named inspector (*visitador general*) by the Spanish Crown. Near the middle of the year, the *alcabala* is again increased, this time from 4 percent to 6 percent. The *aduana* is established at La Paz. Upper Peru becomes part of the new viceroyalty of Rio de la Plata, further disrupting trade patterns.
1777	The first revolt against the La Paz *aduana* is staged in late October.
1778	Joaquín Alós is named *corregidor* of Chayanta. Tomás Catari goes to Buenos Aires seeking justice for his people. The Crown orders *corregidores* to collect the 6 percent *alcabala*.
1779	Tomás Catari is arrested. *Coca,* previously exempt, becomes subject to the 6 percent *alcabala*.
1780	On January 1, riots take place in Arequipa over the *aduana*. Lampoons appear in Cuzco shortly after the Arequipa riot, warning against the *aduana*. In March, there is a riot attacking the La Paz *aduana*.

Catari rebellion begins in late August. In September, the controversial *kuraka* Florencio Lupa is beheaded.

In November, José Gabriel Tupac Amaru's rebellion erupts in Canas y Canchis (Tinta), Cuzco, with the capture and execution of *Corregidor* Arriaga.

1781   In January, Tomás Catari is killed. His brothers Nicolás and Dámaso continue the struggle until they too are killed.

Tupac Amaru, his wife, and others are executed in the main plaza of Cuzco on May 18. Diego Tupac Amaru has already assumed leadership of the rebellion.

Tupac Catari puts La Paz under siege.

November, Tupac Catari is captured and executed.

1782   Bartolina Sisa and Gregoria Apaza, the wife and sister of Tupac Catari, are executed.

1783   Diego Tupac Amaru is brutally executed, along with his mother and others.

1784   Fernando, son of the Inca, is sent into exile in Spain.

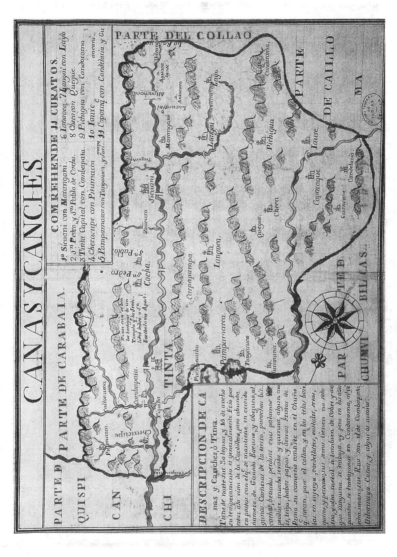

The Province of Canas y Canchis. Tupac Amaru's core towns of Pampamarca, Tungasuca, and Surimana can be seen below Tinta. Archivo General de Indias. España. Ministerio de Cultura. Reprinted by permission.

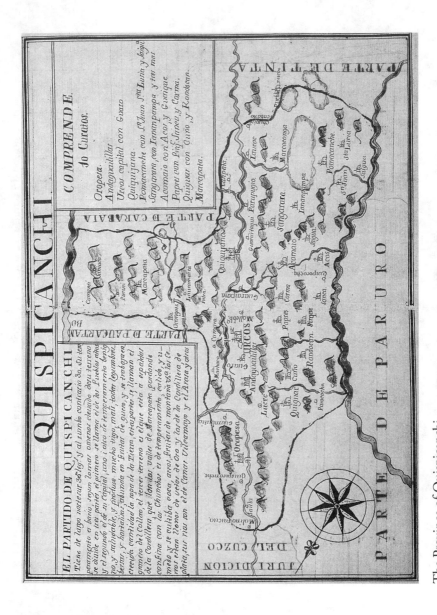

The Province of Quispicanchi.
España. Ministerio de Cultura. Archivo General de Indias. Reprinted by permission.

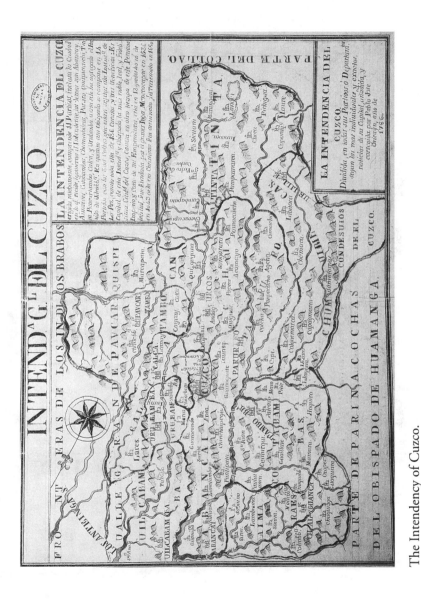

The Intendency of Cuzco.
España. Ministerio de Cultura. Archivo General de Indias. Reprinted by permission.

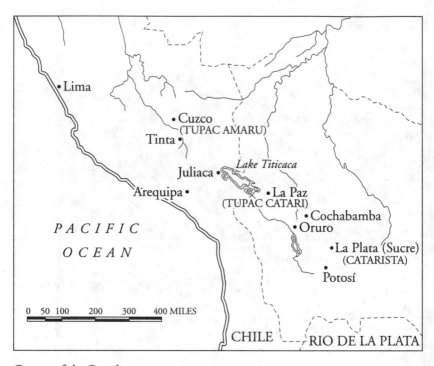

Center of the Revolts

INTRODUCTION

Charles F. Walker

I am honored though saddened to introduce this documentary collection. Saddened because Ward Stavig didn't live to write the Introduction he intended. Ward spent a quarter century researching the southern Andes in the colonial period, producing fine studies on indigenous people of the Cuzco region of Peru. A close attention to how common people lived—their everyday life, struggles, and joys as well as their participation in epic events such as rebellions—characterized his work. Never satisfied with bundling together the Quechua-speaking descendants of the Incas as "Indians," he highlighted differences within villages as well as those between distinct geographical areas. Ward's aptly named *The World of Tupac Amaru: Conflict, Community, and Identity in Colonial Peru* brings the reader into the Andean universe of collective work, *chicha* (corn beer), *coca*, and other elements that the reader will discover in this document collection. Ward died on May 1, 2006, having finished the compilation and translation of the documents as well as his Foreword though not the Introduction.[1]

It's an honor to introduce Ward's work because Ella Schmidt and he have compiled a rich selection of documents that allows the reader to understand the massive uprisings that shook the Andes and reverberated throughout the world in the late eighteenth century, the Tupac Amaru and Tupac Catari rebellions. The selection and translations of the documents reflect Ward and Ella's fine ear for the common people, the *runa*, as well as their understanding of the uprising and the eighteenth century.

In the early 1780s, the Tupac Amaru, Catari, and Tupac Catari uprisings overwhelmed the southern Andes—what is today Peru and Bolivia—threatening Spanish control of its South American colonies more than a quarter century before the Wars of Independence (1808–1825). The documents refer to these three related but unique uprisings. All three were Indian-based rebellions in the Andean region between Cuzco and the silver mines of Potosí. Geography is fundamental for these events and, more generally, the life

---

1. Among other homages to Ward, see those by Arnold Bauer in *Hispanic American Historical Review* (87:1) February 2007, 151–52; and by Luis Miguel Glave in *Colonial Latin American Review* (16:1) June 2007, 145–48. Ward Stavig, *The World of Tupac Amaru: Conflict, Community, and Identity in Colonial Peru*. Lincoln: University of Nebraska Press, 1999.

of Andean people. Narrow valleys cut through the Andes, with only the lowest valley floors dipping below 3,000 meters or about 10,000 feet above sea level. These daunting mountains allowed rebels to heap rocks onto soldiers and provided escape routes. Spanish forces frequently expressed frustration at these guerrilla tactics. In ethnographic terms, Quechua Indians led and backed the Tupac Amaru uprising, whereas Aymaras predominated in the Catari rebellions. Each of the uprisings grew quickly, terrifying Spanish rulers and much of the population. Although each movement had a distinct leadership and geographical center, some individuals participated in more than one, and the leaders at different points attempted to merge. The document collection draws attention to these commonalities as well as differences.

On November 4, 1780, José Gabriel Condorcanqui Noguera, who increasingly used the Inca royal last name Tupac Amaru, had lunch with Antonio de Arriaga in Yanaoca, near Tinta to the south of Cuzco, down the Vilcanota River. José Gabriel was a *cacique* (also called *kuraka*) of the towns of Pampamarca, Surimana, and Tungasuca, a local authority in the Andes who mediated between the colonial state and the indigenous population. Among other duties, *caciques* organized the heavy tax and labor burden placed on indigenous people. José Gabriel claimed descent from "the last Inca," Tupac Amaru, who had been executed by Viceroy Francisco Toledo in 1571. Arriaga was a *corregidor,* the regional authority in charge of collecting taxes, assuring labor for Potosí and other mines, keeping order, and other duties. He was Tupac Amaru's superior, and—as was almost invariably the case—the *corregidor* was a Spaniard and the *cacique* an Indian, often a descendent of Inca lords and thus "royal." Like most *corregidores,* Arriaga had a vast network of economic activities, lending money, selling goods, and collaborating with the more affluent. In fact, he had lent Tupac Amaru money, and they knew each other well enough to share a table. Tupac Amaru left the seemingly amicable meal early, feigning illness, and Arriaga departed hours later to return to Tinta, insisting that he had business to attend. He never made it.

Tupac Amaru and a small group of Indians ambushed him on the steep trail that leads to Tinta. That evening, they took him in chains to the town of Tungasuca where Tupac Amaru and his wife, Micaela Bastidas, demanded that he write his assistants in Tinta and request money and arms. The rebels then seized the money and weapons, imprisoning the officials alongside Arriaga. They also instructed him to convene regional authorities in Tungasuca. On November 9, they hanged Arriaga, claiming that they had orders from the king of Spain (see document 34). Although the actions were not unprecedented—other authorities in the Andes had been treated violently and even killed in recent decades—they shocked witnesses as well as Spanish authorities in Cuzco. Tupac Amaru recruited supporters in nearby towns, attacked haciendas, and ransacked *obrajes,* or textile mills, despised by Indians because of their brutal labor conditions. Tupac Amaru and Micaela Bastidas wrote—or dictated to scribes, including members of Arriaga's retinue—proclamations and letters to Andean towns, calling for the expulsion of *corregidores* and the abolition of despised institutions such as the *mita* labor draft, all in the name of the king of Spain. Their communications excoriated Spaniards but were ambiguous about creoles, Europeans born in the Americas, and were respectful of the Catholic Church (see document 42). The uprising grew quickly, spreading with particular speed in the southern areas toward Lake Titicaca.

On November 13, nine days after the uprising began, Spanish authorities in Cuzco sent a contingent of about 1,000 soldiers, primarily Indians and *mestizos* provided by loyal *caciques,* to arrest Tupac Amaru. They reached the town of Sangarará on November 17. More concerned about an impending snowstorm than a possible rebel attack, they woke up surrounded at four A.M. The troops took refuge in the church, but the Tupac Amaru forces used their slings, the rebels' most common weapon, to bombard them with stones. The exact events are unclear, but the church roof caught fire and much of the building was destroyed. The rebels denied starting the fire and claimed that the Spanish would not allow anyone to leave the church, even when they offered safe passage for women and children. The colonial forces contended that the rebels viciously attacked everyone in or around the holy ground, killing children and raping women. Although they disagreed about who was guilty and who burned the church, both sides agreed on the terrible losses for the Spanish forces: over 500 died, including about twenty Europeans. This statistic reveals that the notion of Spanish or European forces fighting the rebels conceals the fact that Indians were the foot soldiers on both sides and would bear the brunt of the violence.[2]

The rebel victory invigorated both sides. It showed the insurgents that they could defeat a Spanish battalion. This petrified the Spanish, hastening them

---

2. Boleslao Lewin, *La rebelión de Túpac Amaru y los orígenes de la independencia de hispanoamérica.* Buenos Aires: Sociedad Editora Latino Americana, 1967, 447–59; Charles F. Walker, *Smoldering Ashes: Cuzco and the Creation of Republican Peru, 1780–1840.* Durham: Duke University Press, 1999, chapter 2. For historical background, see Kenneth Andrien, *Andean Worlds: Indigenous History, Culture, and Consciousness under Spanish Rule, 1532–1925.* Albuquerque: University of New Mexico Press, 2001; Luis Miguel Glave, "The 'Republic of Indians' in Revolt (c. 1680–1790)." In *The Cambridge History of the Natives Peoples of the Americas.* Vol. 3, part 3: *South America,* edited by Frank Salomon and Stuart Schwartz. Cambridge: Cambridge University Press, 1999, 502–57; Scarlett O'Phelan Godoy, *Rebellions and Revolts in Eighteenth-Century Peru and Upper Peru.* Köln: Böhlau Verlag, 1985. Note that, in these footnotes, I focus on the literature in English.

to take the rebels more seriously. It also allowed them to cast the rebels as heathens or apostates who slaughtered innocent people and burned down churches. Cuzco's bishop, Juan Manuel Moscoso y Peralta, excommunicated Tupac Amaru on the same day as the battle of Sangarará, November 17. At this point, Tupac Amaru led a large group to the south while Micaela Bastidas remained in Tungasuca to monitor allies and enemies. She proved to be an active, clever commander, assuring loyalty and overseeing logistics. Her letters—mostly written by captives who became scribes—capture her sense of urgency in late 1780. She worried that Tupac Amaru was taking too long in his southern campaign, stressing that Tungasuca, Tinta, and Pampamarca, the rebellion's base, were less than one hundred miles from the Spanish stronghold of Cuzco. She urged José Gabriel to return and assault Cuzco, the capital of the Incas and Peru's second city (see documents 52–54). Rebel forces grew, with one calculation putting them at 50,000 by December.

He returned on December 17 and, learning that Spanish reinforcements were arriving from Lima, moved to surround Cuzco. Royalist forces defeated columns led by Diego Cristóbal Tupac Amaru, his cousin, and Andrés Castelo on their way to Cuzco, preventing a pincer movement. Both Spanish authorities and Tupac Amaru and his commanders fretted about what the city's indigenous population, the vast majority of Cuzco's 30,000 people, would do—whether they would join or repel the rebels. Perched on the Picchu mountain on the city's west side, the Tupac Amaru forces negotiated and harassed but did not assault the city. On January 10, under cover of the early morning darkness and a heavy rainfall, they returned to the Vilcanota Valley. Explanations of why Tupac Amaru did not attack Cuzco include the desire to avoid bloodshed (the Spanish had put Indians at the frontline), the fear of being trapped within the city with royalist reinforcements due to arrive, concern about diminishing food supplies, and simple indecision by Tupac Amaru himself.[3] Some documents hint that many of his troops, weakened by the lack of food and the constant rain, suffered from diarrhea and other stomach ailments.[4] The contrast with the events of La Paz in Upper Peru, well documented here and discussed below, is obvious. This siege lasted for months, and thousands died of hunger as a result.

In January and February 1781, Micaela Bastidas and other rebel leaders worried that some of their soldiers, preoccupied with the upcoming harvest and dismayed by the horrors of war, were returning to their town of origin

---

3. Among other accounts, see Lillian E. Fisher, *The Last Inca Revolt, 1780–1783.* Norman: University of Oklahoma Press, 1966.

4. Archivo de Indias, Charcas, Legajo 596, quad. 3, "Testimonio formado sobre el alzamiento de la Prov. de Tinta."

while others were turning the uprising into a caste war, killing anyone associated with the Spanish. Tupac Amaru, Micaela Bastidas, and other commanders had the difficult task of simultaneously motivating and restraining their peasant forces. They could not win without a mass base; they could not incorporate *mestizos,* creoles, and blacks as they planned if their struggle became a caste war. The insurgents also lacked supplies. In early 1781, the Spanish went on the offensive, offering amnesty to Indians who put down their arms (or slings) as well as a large reward for the capture of Tupac Amaru. They abolished two of the most hated colonial impositions: the *reparto* and the customhouses. The *reparto* (also called the *repartimiento*) involved the forced distribution of goods, obliging Indians to purchase or produce European products and thus enriching the *corregidor* and his network of allies (see documents 18–22).

Commander José del Valle led approximately 15,000 troops—divided into six columns—into the Vilcanota Valley, the rebels' base. They captured Tupac Amaru and much of his family on April 6. In a scene that virtually every Peruvian can recount, on May 18, Tupac Amaru, Micaela Bastidas, their son Hipólito, and five other members of their family and inner circle were brutally executed in Cuzco's main plaza. A horse dragged Tupac Amaru to the plaza. After he witnessed the death of his loved ones, executioners cut his tongue and then attached him to four horses to be quartered. His limbs did not detach from his torso, however, and the *visitador,* or general visitor, Antonio de Areche, ordered that he be decapitated. The rebels' body parts were displayed throughout the region, grisly reminders of the supposed defeat of the rebellion and the cost of insurgency (see documents 59–63).[5]

Although much studied, the basic questions about the Tupac Amaru rebellion remain open to debate: what caused it, who supported and opposed it, and what did it seek? Historians agree that the increasing demands of the colonial state, the Bourbon Reforms, on the indigenous population greatly amplified opposition to the Spanish. The hatred for the head tax or tribute, the *mita* or labor draft, the customhouses, the *reparto,* and the fees charged by priests for burials and other services became evident time after time during the uprising. This resentment is explicit in dozens of the documents included here. Indebted by frequent wars with France and England, the Spanish

---

5. Accounts in English include Fisher, *The Last Inca Revolt;* Walker, *Smoldering Ashes;* and the essays in Steve Stern, ed., *Resistance, Rebellion, and Consciousness in the Andean Peasant World, 18th to 20th Centuries.* Madison: University of Wisconsin Press, 1987. Fundamental in Spanish is Lewin, *La rebelión de Tupac Amaru;* see also Carlos Daniel Valcárcel, *Tupac Amaru: El Revolucionario.* Lima: Moncloa Campodónico, 1970.

rulers the Bourbons, particularly Carlos III (who served as king from 1759 to 1788), successfully increased revenues from their American holdings. The Andean rebellions, however, as well as the wars of independence decades later, demonstrated the high price the Spanish paid for this income.

The changes were not only economic. In political terms, the Bourbons sought to centralize power in the colonial state, abandoning the delegation and fragmentation of authority that had characterized their predecessors, the Habsburgs. This "absolutist" campaign replaced authorities who had paid for their position (and whose loyalty thus remained local) with paid officials and bureaucrats, usually Spanish. In the Andes, nonethnic *caciques* slowly replaced those such as Tupac Amaru whose families had ruled locally for decades or centuries. This obviously raised the ire of many *caciques,* and the frustration of Tupac Amaru—who had battled for years to keep his *cacique* position—cannot be underestimated.

Many *caciques,* however, remained loyal, providing troops to fight Tupac Amaru. Some, such as Mateo Pumacahua from Chincheros (outside of Cuzco), saw José Gabriel as an inferior, an upstart whose uprising would only weaken venerable *caciques* such as Pumacahua himself. He mobilized important groups of Indian fighters and supplies for the Spanish.[6] To understand why some *caciques,* towns, and regions backed Tupac Amaru and others did not—our second question of who supported the rebellion—scholars have delved into local power struggles that dated from the first half of the eighteenth century. In this period, individuals and communities flooded the courts with complaints about authorities, illuminating local Andean society for historians. Although these lawsuits reflect growing disenchantment with the Spanish, no single pattern can be found in the nature of the local conflicts. In some cases, *caciques* forged alliances with priests and *corregidores,* whereas in others they were bitter enemies. In many communities, individuals or families fought over the *cacique* position, presenting diverse justifications. This complexity played out in the uprising—*caciques* and priests may be found on both sides. It can be safely said that Andean indigenous people increasingly chafed under and even despised Spanish rule. The reasons and the reactions, however, varied greatly.[7]

---

6. On the role of *caciques* in the uprising, see O'Phelan Godoy, *Rebellions and Revolts;* David Garrett, *Shadows of Empire: The Indian Nobility of Cusco, 1750–1825.* Cambridge: Cambridge University Press, 2005.

7. For outstanding studies that take a long-term historical perspective on the uprisings, see Sergio Serulnikov, *Subverting Colonial Authority: Challenges to Spanish Rule in Eighteenth-Century Southern Andes.* Durham: Duke University Press, 2003; Sinclair Thomson, *We Alone Will Rule: Native Andean Politics in the Age of Insurgency.* Madison: University of Wisconsin Press, 2003; Stavig, *The World of Tupac Amaru.*

Certain broad trends stand out. The heart of the Tupac Amaru uprising lay in the Vilcanota Valley and the Upper Provincias (*Provincias Altas*) to the south, whereas the Sacred Valley remained largely loyal. The bulk of Tupac Amaru's forces came from the towns in that valley and surrounding mountain villages, where he had extensive kinship and commercial ties. In addition, Indians there, active in the Potosí–Cuzco trade route, suffered under the Bourbon Reforms. In terms of sociology, the rebellion cannot be reduced to a Spanish versus Indian battle. Royalists recruited Indians, albeit usually by force, and many indigenous *caciques* despised Tupac Amaru. Moreover, other groups played equally complex roles: *mestizos,* blacks, creoles, and even Spaniards can be found on both sides.

The ideology and platform of the rebellion are also under scrutiny. Did Tupac Amaru intend merely to replace "bad authorities" as Spanish law permitted (although not with such violence), or did he envision himself crowned as some type of Inca king of Peru? Alternately, did he have in mind an Indian revolution that would expel (or maybe even exterminate, to use a favorite verb of the period) all Europeans? Documents supporting each of these positions are included here. Historians will probably never know whether this ambiguity reflected Tupac Amaru's caginess—his effort to buy time and broaden his coalition—his uncertainty, or simply the fact that he never had time to write a program once Arriaga was hanged. It is clear, however, that his movement cannot be subsumed under the category of "precursor of independence," as several generations of scholars asserted. The social base and actions of the rebels varied greatly from those of the Wars of Independence (1808–1825 in South America), as did the period in history prior to the French and Haitian revolutions (1789–1799 and 1791–1804) and the Napoleonic invasion of Iberia (1808).

The Tupac Amaru rebellion did not end on May 18, 1781. José Gabriel's cousin, Diego Cristóbal, took over the leadership and steered the rebellion south toward Lake Titicaca and Upper Peru or Charcas, what became Bolivia. Confrontations turned more violent as the rebel forces ransacked towns and some rebels attacked anyone resembling a Spaniard (see document 70). José del Valle continued to lead the Spanish forces. Although he offered amnesty, his forces executed anyone believed to have supported the rebels. Lines hardened and confrontations became even more brutal. Many people believed during the early phase of the rebellion that they could remain neutral and avoid the violence; however, this proved impossible by mid-1781. For example, del Valle had to escort the remaining population of the city of Puno, which had withstood several rebel assaults, to safety: "Everybody in Chucuito was put to the knife, no living soul being spared" (document 66). In mid-1781, critics deemed del Valle a failure and even a coward for returning to Cuzco without having defeated the rebels (see document 66). The belief that the execution of José Gabriel and Micaela Bastidas meant the end of the rebellion proved false. Nonetheless, in January 1782, Diego Cristóbal Tupac Amaru accepted a Spanish offer of amnesty (see documents 71–72).

The Spanish celebrated but remained cautious, particularly when uprisings took place in areas around Cuzco and even Lima (Huarochirí). They claimed that this broke the terms of Diego Cristóbal Tupac Amaru's pardon and arrested him on February 15, 1783. They sentenced him to a death even more gruesome than that of José Gabriel: not only did he witness the execution of his mother (her body quartered and burned), blazing tongs ripped the flesh off his skin (see document 76). They also imprisoned a vast number of his relatives.[8] The Spanish, however, did not completely succeed in their quest to eradicate the extensive family of Micaela Bastidas and José Gabriel Tupac Amaru. Their youngest son, Fernando, was sent to Spain, never to return to Peru, whereas José Gabriel's half brother, Juan Bautista Tupac Amaru, made it back to Buenos Aires from Spain in 1822 (see documents 78–79).

The Catari brothers and Tupac Catari rebellions took place in Upper Peru, in the area that became Bolivia following its independence in 1825. As Scarlett O'Phelan Godoy noted years ago, this has led scholars to analyze these uprisings and that of Tupac Amaru separately. Following her path-breaking book, however, scholars have begun to probe the similarities, differences, and connections between them.[9] Trouble had been brewing for decades in the Chayanta area of northern Potosí. In the 1770s, community Indians increasingly questioned their *caciques,* as well as certain *corregidores* and priests, and emphasized in the courts these authorities' corrupt ways (this corruption resulted in decreased tax revenues, an argument that caught the attention of Spanish authorities) and their loss of legitimacy in the eyes of locals (see documents 82–83, 122–24). Whereas the Tupac Amaru rebellion was led by a *cacique,* the uprising in Upper Peru emerged from the struggle against these local authorities. Tupac Amaru also claimed royal descent from the Incas, whereas the Catari brothers did not. They based their claim to the *cacique* position on community support rather than lineage.[10]

---

8. See the list in *Colección Documental de la Independencia del Perú,* Tomo II, "La Rebelión de Tupac Amaru." Vol. 3, doc. 284, pp. 368–70, "Rol de los Tupac Amarus arrestados por F. Salcedo, corregidor de Tinta." Lima: Comisión Nacional del Sesquicentenario de la Independencia del Perú, 1971.

9. O'Phelan Godoy, *Rebellions and Revolts.* She has continued this comparative approach in subsequent publications. See, for example, *La gran rebelión en los Andes: De Túpac Amaru a Túpac Catari.* Cusco: Centro de Estudios Regionales, Bartolomé de Las Casas, 1995.

10. Serulnikov, *Subverting Colonial Authority,* 116–18.

In 1778, Tomás Catari, an Aymara from the Chayanta area, pleaded the case of Macha villagers to the high court in Buenos Aires. He won the case but was imprisoned upon his return to Chayanta (see documents 87–89). An armed group freed him. In June 1780, the ten *ayllus*, or moieties, of the Macha community congregated in the city of La Plata to accuse Spanish and indigenous authorities and to demand that Tomás Catari be named *cacique*. Later that month, Catari was imprisoned once again. On August 26, 1780, Indians from throughout the province convened in Pocoata to demand that Catari be freed. The hated *corregidor* Joaquín Alós had prepared the militia. Indians stormed the town, killing approximately thirty soldiers and forcing the rest to take refuge in the church. In early September, the rebels exchanged Alós for Catari (see document 104).

In late 1780, Chayanta saw a unique period of indigenous self-rule in the post-Conquest history of the Andes. Catari sought to change relations between indigenous communities and the colonial state pacifically and never broke off relations with viceregal authorities in Buenos Aires. They, in turn, offered a pardon and tried to bring Catari and his followers back into the fold. Nevertheless, more violence ensued. On September 5, Indians of the community of Moscari killed their *cacique*, Florencio Lupa, and took his head to the outskirts of the city of La Plata (see document 98). Although colonial authorities cast this as proof of the rebels' barbaric plans, the incident reflected a complex local struggle that escalated into the *cacique's* death. It also indicated the limitations of Catari's power—he opposed such violence, to no avail. In mid-December, a militia chief, Juan Antonio Acuña, arrested Catari. In January, peasants attacked the convoy taking Catari to the city of La Plata. Before they could free him, Acuña executed Tomás Catari. The attackers then killed Acuña and his entourage, leaving their bodies unburied and piercing Acuña's eyes (see document 106).[11]

At this point, the uprising lost any semblance of utopic self-government or reformist experiment against bad authorities and became a fierce Indian-based struggle against colonial domination. Tomás Catari's brothers, Dámaso and Nicolás, assumed leadership. They coordinated with other rebellious communities in Upper Peru and led the siege of the city of La Plata in February 1781. They threatened to kill everyone and expressed their desire to link with Tupac Amaru (see documents 111 and 113). Rebels targeted Spaniards and creoles as well as the symbols and mechanisms of colonial exploitation: haciendas, textile mills, and *mestizo* villages. Support for the rebels

---

11. Serulnikov, *Subverting Colonial Authority,* 184–85. See also Thomson, *We Alone Will Rule;* Nicholas Robins, *Genocide and Millenialism in Upper Peru: The Great Rebellion of 1780–1782.* Westport, CT: Praeger, 2002.

among the indigenous people of the area between Potosí and La Paz was massive but not unanimous. As was the case of Tupac Amaru, colonial authorities offered amnesty as well as a reward for the capture of rebel leaders. In late March, Indians from Pocoata captured Dámaso Catari and turned him in to authorities. Nicolás was captured in similar fashion. On April 27, 1781, three weeks after Tupac Amaru's capture and three weeks before his execution, Dámaso and Nicolás were executed in grisly, public fashion in La Plata, their body parts exhibited for all to see (see documents 117–18).

Julián Apaza, an Indian from the community of Sicasica who assumed the name Tupac Catari in honor of Tupac Amaru and the Catari brothers, led the uprising of Aymara communities around the city of La Paz. The Spanish emphasized his low social background (see document 120), belittling him in much of the documentation. This contrasted with the wary respect for the social origins of Tupac Amaru and the Catari brothers. On March 13, 1781, approximately 40,000 Indians surrounded this city, which lies in a crater-like valley 3,800 meters above sea level. They attempted to take the city several times, but their lack of arms and the desperate defense of the Spanish forces and the city's remaining population prevented them. Mariano Murillo, a non-Indian soldier forced into service for the rebels, sabotaged their scarce artillery. When rebels discovered his communication with a Spanish priest and spy, they cut off his arms.[12] Spanish forces broke through the siege and entered the desolate city on July 1, 1781. The Tupac Catari forces remained nearby, harassing those who sought food and other supplies. When Spanish forces left on August 4, the rebels again besieged La Paz. They made life even more miserable by opening a dam and flooding the city. By mid-October, the starving residents had decided to abandon the city, realizing the fate that awaited them; however, days later, Spanish forces arrived and broke the siege (see documents 134–37).

Any semblance of negotiation with the colonial state or the creation of a multiethnic alliance—elements in Tupac Amaru's initial decrees and actions—or of self-rule, as Tomás Catari proposed, had disappeared. The Tupac Catari leaders called for the death of Spaniards, and violence by both sides marked this period (see documents 128–32). In November 1781, Tupac Catari was betrayed by one of his soldiers and captured. Colonial forces sentenced him and his inner circle, including his wife, Bartolina Sisa, and sister, Gregoria Apaza, to brutal deaths; their body parts were distributed as gruesome warnings (see document 139).

The defeat of the Tupac Amaru, Catari brothers, and Tupac Catari uprisings made authorities and the upper classes leery of the Quechua and Aymara

---

12. Lewin, *La Rebelión,* 517–18.

masses, prompting an odd mix of retribution, disdain, and reforms. In the following months and years, colonial officials viciously punished communities and individuals suspected of having supported the rebels. In many towns, military officers forced the men to line up in the plaza and then executed one out of every five, the *quintado*. The violence in no way ended with the 1781 executions. On the other hand, the uprisings had alarmed the Spanish, leading them to abolish or ameliorate some of the more exploitative demands of colonial rule on the Andean people. The Crown understood that these impositions were, if not abusive, at least poorly implemented, and that many of their representatives were extraordinarily corrupt and brutal.

The rebellions' impact did not end with the executions. Not only did they mark the Andes in the coming decades, they became enduring symbols of the radical search for a more just society. Exactly what this meant was not clear then and is no clearer today.

Exploring the Documents

The documents span the eighteenth century and underline the long resistance to colonial impositions, the opposition to heightened demands in the latter half of the century, and the intense struggles over the *cacique* office. They focus on the uprisings themselves, occurring between 1780 and 1782. Readers can use the documents to follow the rise and fall of the different rebellions or to focus on one particular aspect. Many themes emerge that scholars have only begun to examine or have done so insufficiently. First and foremost is the need to compare and contrast the rebellions. Some of the differences appear here. As noted, the role of *caciques* varied greatly within these uprisings, as did the social background of the leaders. The connections between the rebellions or the different phases represent another enticing question. Key questions include how closely Diego Cristóbal Tupac Amaru's forces collaborated with the Cataristas in mid-1781, and whether Tupac Amaru himself served as a key inspiration for the Upper Peru insurgents, particularly after his martyrdom in May 1781. We know that the Tupac Amaru and Tupac Catari forces communicated and that some rebels from the Cuzco-based movement participated in the battles around La Paz. We need to explore, however, how they collaborated, what promoted or impeded this collaboration, and its impact on the rebellions. This collection's fine attention to detail will help solve these riddles.

Certain themes that recur in the documents make for interesting comparisons and potential research projects, big and small. For example, Tupac Amaru repeatedly invoked the king, claiming to act on his behalf. How could he justify the hanging of Arriaga and the uprising itself in the name of the Crown? What was the legal precedent, and what motivated Tupac Amaru? Did the Catari brothers or Tupac Catari do the same or take an equivalent action? On the other hand, how can the references to Tupac Amaru as the Inca king be understood?[13] Were there serious plans to name him monarch? Along these linguistic lines, how did the Spanish treat or denigrate the Indian insurgents? What language did they employ to describe or belittle them? The rich translations permit such an analysis.

For those interested in the imposition, negotiation, and transformation of gender ideologies provoked by the cataclysmic effects of Spanish rule, this collection of documents offers fantastic opportunities to analyze the role of the women involved in these rebellions. How can Micaela Bastidas' importance be explained? Did she truly have "a more daring and bloody character than her husband" (document 51)? What do her letters (documents 52–54) or that of the female *cacique* Tomasa Titu Condemayta (document 50) tell us about the role of women in the rebellion and the period in general (see, for example, document 51)? Was Micaela Bastidas a submissive and subdued woman at the mercy of her authoritarian husband, as she tried to convince her Spanish captors (see document 58)? The documentation seems to show the opposite—that she was a firm and active leader. How does her demeanor compare with that of Gregoria Apaza (see document 125) and other women in the Upper Peru phase? Despite her prominence, Micaela Bastidas has not been the subject of a serious biography to date. This document collection sheds much-needed light on the female leaders and followers (who prove more difficult to study).[14]

Readers will also find many other interesting topics that deserve further consideration. The Catholic Church was an important actor in the events. The bishop of Cuzco, Juan Manuel Moscoso y Peralta, faced accusations that he was a friend of Tupac Amaru (and an enemy of Arriaga) and moved too slowly against him. This hastened him to declare the rebel's excommunication.[15] Although the burning of the Sangarará church led to the depiction of

---

13. Authors who have examined these issues include Jan Szeminski, *La utopia tupamarista.* Lima: Pontificia Universidad Católica de Perú, 1983; O'Phelan Godoy, *La gran rebelión.* On the role of the Incas in Andean social movements, see Alberto Flores Galindo, *Buscando un Inca.* Lima: Instituto de Apoyo Agrario, 1987. For important essays and extraordinary images, see Natalia Majluf, ed., *Los incas, reyes del Perú.* Lima: BCP, 2005.

14. Leon Campbell, "Women and the Great Rebellion in Peru, 1780–1783," *The Americas* 42, no. 2 (1985): 163–96.

15. The two major document collections, well used by Stavig and Schmidt, are the

Tupac Amaru as a "rebellious traitor of the King, Our Lord," he went to great lengths to demonstrate his Catholicism and respect for priests (see document 43). In fact, Tupac Amaru counted on the support of some priests, many of whom also battled with *corregidores* and chafed under the Bourbon Reforms. This balancing act of an anti-colonial uprising that respected Catholicism and priests proved increasingly difficult as events radicalized by mid-1781.

Readers will no doubt find many other subjects of interest. They might be motivated to read some of the secondary literature cited here, to examine the voluminous document collections in Spanish, or to visit some of the places mentioned. I am certain that nothing would have pleased Ward Stavig more. For this, he and Ella Schmidt worked so hard on this valuable collection.

Colección Documental de la Independencia del Perú, Tomo II, *La Rebelión de Tupac Amaru,* 4 vols. Lima: Comisión Nacional del Sesquicentenario de la Independencia del Perú, 1971; *Colección Documental del Bicentenario de la Revolución Emancipadora de Tupac Amaru,* 5 vols. Lima: Comisión Nacional del Bicentenario de la Rebelión Emancipadora de Túpac Amaru, 1980–1982. Also valuable are *Tupac Amaru y la Iglesia-Antología.* Lima: Unidad de Comunicaciones del Banco Continental, 1983; David Cahill, "Curas and Social Conflict in the Doctrinas of Cuzco, 1780–1814," *Journal of Latin American Studies* 16, no. 2 (November 1984): 241–76; Kathryn Burns, *Colonial Habits: Convents and the Spiritual Economy of Cuzco, Peru.* Durham: Duke University Press, 1999.

PART ONE

TUPAC AMARU

I. Early Life, and the Peoples and Geographies of His Natal Territory (Canas y Canchis and Quispicanchis)

1. Descriptions of Tupac Amaru

Tupac Amaru was a well-to-do kuraka *(also called* cacique, *or ethnic leader) who was able to function well in both the indigenous and European Andean colonial worlds. He was descended from the principal line of the Incas who had governed Peru prior to the encounter between the old and new worlds.*

According to most accounts, he was an impressive figure as he led his troops attired in both Spanish and Inca regalia. The first of the following accounts deals with the dress and style of Tupac Amaru and was printed in an Arequipa newspaper that had received the information from witnesses who had seen him as he entered the province of Azangaro en route from his home in Canas y Canchis to the Lake Titicaca basin and the altiplano. *According to this account, the rebel forces were not only large, but Tupac Amaru seemed to have foreign help. As the newspaper put it, "The army was considerable in number, and besides the infantry, they had over a thousand men in the cavalry, and on the left and right hand side of Tupac Amaru . . . were two very good looking blond men who appeared to be English." Then, as now, those in power tended to view opposition forces not just as illegitimate but as being spurred on by "foreign" help or support. They wished to believe that their rule was just and that the common people under their control would not engage in such upheavals without a catalyst in the form of outside agitators or troublemakers like Tupac Amaru. The second description of the Inca is that of a military officer who had been acquainted with Tupac Amaru before the rebellion. The final description of the rebel leader is that of a priest and reflects considerable admiration for the Inca.*

Document 1. A Newspaper in Arequipa, January 4th, 1781
Tupac Amaru was riding a white horse [garnered] with embroidered and embossed trappings, a pair of large blunderbusses, pistols and a sword. [He was] . . . dressed in blue velvet [embellished] with golden braids; his cloak in the same style was scarlet . . . with golden braids on the front. [He also wore] . . . a three-cornered hat, and over his attire a shirt or "*unco,*" like a bishop's rochet [a close-fitting linen vestment], sleeveless and richly embroidered; and around his neck there was a gold chain and hanging from it a sun of the same metal: insignia of the princes, his ancestors. [*CDIP,* 119. 1781-I-4]

Document 2: Description of Tupac Amaru by Colonel Pablo Astete
[Tupac Amaru was] . . . a man five feet, eight inches tall; a thin body with the features of an Indian: aquiline nose, dark and lively eyes larger than Indians normally have. In his manners he was a gentleman, a courtier; he carried himself with dignity around his superiors, and with formality among the Indians. He spoke the Spanish language perfectly, and Quechua with a special grace; he lived in luxury, and when he traveled he was always accompanied by many servants and sometimes by a person to say mass. . . . When he resided in Cuzco, his clothing generally consisted of a coat, short black velvet pants that were then the fashion, silk stockings, buckles of gold at the knees and on his shoes, a Spanish beaver hat that was then worth twenty-five pesos, an embroidered shirt and a vest of gold cloth worth seventy or eighty pesos. He wore long hair . . . down to his waist. He was very well esteemed by all classes of society. He was generous and especially his magnificent remuneration of a doctor who accompanied him on his return to Tungasuca from Lima where he returned sick of body and perhaps wounded in spirit from the fatigues and deceit that the members of the Royal *Audiencia* caused him. [*RTA,* 394–95]

Document 3. Description of Tupac Amaru by D. Vicente de Jaras, Priest
Tupac Amaru is not an idiot Indian, as they think in this City. I do not know him, but I know that he is quite capable and that he does not compromise in order to achieve what he wants. He shows himself to be generous with those who follow him, and even with travelers. He behaves in a pious manner, and still wants to persuade the heavens to favor him. [*RTA,* 394–94]

2. Descriptions of the Indigenous People of Quispicanchis and Canas y Canchis (Tinta)

Descriptions of the peoples of Quispicanchis and Canas y Canchis during the colonial period are not abundant, but a few, often reflecting the writers' own lenses and beliefs as much as mirroring the observed, do exist. The first description is by the insightful and generally accurate chronicler Pedro de Cieza de Leon. In it he gives a straightforward account of the ancestors of the people who lived in the region that was the heart of the rebellion in the mid-sixteenth century.

In the late sixteenth or early seventeenth century, the indigenous chronicler Guamán Poma, whose work, El Primer Nueva Corónica y Buen Gobierno, is one of the most important documents of the colonial period in the Andes, recorded his impressions of the Canas y Canchis people. Guamán Poma, perhaps influenced by Spanish observations but perhaps reflecting his own perceptions as well, used skin color as a factor in his descriptions. According to Guamán Poma, the peoples of Quispillacta (Quispicanchis) were "somewhat white and gentlemen (gentilhombres)," *whereas the Canas were "somewhat dark* (moreno) *and tall of stature."*

Almost two centuries later a Peruvian newspaper, the Mercurio Peruano, *provided another portrait of the Canas y Canchis. This description reflects the distancing of the indigenous and nonindigenous worlds, as viewed by Euro-Peruvians, in the aftermath of the Tupac Amaru rebellion. Indigenous people appear to be more alien, more the "other." Many of the older stereotypes of indigenous people that were prevalent in the era of conquest reappear. These were the attitudes that many people of European and mixed descent took with them into the independence period and that influenced their treatment of indigenous peoples. What follows are the descriptions of people by Cieza de Leon and the* Mercurio Peruano.

Cieza de Leon

[The Canchis were] intelligent and domestic Indians, without malice, and always skillful in working, especially gold and silver. They also had large flocks of sheep (*ovejas y carneros*). Their villages are like those of their neighbors; they wear the same clothes, with black . . . [braids] round the head, the ends of which hang down as low as the chin. The Canas all wear clothes, both men and women, and they have large, round, high woolen caps on their heads. Before they were subjugated by the Incas, they had their villages in the mountains, whence they came forth to make war; afterward they descended into the valley.

Mercurio Peruano

[The Canas] were distinct in character as well as customs and dress. They were very arrogant, serious and melancholic, their music was mournful and very slow, and even their attire was doleful: their shirts, and their blankets and capes were black. . . . The Canchis were happy, festive and lazy, but very poor; therefore they dressed in rags and skins.

The Canchis are medium of height, and very bold, fickle, restless, disloyal and deceitfully obedient; for when they can get away with not observing . . . orders . . . with impunity, they do so. They are hardworking and not at all lazy. . . . The Canas, even though of darker skin, are corpulent and better shaped: they almost have the same proportions as the others; they . . . ride horses and have their houses adorned with tiles, tables, and other furniture.

But for the most part, all of them are dull and faint-hearted, taciturn and lovers of solitude: they build their huts in the most rugged and remote of mountains: at the sight of travelers they flee like wild beasts: in their conduct they are harsh, and are even curt with their own wives; and they have a great tendency towards the most ridiculous superstitions. [*WOTA*, 10, 12]

3. Two Population Documents of Rural Cuzco

The following two documents provide different views of the segments of the indigenous population of Canas y Canchis and Quispicanchis that were subject to Spanish colonial exactions in the eighteenth century. The first focuses on the population of adult males responsible for tribute payment and the percentage of these men subject to the mita *of Potosí (gruesa). The second document provides the population of people born into the community with rights and obligations (originarios), and those without legal access to lands who were not subject to community obligations (forasteros). Because women were not legally subject to most state labor drafts, they—and the children—are not included in these counts.*

1733 Tributary and *Mita* Populations of Quispicanchis and Canas y Canchis [*WOTA*, 195]

Community	Tributaries	*Originarios*	*Forasteros*	Service to Church and State	*Mita Gruesa Ordinaria*	
Quispicanchis						
Cullupates	160	127[142**]	18	15	18*	6
Papres	93	83	10	13	10	3
Pomacanchi	240	74	166	28	6	2
Guayqui	53	46	7	12	4	1
Totals					38	12
Canas y Canchis						
Sicuani	288	272	56	14	30	10
Senca	250	167	83	7	22	7
Lurucachi y Marangani	115	74	51	25	5	1

(*continued*)

Community	Tributaries	Originarios	Forasteros	Service to Church and State	Mita Gruesa Ordinaria	
Coporaque	168	101	67	16	12	4
Ancocava	97	46	51	25	5	1
Yauri	252	153	99	26	18	6
Checacupa	250	84	166	26	8	2
Layosupa	166	136	30	26	15	5
Languisupa	186	169	17	17	21	7
Pichigua	531	490	41	33	65	21
Checacupi	227	121	106	15	15	5
Pitumarca y Cangalla	29	27	2	6	3	1
Cacha	176	93	83	27	9	3
Charrachape	76	34	42	12	3	1
Tinta and Tungasuca, Sumimana, Pampamarca, and Urinocas	—	405	—	34	53	17
Combapata	190	152	38	19	19	6
Totals					318	102

* Two extra, or *remuda*, go with the *mita*.
**[There appears to have been a mistake made by the person who composed the document]

Population of Canas y Canchis in Late Colonial Period: Originarios (O) and Forasteros (F) [WOTA, 229]

Community	1728		1785		1796		1812	
	O	F	O	F	O	F	O	F
Sicuani	232	56	1003	95	1148	182	1162	446
Lurucache	167	83	175	1	193	22	179	29
Marangani	64	51	168	2	162	10	200	—
Cacha	93	83	430	1	541	5	445	1
Charrachapi	34	42	114	2	115	2	129	—
Tinta	149	—	371	4	409	2	441	10
Pampamarca	182	74	135	12	209	40	207	38

(*continued*)

Community	1728		1785		1796		1812	
	O	F	O	F	O	F	O	F
Combapata	152	38	196	—	218	4	241	16
Checacupe	121	106	135	67	235	1	211	3
Cangalla	27	2	368	2	497	3	368	22
Yanaoca	144	50	227	44	456	130	350	101
Coporaque	111	67	453	31	489	33	393	29
Ancocahva	47	51	222	16	271	16	172	14
Yauri	153	99	700	45	790	182	51	530
Pichigua	492	41	552	12	616	40	510	46
Checasupa	179	153	494	—	599	3	515	4
Languisupa	169	17	198	18	188	35	157	40
Layosupa	136	30	270	19	365	23	239	99
Canchis	1221	535	3195	186	3727	271	3583	566
Canas	1431	508	3116	185	3774	462	2987	683
Province	2652	1043	6311	371	7501	733	6570	1249
Total O & F	3695		6682		8234		7819	

4. Geography of Quispicanchis and Canas y Canchis

In the preindustrial world, people lived off of the resources they wrested from the environment, though they often supplemented these items by trading them for other goods. This was especially true of rural indigenous peoples, such as those living in rural Cuzco. Almost everyone worked in agriculture and depended on their harvest to maintain their physical existence and provide them with the means for their cultural reproduction. Canas y Canchis—due to climate, distance from Cuzco, and smaller concentrations of fertile soils—was not as attractive to Europeans as Quispicanchis. However, Canas y Canchis was an important trading center with annual fairs that attracted people from much of the southern Andean highlands. It was also an important center of wool production—sheep and alpaca—that the many textile mills (obrajes) and workshops (chorillos) used, depending on indigenous labor to produce cloth and clothes for sale throughout the southern Andes. In addition, it was a center of transportation; the packers (or muleteers) used the abundant llamas for this purpose in the early colonial period and later evolved to the use of many more

mules. Tupac Amaru was the owner of pack mules and llamas, and the trans-
porting of goods throughout the southern Andes was an important part of his
business. There were relatively few Spaniards in the province, and those who
did live there had indigenous peoples for the overwhelming majority of their
neighbors.

The province of Quispicanchis, where many of the Cuzco elite had lands
and homes, was a different story. The rich lands, the valley bottoms, the possi-
bility for irrigation, and the proximity to Cuzco made the region an important
center for Spanish land holdings and for the supplying of the city of Cuzco, as
well as more distant regions. This made these lands profitable and desired. Here
the Spanish hand was stronger and their numbers greater, but for all their
power they were still very much a minority living in the midst of indigenous
communities and dependent on indigenous laborers to work their lands and
produce their wealth. The late colonial traveler and geographer Cosme Bueno
scrutinized rural Cuzco with his keen eye for the economic underpinnings of
life. The following are short descriptions of the region written by Cosme Bueno.

Canas y Canchis

Because there are many snow-covered mountains, its climate is extremely cold
most everywhere. Nevertheless, wheat, barley, corn, potatoes, *ocas* and *quinua*
grow there, and in warmer regions—ravines near the rivers—some fruit although not in abundance. In the higher regions where pasture is abundant,
cattle are raised as well as great numbers of *vicuñas, h(g)uanacos, vizcachas*—
that are similar to hares or rabbits—deer (*ciervos*) and partridges. In the rivers
large *bagres* are caught. There are many lakes on which aquatic birds such as
ducks . . . breed. . . . Many silver mines are found in this province, but they
are not worked at present due to flooding in some and cave-ins in others.
Those of Condoroma, that have suffered the first accident, are an exception. . . . In the jurisdiction of . . . Yauri there are two copper mines that are
worked. There are also some gold mines; but not of consequence.

Quispicanchis

Its climate is diverse. The climate of the valley of Oropesa, which is the closest to Cuzco, is temperate and desirable. It is for this reason that many distinguished *vecinos* from Cuzco and members of religious orders have haciendas
where they grow corn, wheat, and other grains, fruits and vegetables. . . . Almost all the rest of the province is cold although wheat, corn, and other crops
(*semillas*) are also grown; in the higher regions there are several *estancias* that
supply Cuzco with cattle and other livestock (*ganados mayores y menores*) especially towards the east of the province where the Cordillera (mountain

range) de Vilcanota runs. . . . Passing the *cordillera* one finds the *montaña* of Andes de Cuchóa where a broad river, named Araza, flows. . . . On a mountain named Camanti near this river there is a gold mine, and in the surrounding region various *coca haciendas* where bananas, pineapples, papayas, limes, granadillas and other fruits of the *montaña* are harvested. Also various poisonous insects live. For protection against barbarous Indians, those with interests in the mine continually maintain some armed guards.

This province is irrigated by two notable rivers, with some fish and many arroyos—among these the Huatanay that passes Cuzco . . . [and] flows into the Vilcamayo river that exits in the north of the province . . . and it enters from Canas y Canchis. The other notable river [is the] Apurímac. . . . A half league from Oropesa . . . there is a lake that today is named Mohina . . . where many reeds . . . some fish and water birds grow. . . . There are some other small lakes and also a large one named Pomacanchi. [*WOTA*, 8–10]

5. Marriage Certificate of Tupac Amaru and Micaela Bastidas

Many Andean couples lived together for long periods before they were married as part of the development of a strong relationship. This practice, known as sirvinakuy, was designed to ensure an enduring, stable marriage and to produce a couple who would be good, dependable members of the community. However, by the late colonial period most couples in the area of rural Cuzco desired to be married by the church. This was especially true for elite Indians who did not consider themselves fully married until they were blessed by the church.

The following marriage certificate shows that Micaela Bastidas, recognized as a Spaniard, married Tupac Amaru in the community of Surimana, one of the three communities over which the rebel leader ruled as kuraka (the other two were Tungasuca and Pampamarca). They were married by the priest Lopez de Sosa, who was like a surrogate father to Tupac Amaru after his own father died. Tupac Amaru was sixteen years of age at the time of their marriage.

Year 1760. In the town of Surimana on the Twenty-sixth day of the month of May of 1776 and having had published the three marriage bans as ordered by the Holy Council of Trent during the three holidays and during the Main Mass and not having resulted in any objections and proceeding by mutual consent of those contracting marriage I Doctor Don Anthonio Lopez de Sosa priest and vicar of said town, married and blessed, which make their marriage true and legitimate following the orders of our Holy Mother the Church, Joseph Thupaamaro [*sic*] single, legitimate child of Don Miguel Thupa Amaro and Rosa Noguera with Micaela Bastidas, single, illegitimate daughter of Don Manuel Bastidas and Josepha Puiucahua Spaniards of said town. Acting as godparents Andrés Noguera and Martina Oquendo. Acting as witnesses Diego Castro and Andrés Castro which I registered through my signature.

Don Antonio Lopez de Sosa [*CDIP,* 4. 1760-V-25]

6. Death and Birth Records of the Parents, Uncle, and Children of Tupac Amaru

Rosa Noguera (Mother of Tupac Amaru), Death
In the pueblo of Surimana on the 11th of October of 1740, I D. Santiago Lopez, Priest of the Parish of Pampamarca, and its Annexes, buried the body of Doña Rosa Noguera, legitimate wife of Don Miguel Tupac Amaru, governor of this said pueblo, who appeared to be about thirty years old, in the Church. She left two male children named Clemente and Joseph; she died without sacrament because she died all of a sudden. She was buried in the Church with the cross . . . mass . . . the body present, and four responses: thirty pesos were given for the funeral fees. . . .

Santiago Joseph Lopez [*CDIP,* 2. 1740-X-11]

Miguel Tupac Amaru (Father of Tupac Amaru), Death
Ayllu Callca. Miguel, 48 years old. Fees 25 pesos.
In the pueblo of Surimana, annex of Pampamarca, Province of Canas y Canchis on the 30th of April, 1750, I . . . Don Julian Antonio de Vargas y Céspedes, deputy (*Theniente*) of the *cura,* buried the body of Don Miguel Tupac Amaru, Indio Principal of said pueblo, married . . . according to the order of our Mother the Church with Doña Bentura Monxarras, Spaniard of this said pueblo in the *ayllu* of Callca. He died having confessed with me and receiving the Sacred Sacrament of the Eucharist . . . and extreme Unction; of the age of forty eight. . . . He left four children. He was buried in the Church with the accompaniment of the Cross . . . incense, six responses and mass . . . with the body present. Funeral fees of twenty-five pesos were paid and one peso for ecclesiastical building funds. . . .

Julian Antonio de Vargas y Céspedes [*CDIP,* 3. 1750-IV-30]

Mariano, Son of Tupac Amaru, Birth
In the pueblo of San Felipe of Tungasuca, annex of the Parish of Pampamarca, Province of Tinta, . . . Revered Friar Isidro Rodríguez, deputy priest of this Parish, on the 18th day of the month of September of 1762, I baptized and put the oil and *chrisma* on a child of one day of age, and I named him Mariano, legitimate child of Joseph Tupac Amaru and Doña Micaela Bastidas. His Godfather was Doctor Antonio Lopez de Sosa, Priest of this Parish and that it be registered I signed it, I the priest Don Antonio Lopez de Sosa. [*CDIP,* 6. 1762-IX-18]

Fernando, Son of Tupac Amaru, Birth
In the pueblo of Our Lady of the Ascension of Pampamarca, province of Tinta, on the 3rd of April, 1769, I Doctor Don Antonio Lopez de Sosa, Priest of the same . . . put the oil and *chrisma* on a child of ten months and three days who I baptized . . . and named Fernando, legitimate son of Don Joseph Tupac Amaru and Doña Micaela Bastidas. His Godfather in the water was Antonio Noguera and in the oil Doña Michaela Capactinta. And that it be registered I signed

Don Antonio Lopez de Sosa [*CDIP,* 7. 1769-IV-3]

Marcos Tupac Amaru, Uncle of Tupac Amaru, Death
In the pueblo of Our Lady of the Purification of Surimana, annex of the Parish of Pampamarca, province of Tinta, on the 20th of May, 1769, I, Doctor Don Antonio Lopez de Sosa, Priest of the same and vicar of this dioces, buried the body of Don Marcos Tupac Amaru, husband of Marcela Castro and resident of this pueblo: who died at more than sixty years (of age) and having received all of the necessary sacraments. Because it is recorded I signed.

Doctor Antonio Lopez de Sosa [*CDIP,* 8. 1769-V-20]

7. Education at San Borja in Cuzco

The young Tupac Amaru, in line for assuming the office of kuraka, was sent to Cuzco to be educated at the school that was dedicated to teaching future kurakas. *Thus, Tupac Amaru became a literate man who knew some Latin as well as Spanish and Quechua. The following is a description by Dr. Ignacio Castro of the school, San Francisco de Borja. The school was run by the Jesuits until their expulsion in 1767.*

San Francisco de Borja was founded for the sons of Indian nobles and *caciques;* there are usually more than twenty-five of them. The dress is a short green cape with an interior short wide-sleeved shirt of the same color, a red sash with a silver emblem of the Royal Arms, and a black hat; they wear their hair cut to the shoulders. The education they receive is limited to the rudiments of Christian Doctrine, reading and writing. They are given board, paper, pens and ink. The Jesuits were in charge of their care. After [the expulsion] there have been Prebendaries in charge of its [the school's] administration. The house is beautiful, with gardens, patios, covered walkways, attractive rooms and a Chapel. [*RTA,* 386]

II. Early Eighteenth-Century Discontent, Violence, and Plagues

8. Impact of the Great Epidemic of 1719–1720

Although the epidemics of the early colonial period are those that are best known for their devastation of indigenous communities, a terrible epidemic worked its deadly way through the Andes in 1719–1720. One of the impacts of the epidemic was to disrupt the structure of traditional leadership in many communities. This meant that new kurakas, *sometimes not from traditional ruling families, were put into office, and sometimes these* kurakas *had more allegiance to the* corregidores *who appointed them than was healthy for the community whose interests they were supposed to uphold. The death of traditional* kurakas *also had the potential to open up existing tensions in communities that might not have come to the surface had the traditional order been in place. The communities of rural Cuzco, like everywhere else, were hit hard by the plagues of 1719–1720. In the Quispicanchis community of Quiquijana, almost all of the officeholders died. A witness gave the following account to the* corregidor *that shows that almost none of the men of authority and respect survived.*

Don Francisco Niño, Don Martin Tiraquimbo, Don Melchor Guamansauni, Don Thomas Ramos, and Don Alonso Orcoguarana who were *caciques principales* and *governadores* of this pueblo, are dead, they died in *la peste* . . . and of the same fate all the *segundos* and *mandones* have died, such as Francisco de Estrada who died without one member of his family remaining, and in the same manner Matheo Pichu with all his family, Don Gavriel Cusigualpa,

Agustín de Rado, Don Ygenio Ninamalco and others, and Don Blas Chinche who was *alcalde* with the said Don Melchor Guamansauni, and those that were placed after by your mercy, Señor *Corregidor*, they also died, as did all the *regidores* and *ministros de justicia,* and the only *mandones* (authorities) that remain alive are Don Miguel Quera and Don Fernando Vitorino. [*WOTA,* 230]

9. Huarochirí Revolt, 1750

As tensions mounted in the mid-eighteenth century, Spanish officials slowly became aware of minor revolts and conspiracies that began to grow in numbers. One of the most serious of these was a plot in the region of Huarochirí, bordering on Lima; the targets were the viceregal government in Lima and important Spaniards. The plan of the Huarochirí rebels included freeing the slaves and taking control of the prisons, seemingly with the plan to liberate the prisoners. Although the conspiracy was discovered, the threat of such a revolt—with its implications for political disorder, social change, and upheaval—served as a "shot across the bow" for some Spaniards. It confirmed their worst fears about the true nature of the lower orders of the society over which they ruled. The majority of people of European descent, including those in government, did not heed this warning and continued down the path that would lead to open rebellion, ignoring other serious upheavals such as that of Juan Santos Atahualpa in the Amazon basin. The following document is testimony taken from the Huarochirí plot.

At midnight they would set fire to the ranchos that surrounded the city, and afterwards open the dam of Santa Catalina. In the meantime the church's bells would be rung as an alarm, and when the frightened people tried to reach the streets, the floodwater would obstruct them. Later, 500 men would be sent to the government Palace to kill the Viceroy, his family and his guards; and after seizing the Palace, another 500 men would be dispatched to El Callao, to take control of the city's prison. Fifty men were also to be sent to guard the corners, and they would be ordered to kill all the *chapetones* ministers, and anyone who killed a *chapetón* would be allowed to keep all the dead man's titles. And they would free all the slaves, so that they would not oppose them but rather support them, and they would appoint one of them [slaves] to an important position. But they would be neither against the Catholic Church nor against the priests as they would allow a number of clergymen from each Religious Order to stay. And they also wanted to appoint a King, and some suggested that they crown the *indio chuncho* [Juan Santos Atahualpa] as King, but others did not agree with this idea, and they intended to discuss their plans further, on Saint Peter's day [29th of July] but before they could do so, the imprisonments took place. [*RR*, 93–94. Translated by Scarlett O'Phelan Godoy]

10. Sentence against Farfán de los Godos and His Comrades

Early in 1780, a conspiracy was uncovered in Cuzco that implicated mainly criollos and one cacique *from the pueblo of Pisac. This conspiracy, known as the Farfán conspiracy, might have served as a warning to the government that the situation was reaching critical levels and that a wide variety of the crown's subjects were discontent with the changes being made in the economy, but apparently it did not. The officials dealt with the conspiracy as an isolated event, and they hanged all conspirators except the* cacique. *However, the* cacique *was hanged shortly thereafter—once word of the Tupac Amaru insurgency reached Cuzco—for it was reported that the Inca was coming to save his fellow* cacique. *Thus, 1780 proved to be a fateful year. As the Farfán conspiracy, the Juan Santos Atahualpa rebellion, and the Catari uprising in Alto Peru (Bolivia) showed, Tupac Amaru was far from alone in his challenge of the colonial state. The Bourbon reforms, which included new and higher taxes, affected many people—especially the indigenous people who already lived on the margin. The following is a brief description of the Farfán conspiracy.*

Around the month of May of this year that is ending [1780], several lampoons appeared in Cuzco. For two full months the militia corps dedicated themselves to going around the city [looking for lampoons], and the judges to conducting investigations to learn who the authors were. These activities resulted in the apprehension of Juan de Dios Vera, Diego Aguilar, Asensio Vergara, Ildefonso Castillo, Josef Gomez, Lorenzo Farfán, Eugenio Ricas, Felipe Unda, and Jose Verzera, who together with the *cacique* of the pueblo of Pizac in the Province of Calca, Bernardo Tabuazo who couldn't be found, met several times to plan an uprising as they indicated in their confessions, which were included in the warrant regarding these issues. The sentence of death on the gallows was pronounced for the first seven executions and the last three were condemned to ten years in the prison of Valdivia. The sentence was carried out on June 30th. After this, the *cacique* was offered a priest [to confess] and while they were trying to figure out whether he should be granted immunity, the news about Tupac Amaru [came to light]. . . . Because it had been rumored around Cuzco that he [Tupac Amaru] was coming to free him, it was decided to hang him and this was done. It is said that because of this event he took it upon himself to avenge him, moving forward with the machination of his ideas which have caused so much consternation in the Kingdom. [*RTA*, 781–82]

III. Colonial Exploitation and Demands

11. List of Prices (*Arancel*) Charged by Priests for Services

Priests and friars not only looked after the spiritual well-being of their parishioners, they sometimes provided advice and support to the indigenous communities. They were largely responsible for informing local villagers about Spanish government, culture, beliefs, and lifestyles. Some priests, however, exploited their communities, worked with Spaniards to the disadvantage of indigenous communities and individuals, and served as informers in times of trouble. Information given to priests in confession was not necessarily kept secret, particularly if it related to issues of security or violence.

As people became faithful believers, they usually desired to have the sacraments performed for them and to participate in church fiestas such as Christmas and Easter. The priests charged for their services. The following arancel, *or list of charges for services, shows the official prices charged by parish priests for their services to* naturales *(Indians), which also extended to* mestizos, mulattoes, *and* Negroes.

Many priests charged more than the costs shown in the list, but some charged less or even nothing in times of emergency or lack of funds. However, it was all too common for priests to refuse to perform services—including burials—if they had not received payment. Even if the priest meant well, such created desires as the sacraments were indirect forms of economic coercion in which people were obliged to labor in the European economic sector, or provide goods for that sector, to meet needs that were a part of their new belief system. Thus, the church and priests were not just spiritual guides. They were also part of the economic arrangement that helped drive the colonial economy. Priests' fees were just one of the ways that Spanish colonialism enlisted people to work for them without having to rely directly on coercion.

Sacrament	Costs
Low mass (*misa rezada*)	2 pesos
High mass (*misa cantada*)	4 pesos
High mass and procession (*misa solemne y procesion*)	12 pesos
Mass on sacred feasts (*misa de Fiestas*)	10 pesos (at Potosí, 14 pesos)
Misa de salud	16 pesos
High burial for *mestizo* (*entierro cantado con pompa de mestizo*)	40 pesos
Low burial for *mestizo* (*entierro rezado de mestizo*)	at church, 10 pesos / at convent, 13 pesos
Low burial for *mestizo* child (*entierro rezado de mestizo menor*)	at church, 8 pesos / at convent, 10 pesos
High burial for mulatto or Negro slave (*entierro cantado de mulato o negro esclavo*)	at church, 14 p/at Potosí, 18p / at convent,18 p/at Potosí, 24p
Low burial for mulatto or Negro slave (*entierro rezado de mulato o negro esclavo*)	at church, 9 p/at Potosí, 11p / at convent,12 p/at Potosí, 14p
Low burial for slaves	at church, 8 p/at Potosí, 10p / at convent, 10 p/at Potosí, 13p
High burial for slaves	at church, 6 pesos / at convent, 8 pesos
Burial at the cemetery	4 pesos/at Potosí, 8p
High burial for *indio criollo* at Potosí	12 pesos
Burial at the cemetery for *indio criollo* in Potosí	*rezado:* 6 pesos / *cantado:* 8 pesos
Funeral mass for *mestizo* (*misa de velacion de mestizos*)	10 pesos
Funeral mass for free mulatto (*misa de velacion de mulatos libre*)	6 pesos
Funeral mass for slave (*misa de velacion de esclavos*)	4 pesos

[*RR*, 115. Translated by Scarlett O'Phelan Godoy]

12. Description of Work in Potosí Mines by Father Acosta

The forced labor system of the mita *was not only very disruptive, it endangered the lives of the Andean peoples who were ordered to leave their homes and travel—sometimes hundreds of miles, as in the case of Canas y Canchis and Quispicanchis—to work in Potosí. In the following account, Father José de Acosta (the author of the* Natural and Moral History of the Indies *and a keen observer of colonial life) describes labor conditions in the mines of Potosí as they were a couple of centuries before the rebellion. By the late eighteenth century, however, mines were much deeper, labor demands harsher, and forced labor more frequent. We have chosen an early English translation of Acosta to give the reader the flavor of the English language used in an earlier period.*

They must descend [great depths] to labor in the mine. . . . They labor in these mines in continual darkness and obscurity, without knowledge of day or night. And forasmuch as those places are never visited with the Sun, there is not only a continual darkness, but also an extreme cold, with so gross an air contrary to the disposition of man, so as such as newly enter are sick as they at sea . . . which happened to me in one of these mines, where I felt pain at the heart, and beating of the stomach. Those that labor therein use candles to light them, dividing their work in such sort, as they work in the day rest by the night, and so they change. The metal is commonly hard, and therefore they break it with hammers, splitting and hewing it by force as if they were flints. After, they carry up this metal upon their shoulders, by ladders of three branches made of neates leather twisted like pieces of wood, which are crossed with staves of wood, so as by every one of these ladders they mount and descend together. They are ten *estados* [one *estado* equals 2.17 yards] long a piece, and at the end of one, begins another of the same length, every ladder beginning and ending at platforms of wood, where there are seats to rest them like unto galleries, for that there are many of these ladders to mount by one at the end of the other. A man carries ordinarily the weight of two *arrobas* [one *arroba* equals 11.5 kilograms, or about 25 pounds] of metal upon his shoulders, tied together in a cloth in the manner of a skippe, and so mount they three and three. He that goes before carries a candle tied to his thumb, for as it is said, they have no light from heaven, and so go they up the ladder holding it with both their hands; to mount so great a height which commonly is above a hundred and fifty *estados,* a fearful thing and which breeds amazement to think upon it, so great is the desire of silver, that for the gain thereof men endure any pains. [*WOTA,* 186–87]

13. Late Seventeenth-Century
Description of Potosí by Acarete du Biscay

Occasionally, non-Spaniards made their way to Potosí and glimpsed the life and working conditions of the indigenous labor force. In the late seventeenth century, Acarete du Biscay observed conditions in the mines. What he saw and recorded, as follows, confirmed the continuing horrors of this work. The reader will note that, at this point, the workers were forced to work all week in the mines instead of leaving the mine every day, as Viceroy Toledo had originally ordered. Workers were paid at the end of the work week; the bodies of those who had been killed or were overcome by illness or weakness were brought to the surface at the end of the week.

After six days of constant work, the conductor brings 'em back the Saturday following to the same place, there the *Corregidor* orders a review to be made of 'em, to make the owners of the mines give 'em the wages that are appointed 'em, and to see how many of 'em are dead, that the couraces [*kurakas*] may be olig'd to supply the number that is wanting: for there's no week passes but some of 'em die, either by divers accidents that occur, as the tumbling down of great quantities of earth, and falling of stones, or by sickness and other casualties. They are sometimes very much incommoded by winds that are shut up in the mines. [*WOTA*, 187–88]

14. Abused *Mitayos* from Coporaque
Flee Potosí and Return to Their Community

Because completion of mita *service was important to keep the community in good standing with the colonial state, most communities in the region of rural Cuzco worked to make their people comply with the* mita. *Even though they resented this disruptive and oppressive service, which often took them away from their community for more than two years, the survival of the community was even more important. However, it placed a tremendous burden on villages: not only did they try to supply goods for the* mitayos *but the wives and children almost always accompanied the male* mitayo. *The severity of the work led many to flee their communities. This made life even harder on those who remained; the state did not always make regular counts of the population, which forced these communities to contribute a higher percentage of their people to mine work.*

When Tupac Amaru went to Lima to be recognized as heir to the Inca
throne, he sought an end to the mita *because of its destructive impact on his*
people. His uncle had been wiped out financially for not being able to send
the required number of mitayos *to Potosí when he was* kuraka. *This made the*
issue very personal to Tupac Amaru, as well as an issue of deep and generalized
concern for almost all indigenous peoples who were subject to this colonial labor
exaction.

The following document discusses mitayos *from the Canas y Canchis com-*
munity of Coporaque who left Potosí and returned home before their time of
service was complete. They did this because they were suffering abuses at the
hands of the mine owner to whom they were assigned, not just because of the
harshness of the work. As a result of the mine owner's reputation for abuse, and
because of the good reputation of the mitayos *in the community, the* kuraka
supported his people and wrote to the corregidor *on their behalf.*

The following document is from the kuraka's *letter. He was able to convince*
the corregidor *that the* mitayos *should not be punished, but this was not al-*
ways the case. Communities did not necessarily support people they suspected of
fleeing just because the work was terrible, and not all corregidores *believed the*
mitayos *or their* kurakas. *Overall, the* mita *was incredibly destructive to the*
communities and was one of the causes of the rebellion.

[The *kuraka* noted that] . . . they had experienced very bad whippings and
affronts on the part of the head carpenter and other administrators of the re-
finery of Dn. Bernardo Zenda and that not being possible for them to endure such inhumane treatment they returned, obliged by the conservation of
their lives to seek refuge, abandoning their pack llamas, their sleeping gear
and their prebend of food; that a few days earlier for the same reason two
other *cédulas* [another term for *mitayo*] of the said *mita* did the same, abandoning their wives and children: that when the women with their weeping
[asked] said administrators not to mistreat thusly their husbands, they also
mistreated them with blows, afterward locking them in a chapel, and that
lately the cruelty of said administrators is so great that . . . they have forced
the wives of these Indians to work in place of their husbands. The two aforementioned Indians, especially the *enterador* [community member responsible for getting the *mitayos* to Potosí from their home community], are known
in these *ayllus* for being of very good repute, for which reason we cannot presume that they have come back fleeing, but obliged by grave motives. . . . We
assure Your Majesty that we received continual complaints . . . for some years
from the captain *enteradores* and *cédulas* that return from said *mita* [and] they
do not pay the *leguaje,* nor justly [pay] the daily wages and that they oblige
them to work more than physically possible and as a result many Indians

return with chest injuries and they die here then asthmatics, for this reason everyone has the greatest horror of said *mita*. Although we have tried to persuade the two Indians to return to complete their *mita* time they absolutely resist and we do not have [means] to remit them by force a distance of more than two hundred leagues. . . . Captains have also complained on other occasions of violence. . . . We implore Your Majesty . . . for a remedy of the referred excesses that we bear and for which we ask justice. . . . [*WOTA*, 205]

15. Tupac Amaru Protests the *Mita* to the *Audiencia* of Lima

The provinces of Canas y Canchis and Quispicanchis were part of the mita *system established for the mines of Potosí by Viceroy Toledo in the late sixteenth century. The peoples of these provinces suffered even more than those in other provinces due to their distance from the Cerro Rico (Rich Mountain, Potosí); they often served two years instead of one and lost a great deal of time traveling to and from the mines. In the following document, Tupac Amaru presents his demands to royal officials in Lima that the* mita *be eliminated for the people of his province, Canas y Canchis, because of the suffering it created and the depopulation of the province that resulted from people fleeing their homes or not returning following their service in Potosí. The* mita *became one of the sources of concern around which support for the rebellion Tupac Amaru was able to congeal. The future Inca also grew in stature among the indigenous people of his region because of his opposition to the* mita. *Note that Tupac Amaru refers to sections of the colonial law and older orders by the Crown to support his argument that the indigenous peoples from the provinces should be removed from their service in the* mita *and replaced by resident labor and slaves. He also implores that laws providing for travel payment, known as* leguaje, *be enforced. Thus, in his petition Tupac Amaru not only deals with the abuses and deteriorating social and economic conditions fostered by the* mita, *he also uses colonial laws and royal proclamations to enhance his case. Use of the colonial legal structure was quite common; in general, violence ensued only when legal options had failed or been exhausted.*

Honorable Sir: I, José Tupac Amaru, *Cacique* of the pueblos of Surimana, Pampamarca and Tungasuca in the Province of Canas y Canchis (alias Tinta) and in the name of the *Caciques* of the other pueblos of said provinces, and in virtue of the powers that I duly represent, I put myself at the feet of your

Excellency with the utmost respect and say: that the supplicant [Tupac Amaru], on behalf of the Pueblos, humbly presents himself to Your Excellency on behalf of those Indians, who are your subjects, due to the imponderable toils that they suffer in the *mita* of Potosí, more than 200 leagues distant; and what is more, the grave damage that the uprooting of these Indians from their villages visibly entails. Who, forced to travel to such a distant mine, take their women and their children with them and make a painful farewell to their relatives and their home [*patria*]; because the harshness and ruggedness of [living on the] road kills them, annihilates them; the strange nature and heavy work of Potosí, or their dire poverty, does not afford them the means to return to their pueblos when the calamity [of the *mita*] has not already taken away their lives.

The other pueblos of the Province suffer the same misfortune, and all of them call for relief from the unbearable toil. The province has always been big [large in population], but in earlier times there were many more Indians, and they could take turns going to the *mita* with some time in between for rest. What happens now happened then, but somewhat differently. Back then Indians died or deserted, but the pueblos were still more populated and their absence was felt less. Today due to the extreme decline in which [the pueblos] find themselves, it is almost impossible to comply with the *mita* because there are not sufficient Indians who can serve, and it is necessary that the same ones return or that the *caciques* are forced to make it palatable for outsiders to serve [in their place] paying them with their own money whatever they require.

Thus, there is a lack of people who can work the rich mines to remove the ore for the public benefit and fulfill their service to the King as humble subjects in a matter so important to the Royal Crown and the Kingdom. Today, full of despair, they go to serve those who in name only are miners. The deficiency of ore has transformed the *mita* into a "family business," that includes the mine owners renting the Indians of their *repartimiento* to others or occupying them gathering ore from the tailings [*broza*] of the mining process that is called "to venture." And after having done the job well they are forced to work with the ore as if it were ready to be hauled, thus forcing them to work three days to accomplish what in other circumstances would be done in one.

The attention that Your Majesty has benevolently shown in the multiple laws and regulations is none other than that of good treatment and conservation of the Indians. Even as far as the *mita* is concerned, your Royal preference is for mercy, ahead of the utility gained from the extraction of ore and other riches; because they [the riches] would be of little importance as the extinction of the Indians would make . . . [such benefits] short lasting. For if there are no Indians, there are no riches either. . . . [T]he population of the Cerro de Potosí could provide the workers, instead of bringing them from remote provinces like Canas y Canchis that are more than 200 leagues away from Potosí. We would ask Your Excellency to consider what a turn of events this is, and what type of roads these miserable Indians are forced to walk. Now you can see the gravity of their work, their vexations and their grievances.

In addition to the time that they must spend in the journey, they arrive totally ruined, incapable of suffering the hardships of the work in the *mita*. The vexations they suffer during their residence are not any less, as it seems that bad treatment of the Indians has become the nature of things . . . at the same time that they [the *mitayos*] are considered to be so necessary and useful. The work that they are forced to do, the tasks that they are forced to comply with, and all the other abuses that they suffer have been recorded. . . . These complaints have been duly submitted to the Superintendent because, even though the truth of Indians is not held in esteem, they are, after all, the unfortunate ones and carry the weight [*trabajo*] and the worst aspects of their humble condition. . . . Wickedness [is done in] hiding the wrongs against some *naturales* that merit Your Majesty's and Your Excellency's compassion. [This is done] in order to give a different color to everyday occurrences, so that complaints about their grievances are not believed.

This, however, is not the primary subject of this present petition. It confines itself to exposing the impossible situation in which this province finds itself in continually complying with the Potosí *mita* due to the extreme decline [in population] that prevents the very small number of Indians remaining from meeting *mita* demands as they conform to the Royal Laws and Ordinances; and all this in circumstances such that the Indians come from great distances and are fatigued [while at the same time] there are a great number of workers who have established themselves in said Cerro of Potosí and who could work in the mines without need of the *mita*, even if they [the mines] were thriving.

With the Ordinances contained in the Book 2, F.18 to Ch.10, dealing with the conservation of these provinces that depend on labor and the refining of the mines, and the limited need of the Indians' industry, Your Majesty expresses great desire that those provinces be relieved from their duty as soon as possible and that there should be no *repartimiento* for them. In the meantime the miners should supply themselves with Blacks [one assumes he means slaves] or voluntary day-laborers; Chapter 12, dealing with the ore of Potosí, mandates that to expedite work, labor should be supplied through the best way and form possible, [through] the *mitas* of those Indians who live in the settlement or nearby territories; Chapter 14 deals with the punctual and adequate day-wages that they should be paid, and the particular care of their health and spiritual and material well being, and that the travel costs of those who serve in the mines from outside the settlement should be reimbursed going and coming.

In Ordinance 2, Chapter 2, it is repeated that miners should buy slaves in order to help alleviate the [burden of the] Indians; Chapters 4 and 8 require that settlements be built around the mines so as to lighten the burden of *mita* and "*repartimientos*" and avoid bringing them [*mita* workers] from outside. Chapter 5 requires that the *mita* and *repartimiento* do not exceed one-seventh of the population (adult male tribute payers) of each town at the time of said *repartimiento;* because the extraction of gold and silver should not be given more attention than the conservation of the Indians. And finally, Chapter 13 (requires) punishment of those *caciques* who send to the second *mita* the same Indians that were sent to the first.

These Ordinances are in compliance with the laws included in Book 6, F. [Folio] 12 of the Recompilation of the [Laws of the] Indies. According to them, in all circumstances the claims of the provinces of Canas y Canchis are just. The main reason is because of the decline of Indians who, reduced to miserable numbers, cannot find respite [from the *mita*]. And against [the expressed desire of] those Ordinances, they who went first [to the *mita*] go a second time as otherwise the *mita* requirements cannot be met. Whether the limits of one-seventh of the population are being met cannot be determined, as we hardly have one-seventh of our population left as can be demonstrated with little difficulty. . . .

The *Corregidor* of the Province sees and experiences the decreasing numbers and the difficulty it takes for *Caciques* to deliver said *mita,* but they do not cease in always informing them that it is necessary. Distance is a grave inconvenience, more than 200 leagues of journey and same amount to come back merits serious concern over the suffering. . . . They say their farewells as if they were dying or never returning to their homeland [*Patria*]; they sell their huts and their furniture in painful transactions due to the strong disposition Indians have towards their people, their furniture, and their animals. Loaded with their women and children, each Indian *mitayo* who leaves the pueblo takes a whole family with him, preventing the propagation of the community. Thus they take to the road which is more than two hundred leagues of rugged terrain, rivers, mountains and *punas*. And if they suffer going to the *mita,* they suffer even more when deciding to go back especially when, as regularly happens, they do not foresee having the work to maintain themselves and [for this reason] they never return.

When Indians were indispensable to the *mita,* their conservation was given more attention due to their poverty, it now is beyond understanding that when the need for labor has decreased and the availability of labor has increased in Potosí, poor Indians of these distant provinces of Canas y Canchis would not be relieved of such *mita* in conformity with the expressed literal context of said Royal Ordinances. That, responding to the present case, the miners should opt to hire those large numbers of Indians who have become part of the indigenous barrios and have located themselves in the Cerro of Potosí and who voluntarily contract themselves out to work. This would end the problem of lack of workers that made the *mita* necessary in the first place. The miners know this situation very well, but they still want the *mitayos* because they can treat them worse than slaves; because they pay them less, and use their privilege as miners as a pretext and to feign difficulties in the extraction of ore as a pretense to preserve the *mita* so that they can abuse the Indian labor, regardless if those Provinces are being annihilated, reducing the Royal Treasury of Your Majesty through the innumerable lost tributaries. Miners are so engrossed with getting immediate returns from the *mita* that even though they are required to pay the *leguaje* [travel payment for *mitayos* ordered by the Crown] covering the Indians' travels to and from their communities, this is the last thing they think of doing, so much so that the Superior Government issued a decree on August 25th, 1768, to the Governor of Potosí ordering him to require the payment of the *leguaje* by the miners at the request of the Indians of the province of Lampa. This [law] cannot be enforced and the miserable Indians embark on their long journeys without the support that is due to them. . . . [E]ven if they were in the same numbers as previously, it would always be fair that they get paid their *leguaje* and be offered support both ways. Without [this payment] they should not be found guilty if, lacking that support, they decide not to comply with the *mita*. It is in these conditions that I ask and beg you that, having presented to you such written authority and instruments of representation, you would deign to declare the Indians of said province of Canas y Canchis exempt from the *mita* of Potosí due to the decline in which they find themselves and other just causes that I the petitioner have presented. I beg for mercy which we expect to justly attain from your powerful hand. Lima, 18 of December 1777.

—José Tupac Amaru [*CDIP,* 17. 1777-XII-18]

16. Three Documents Related to the Potosí *Mita*

The first of the following documents deals with mita *workers leaving for service in the mines of Potosí, as described by the newspaper* Mercurio Peruano *in 1792. This description could have come from nearly any community that was subject to the* mita *at any point during its long history. It gives a sense of the sadness of the situation and its impact on the people leaving, as well as on those who remained in the community.*

The process of forced migration began in earnest when the corregidor *or his representative notified a community and their* kuraka *of their obligation to serve in the Villa Imperial (Potosí) and the date of their departure. The* kuraka *was normally required to bring his people to a designated point of departure. In the case of Pomacanche, this was the central plaza; near Quiquijana, there was a special location—Antucota Pampa—where people gathered.*

The second document addressed the provisions the mitayos *and their families took with them. The* kuraka *was responsible for making sure that his people traveled with enough goods, such as* coca, *to support their journey to—and hopefully some of their stay in—Potosí.*

One of the most serious consequences of the mita *was the separation of families. Children from rural Cuzco often accompanied their parents to Potosí, but this was not always the case. Communities—and the parents within them— had different customs. Some took their children, whereas others did not. When the contingent from Papres departed in 1687, many* mitayo *couples left their children behind: Agustin Quispe and his wife bid farewell to three children; Mateo Masi and Isabel Poco had to leave "one young* (tierno) *son"; and Melchor Canaya, who had been selected as a backup worker* (remuda), *and his wife, Juana Caya, left two "hijos tiernos." A list of* mitayos *from Papres does not mention children either being left behind or going. In the same year, twenty-one* mitayos *from Acopia included no children accompanying their parents to Potosí, whereas the same document recorded that couples from Pomacanche had children with them. Pedro Chuchocane and his wife, Juana Micayla, took their two sons—ages seven and nine—and Gabriel Quispe and Ysabel Ticlla took one child. In a 1689 survey of parishes in Quispicanchis and Canas y Canchis, some priests mentioned the Potosí* mita, *and others did not. Almost all of those who did, such as those of Sicuani, Langui, Layo, San Pedro de Cacha, and San Pablo de Cacha, noted that the families accompanied the men.* Mitayos *from Cuzco almost never went alone. Thus, the* mita *was, in reality, a family* mita. *If there was no spouse, another female was often sent to accompany the* mitayo. *When Diego Choque left Pomacanche for Potosí, his mother went with him. When Juan Pacha departed from Sangarará, the-eight-year-old daughter of Aria Rosa was sent along to assist him.*

The third document discusses the compliance of the communities of Canas y Canchis and Quispicanchis with the mita *and compares them to the nearby province of Chuquito. The peoples of Canas y Canchis and Quispicanchis strictly complied with the imposed colonial obligation of* mita *service, unlike the peoples of Chuquito. This is especially interesting because the* mitayos *were to be paid for their travel to and from Potosí. Payment* (leguaje) *was, however, a matter of continual contention—not only between* mitayos *and miners, but also between the Crown and the mining sector. Despite repeated royal orders, colonial officials lacked the will, or perhaps the power, to enforce payment. Because it was against the Crown's interests to suspend the* mita *if the* leguaje *was not paid, the position of those authorities who were inclined to enforce payment was weakened. Thus, the* leguaje, *instituted to help* mitayos *and those left behind to survive, was nonexistent or inconsistent for most of the colonial period. For Cuzqueño* mitayos *this meant that one half year of service—three months each way—typically went uncompensated. As seen in the petition of Tupac Amaru concerning the* mita, *in the late 1770s mine owners were still avoiding the payment of* leguaje.

In addition to the other difficulties, the sheer distance to Potosí was a significant problem. A Sicuani priest reported that the number of community members continued to decline: "It is rare that [the mitayos *and their families] return for lack of provisions and for the very great distance that they are from Potosí and because the Royal ordinances are not complied with." Mitayos were supposed to serve one year in Potosí, but the great distance and travel time influenced the communities of Canas y Canchis and some other distant regions to develop a policy of two years of service. Thus, the burdens and separations forced on the peoples who came from villages in these provinces were even greater than for those who lived closer to the Cerro Rico. A Canas y Canchis priest, sensitive to the impact of colonial exactions and abuses, complained that the communities were "dissipated" by pressures from* corregidores *"and principally the* mita *of Potosí, where each two years they dispatch from each parish more than twenty Indians, that are entire families." For all of these reasons, it is no wonder that Tupac Amaru tried to lift the burden of the* mita *from his people.*

Document 1: *Mita* Workers Leave for Potosí

The Indians that go to Potosí and its refining mills leave their homeland with great mournfulness. . . . The day of their departure is very sad . . . [After mass] they pay [the priest] in order to entreat from them all-powerful success in their journey. Then they leave for the plaza accompanied by their parents, relatives and friends; and hugging each other with many tears and sobs, they say goodbye. Followed by their wives and children, they take to the road preoccupied with their suffering and depression. The doleful and melancholy nature of this scene is augmented by the drums and the bells that begin to signal supplications.

Document 2: List of Goods Taken by *Mitayos* to Potosí from Pomachape

Goods Taken to Potosí by Indians of Pomachape

Name	Goods Taken to Potosí
1. Joseph Lope, *capitán de mita* and Josepha Asensia	6 llamas loaded with *chuño,* wheat, corn, *coca* and shelter (*toldo*).
2. Joan Vilca Poma, with *enterador*	3 llamas loaded with corn, *chuño,* wheat, a *burrico coca* and shelter.
3. Martin Choque, *cédula* and Josepha Malque	6 llamas loaded with corn, *chuño,* wheat, *coca* and shelter.
4. Joseph Alvarado, *cédula* and Teresa Sisa	4 llamas loaded with corn, *chuño,* wheat, *coca* and shelter.
5. Joan de Mendoza, *cédula* and Jacoba Poco	5 llamas loaded with corn, *chuño,* wheat, *coca* and shelter.

Document 3: Spanish Evaluation of Community Compliance with the *Mita*

Reputation for *Mita* Delivery in Cuzco and Chuquito

Community and Province	*Mita Ordinaria* (number of *mitayos*)	*Buenos, Medianos, Malos*
Canas del Cuzco		
Siquane	19	*buenos*
Singa y Lurucache	15	*buenos*
Marangani	5	*buenos*
Coporaque	11	*buenos*
Yaure	31	*medianos*
Checasupa	15	*buenos*
Layosupa	11	*buenos*
Pichigua	43	*medianos*
Cacha	17	*buenos*
Charrachape	2	*buenos*
Ancocaba	1	*bueno*
Llanguisupa	12	*buenos*
	185	
Tinta Canches		
Checacupi	21	*buenos*
Cangalla	5	*buenos*

(*continued*)

Community and Province	*Mita Ordinaria* (number of *mitayos*)	*Buenos, Medianos, Malos*
Tinta Canches	24	*buenos*
Combapata	7	*buenos*
Combapata de D. Ant.	5	*buenos*
Yanaoca	29	*buenos*
	91	
Canches Quispillactas (Quispicanchis)		
Pomacanche de Rios	19	*medianos*
Pomacanche de P. Arias	6	*buenos*
Sangarará	13	*buenos*
Collopata	8	*buenos*
Acopia	7	*buenos*
	53	
Chuquito		
Chuquitos	116	*medianos*
Acora	90	*buenos*
Hilave	83	*medianos*
Jule	105	*medianos*
Pomata	93	*malos*
Yunguyo	61	*malos*
Cepita	70	*malos*
	618	

[*WOTA,* 174–76, 182–83].

17. A Communal Strategy to Maintain Compliance with the *Mita* and Other Demands

The mita *did great harm to the communities, but at the same time the* naturales *in Quispicanchis and Canas y Canchis developed strategies to preserve their communities and minimize the damage of the* mita *as much as they could, while forcing people to render this obligation to the Crown. The degree to which they succeeded is evidence not only of their tremendous will to maintain their communal way of life but of their ingenuity. Using the legal system, the* naturales *denounced abusive treatment in Potosí and attempted to abolish* mita *service entirely, as witnessed in the actions of Tupac Amaru. This was often done with the support of Spaniards in the home provinces who did not benefit*

from the mita *and saw it as a diminishment of their labor pool. A priest of
Yanaoca (Canas y Canchis) argued the case against the* mita *more succinctly:
"Your Excellency the state in which these miserable Indians are found most
probably [is] caused by said* mita. *"*

Complaints by Canas y Canchis caciques against the mita *in the 1700s
mirrored those made two centuries earlier. The travel stipend, or* leguaje, *was
not being paid. People had to sell many of their goods just to provision themselves for the journey. When they returned to their communities, nothing
awaited them—"Their houses [were] destroyed, their fields . . . [were] un-
cultivated"—except the "payment of five or six* tercios *[tribute for two and
one-half or three years] that they have fallen behind during their absence in
Potosí." The caciques continued to be charged tribute and, one of them argued,
"[as] we caciques do not have the means to replace this money, it is necessary to
charge them [the* mitayos] *upon their return. This is the cause why more do not
return to their Pueblos remaining vagabonds." Such situations hardly enhanced
communal solidarity or goodwill for the* corregidor; *however, they were beneficial to the state's treasury. In addition to tribute problems,* kurakas, *like the
priests, complained that those* mitayos *who did come home often suffered from
pain, lung problems, injured chests, were unfit for work, and died within a
short time.*

The caciques of Canas y Canchis summed up their despair over the mita,
*and their desire for government help to change policies, in the first few lines
of their petition when they wrote: "The caciques of the entire province of Tinta
in voice and name of our respective communities . . . say that when evils frequently become unbearable, hope has no other asylum than the recourse, and
the humble representation of them, to our superiors."*

Although individual colonial officials sympathized with the naturales, *or
perhaps supported them for their own reasons, Crown policy maintained the*
mita *throughout the colonial period. The communities of rural Cuzco continued to complain about the* mita *until it was finally abolished amid the turmoil
of colonial rebellion in 1812.*

To ensure compliance with the mita *and other governmental demands under
these difficult circumstances, the* naturales *of* ayllu *Suio in Sicuani developed a
strategy to govern their communal lives. Thus,* ayllu *Suio used the Potosí* mita
*and other demands that threatened solidarity to strengthen the community by
turning compliance into steps on a ladder that led to positions of honor within
the community. They protected their social reproduction and safeguarded their
compact with the king and state through internal and agreed-on means. The following document, from after the great rebellion, gives a sense of the effort and
strategy used by communities to stay on good terms with the colonial government. When this commitment was eroded by excessive demands, as happened almost two decades before this document was written, rebellion became possible.*

That being the ancient and established custom we gather every year in a certain place that we are accustomed, in the semester of San Juan, in order to deal with the things pertaining to the Service of God, of the King, and the public good, and on the same day we elect from one year to another the officials of Alcalde, Seconds, Captain *enterador, cédulas,* and the other obligations. . . . [In the *mita*] we are subject to go first as *cédulas,* [and then as] *enteradores,* this is after serving the personal obligations and menial positions (*serviles*) of Second, local mita service, mail carrier . . . and the rest . . . all of these obligations serve as steps for us . . . [and those who complete them can then fill] the honorific posts that distinguish loyal and true subjects of Your Majesty. [*WOTA,* 201–2]

18. A Priest from Quispicanchis Gives an Account of the *Reparto*

In the mid-1750s, the Bourbon government legalized and set quotas for what had been an informal system of forced distribution of goods to indigenous peoples and, in some instances, to mestizos, criollos, *and Spaniards as well. The idea was to force indigenous people to participate more fully in the European economy either by forcing them to work for the Spanish or by producing goods for Spanish consumption to pay for goods brought in from the outside, which the indigenous people were then forced to buy. Sometimes these goods were useful, but often they were not.*

The reparto *was also disliked because the goods sold often cost much more than the market price for the same materials. Thus, merchants in centers like Lima, who had the ear of government officials, supported the local* corregidores *in the business of the* reparto. *People could not refuse what was offered, and, if they did not pay, they might find themselves in jail or in a textile sweatshop trying to work off what they "owed." The* reparto *became a leading cause of complaint in the period before the great rebellion, as individuals and communities resisted or complained about being "forced" consumers and all that this implied for their freedom and the way they lived. To provide a modern example, imagine that the state sponsored a private company—such as Sears or Macy's or Ace Hardware—that came to your home and forced you to buy goods you may or may not have use for, at prices that were higher than their normal sale value, knowing that the state would jail you or put you to work at hard labor if you didn't pay for the goods in full within a few months.*

Right after the *corregidores* arrive in any town of their province, they send their servants to the *alcaldes* and *alguaciles* so that they will, from house to house and hacienda to hacienda, notify Spaniards and Indians (of whom they have a list) to come and present themselves in front of them to get the *repartimiento,* and their cashiers distribute them not the items that they have asked for but whatever they want to give them, without even telling them nor negotiating the prices with them, they give them the bundles and write down the amounts owed. They [*corregidores*] break the tariffs set by law, that having been told that [the *repartimiento*] should not be more than 140,000 pesos, mules and clothes included, in this province of Quispicanchi during their five years in office, it is well known that one distributed more than 300,000 pesos, and that this could not have been possible without excessively charging provincial Indians and Spaniards. The source of this is that the tariff is assigned by province and then nobody knows how much each of the villages in the *repartimiento* has to be allocated. [*WOTA,* 216]

19. Tupac Amaru and Troubles over the *Reparto* with Geronymo Cano, *Cobrador* (Tax Collector)

It was not just through the exploitation of poorer community members that Tupac Amaru experienced the oppression and greed of the forced sale of goods known as the reparto. *Even in his position as a relatively well-to-do* kuraka, *he experienced difficulties meeting payments. Many others were also aggravated by not receiving the goods they had to pay for, or by getting goods that were not needed. Although the* corregidor *was in charge of the* reparto, *someone who worked for the* corregidor *usually was directly responsible for the distribution of goods and the collection of payment. In the following case, it was a tax collector named Cano who aggravated Tupac Amaru. Many* cobradores *were harsh in their methods of collection, verbally and physically abusing people or having them sentenced to hard labor to work off debts. In the following document, Tupac Amaru complains of not getting the materials he was supposed to receive, and then having the* cobrador *take extra monies or goods as well.*

Demand against Mr. Geronymo Cano.
I, Sr. Joseph Tupac Amaru, *Cacique Principal* and Governor of the Town of Pampamarca of this Province of Canas y Canchis, appear before you by right,

and express that Mr. Geronymo Cano, collector of the *Repartimiento* of this Province, had noted in the book of the *repartimiento* that he had given me two and one-half *arrobas* [one *arroba* equals 25 pounds] of iron at six and a half *reales* per pound, or what amounted to fifty pesos and six *reales:* which belonged to General Gregorio Viana, *Corregidor* who was from this Province and by whose order I was being charged those fifty pesos and six *reales.* Mr. Baltazar Calvo (a collector who worked for Cano) collected this amount with notable efficiency, even without my having received the aforementioned iron. This I paid only to avoid the embarrassment of the prison term with which he was threatening me. And due to this wickedness he [Cano] owes me those fifty pesos and six *reales.*

He also owes me 150 pesos in rent for the land belonging to the *Casicasgo* [estate] that I was given by Your Majesty. . . . [E]ven though it is customary that when a new *Cacique* starts in office he needs to harvest the produce available to help defray the costs of his office, you determined that the above mentioned Mr. Geronymo Cano should harvest the produce so that the tribute could be paid, and that I would only charge for the renting of the land. Without regard to such just determinations, he nonetheless cashed for himself those 150 pesos, if not more . . . and that with the 50 pesos and six *reales* cited above, he owes me 200 pesos and six *reales.*

In addition he took six loads from the harvest of the potatoes that I planted, valued at more than sixty pesos and he should have informed me of this. He took them with him, as if daring me, a deed witnessed by past *Alcaldes,* to whom I will protest; these together amount to an additional sixty pesos. [Taken all together] the three complaints amount to 260 pesos, six *reales.* This sum is sufficient for you to order an embargo on all the goods and properties that apparently belong to the said Geronymo Cano of the town of Tungasuca, and some of his potato harvest, so that I can be fully reimbursed for the entire amount . . . and that a date should be fixed so that those items be put under the custody of a trusted person until the transactions and auctions of same can proceed.

Thus, I ask and beg you, based on what I have presented, that you order this restitution be made as it is fair and legal, and I swear before God and the [Holy] Cross that what I have charged against Sr. Geronymo Cano is certain and truthful,

Joseph Tupac Amaru [*CDIP,* 6. 1768]

20. A Tupac Amaru Proclamation Concerning the *Reparto*

One of the efforts undertaken by Tupac Amaru was to win the support of those who would benefit from the changes he proposed, such as ending the hated reparto. However, due to doubts about the success of the rebellion or about joining the rebellion, not all indigenous people were quick to follow the rebel leader's admonitions. In the following proclamation, the liberation from colonial exactions carried with it an implied threat that the indigenous people must support the insurrectionary program or face the consequences.

Don José Gabriel Tupac Amaru, ["From:] Don Joseph Inca of Royal Blood, descended from the principal trunk of the Royal Family Tree. It has come to my attention that the inhabitants from the *doctrina* [parish] of Asillo have not yet participated . . . in the enterprise that I have at hand, which is to remove all the encumbrances coming from the *reparto,* taxes, customs and other perverse impositions. To this end, it is beneficial that all should be willing to help me by joining my troops, so that we can apprehend the *corregidores,* and all those who are their allies, so that we can give them sentences that match their Deeds; for it was they who oppressed the provinces with their *repartos.* And, if scorning my reasoning, they do not comply with my decisions, I will make them pay for their omission with their lives, as I am working for their own good and commissioning Don Genonimo [*sic*] Guampo Tupa and Don Francisco Diaz to explain [to the people] what I have verbally communicated to them. Done in Ayaviri. On December 6th, 1780.

Don José Gabriel Tupac Amaru, Inca [*CDIP,* 93. 1780-XII-6]

21. Proclamation Published in Lima to Take the *Repartimientos* away from the *Corregidores*

Spanish officials, alarmed by the rebellion and aware of the continual complaints against the reparto *and the frequent abuses of those who profited in one way or another from the* reparto, *acted quickly to end this system of forced sale of goods. Undoubtedly, the royalist officials hoped that this lessening of their burden would deter indigenous people from joining the rebellion, or induce some of those who had rebelled to abandon the uprising.*

Don Agustín de Jáuregui and Co. Taking into consideration the pity with which our Catholic King, mindful of the well-being and utility of the Indians of this Kingdom, gave permission and license to the *Corregidores* and Governors . . . of the Provinces to distribute *repartimientos* to said natives. [The *reparto* consisted] of mules, clothing, and other items that were needed for their traffic and commerce, to cultivate their crops, and other necessary items for their clothing and comfort; under [the conditions that] assure the liberty of the Indians in this type of transaction, the legitimacy of the prices, and the fairness in collecting them. To this end a Board of *Oidores* [Judges] of the Royal *Audiencia* was created in order to set the tariffs or taxes so that those items that were distributed in each Province, according to their need and convenience as well as the prices to be charged, without exceeding . . . [need or price] under grave penalties. And just in case said *Corregidores* might commit abuse or excess might as to the quantity or quality of the items, or over their value, or the mode of collection; this Royal *Audiencia* should be informed so that it can compensate the natives. And even though all safeguards that seem just and convenient . . . have been set in place by the Supreme Government and said Tribunals to enforce them, the favorable effects promised and expected by these regulations have not been effective. Much to the contrary, the *Naturales* have experienced generally dark consequences through the abuses the *Corregidores* have imposed on them, causing grave harm and damage to the Indios themselves, who were supposed to benefit from the supposed safeguards. For these reasons . . . and taking into consideration all the matters expressed in the tribunal, it was unanimously agreed to . . . extinguish all *repartimientos* of all the *Corregidores*. Thus, I declare that from now on all *repartimientos* should be abolished and extinguished and considered to be so in all the provinces of this Kingdom. And it is ordered that not one of them try to carry on [the *reparto*] under any circumstance; in small or large quantity, nor for any items or things even though they might claim that they are useful to the Indians of their jurisdiction, or are given for a very small price, or are distributed following their wishes, their consent or their request. None of these actions, or any others whatsoever, will excuse a transgression, nor will they exempt any of them from losing their jobs, their property and anything else that might be deemed necessary depending on the circumstances. Penalties will be enforced against any *Corregidor* or Governor who shall serve in the provinces of this Kingdom if it can be proven that they imposed a *repartimiento* on the Indians. Only those who have concluded a *repartimiento* or have it mid-way are allowed to finish it and collect what is just, with the precise understanding that there will be no abuses, excesses, or harm done towards the Indians. Transgressions will be examined and severely punished by a court of this Royal Audience composed by ministers that I will name, who are professionals who know about these matters and will compensate the Indians so that justice may be done and pity expressed to them. . . . Any new *Corregidor* entering the provincial government must know that they will not be able to benefit from the *repartimiento*. . . . And so that this information can be distributed to all, it should be published in all cities, pueblos and villages of this Kingdom and enough copies are to be printed so that the *Corregidores* and Justices can be given sufficient copies to affix in public and customary places to this end. Dated in the City of Kings of Peru on December 9th, 1780.

—Don Agustín de Jáuregui
—By order of his Excellency, my Lord.
—Simón de Dolarea [*CDIP,* 99. 1780-XII-9]

22. Edict Due to the Revolt of José Gabriel Tupac Amaru to End the *Repartimientos* and Some Other Established Contributions

Officials in Cuzco were especially concerned with neutralizing indigenous sympathy for the rebellion as much as they could, and with making appeals to mestizos and other castas to support the loyalist effort. In the following document, produced just days after the execution of Arriaga, the corregidor *of Cuzco and the Junta de Guerra make it clear that the* reparto *is to be done away with. At the same time, they encourage people to engage in trade by removing certain fees and hindrances, because they know that their survival depends on the supply of food as well as their military force. They also abolish various taxes. The officials appeal to a sense of loyalty to the Crown—as well as to faith—to keep people in line. Additionally, they offer amnesty to the rebels and encourage people to join their military forces.*

I, Dn. Fernando Ynclan y Valdes, Knight of the Order of Santiago, Lieutenant Captain General, *Corregidor* and *Justicia Mayor* of this great city of Cuzco and its jurisdiction, for the sake of your Majesty. I say: As it is of the utmost importance to sustain by any means available to us the Catholic Faith that we all profess due to God's almighty mercy, as good Christians we profess to live and die by it [our faith] . . . worshiping the Divine Cult and sacred images that, as we all know, have been desecrated by José Gabriel Tupac Amaru and his allies. [This] fact can be verified by the events that took place in the Church of the Pueblo of Sangarará, which with disrespect and notorious irreverence was set on fire even while the Sacred Sacraments were there and it was polluted with all the blood of those who were inside and in its Doors and Cemetery and were . . . wounded or killed on the 18th of said month, by a multitude of people who attacked the Spaniards. . . . This being a crime of detestable nature and therefore banned and punished by Canonic and Royal Laws with heavy penalties, which said Tupac Amaru . . . is deserving, as well as those who collaborated in the sacrilegious activities. . . . [B]earing in mind that said Tupac Amaru has raised the Pueblo of Tungasuca in rebellion and conspired against our Lord the King (God save him), his operations give ample proof of his criminal actions. . . . [He also] put *Corregidor* Dn. Antonio Arriaga to death . . . and is planning to execute others. Hidden behind the mask of piety, he has offered to free the Indians of that Province from tributes, . . . and sales taxes, customs and other contributions, without having the authority to do so, and using the supposition that he has superior orders for which he has not produced any proof nor will be able to do so.

Therefore I should order, and I do order, that this Edict be published as a Notice of War so that the news reach everybody, not only in this City and District but in all Provinces subject to its Royal Treasury, doing this in the name of the King our Lord, so that all Indios and other provincials will defend, as is expected, the Dominions against the Rebel and his followers by any means available so as to make clear their loyalty and faithful adherence to the Sovereign. And taking into consideration the piety and benevolence with which these Indians have been treated by our Catholic King, as his Laws and Royal Ordinances attest, we protest in his Royal Name that their privileges are being punctually and exactly safeguarded through the compliance of His Majesty's decision of not having them pay the tithes in this episcopate. This was done in accordance with the rulings of the . . . Royal *Audiencia* of Lima and later confirmed by His Majesty, and as it is attested in the books of this municipal council. Moreover, they will also be free immediately from the *Corregidores' repartimientos* and will not need to pay for anything those *Corregidores* have distributed to them, and will not, under any circumstance, be imprisoned in Obrajes. . . . [T]he *Mestizos* are promised the benefit of not having to pay taxes, nor custom charges, and that they will benefit from this freedom and exemption as well as their children and their children's descendants.

. . . [T]hose who cooperated in the present excesses are pardoned and given general Amnesty. They will not be prosecuted in any way and will not be treated as rebels, but those who label themselves as rebels . . . will pay with their lives. Finally, they [the Indians] will be given a new distribution of lands and they will be given enough land so as to be able to support themselves, having experts supervising the distribution and assisted by appointed Protectors. All this will be approved by our Excellency the Viceroy of these Kingdoms, the Lords of the Royal *Audiencia,* and the *Visitador General* without any discussions. And this will be confirmed by our Lord the King as his royal intention is to benefit his Subjects from whom he expects them to show their courage and strength to catch the Rebels so that our armies have the laurel of victory, for our glory, the good of the nation, and in service to God and our King. And this edict will be made known to the Royal Officials so that they will not, under any circumstance, charge taxes or custom duties to the Indians and *Mestizos*. They (the Indians and *Mestizos*) can bring their loads and commercial products coming from their harvests, husbandry, and farming so that they can sell them. The Guards of the *Visita* and *Camineros* are to be made aware of what has been agreed to so that they allow these loads to come in freely, without causing or charging the most minimal expenditure under penalty of death. Thus, I, the present *Corregidor*, have provided, ordered, and signed with the approval of the members of the War Council who also signed it in the said City of Cuzco on the 20th of November of 1780, which I attest. And in this situation the said *Corregidor*, after consulting with the Council also ordered it to be published that all those *Mestizos* and other peoples who would enlist under the Banners of the King be paid a daily salary of two *reales* or more, depending on the rank they are given, as is being done with all those who are presently working for them and in the service of the King. Don Fernando Ynclan y Valdes, Don Marco Antonio de la Camara y Escudero, Don Sebastian Josef de Ocampo, Dn. Miguel Torrejon, Dn. Joaquin Calcarcel, Don Pedro Josef Veles, Dn. Francisco Javier Olleta, Dn. Josef de Saldivar y Saavedra, Dn. Matias Baulen, Dn. Ysydro Guizasola. By orders of their Mercies, Miguel de Acuña notary public and of His Majesty. [*CDIP,* 77. 1780-XI-20]

IV. The Breakdown of the Colonial Order

23. The *Kuraka* of Lurucache, Canas y Canchis, Abuses His Community

One of the factors that caused tensions in the indigenous villages was the mistreatment and exploitation of community members by the kuraka *(cacique). Although this was not nearly as common in Quispicanchis and Canas y Canchis as it was in the regions that rebelled in Alto Peru (Bolivia), there certainly were cases of abuse. One of the* caciques *from Canas y Canchis who abused the people under his control was Santos Mamani of Lurucache. Prior to being elevated to the position of* kuraka, *Mamani had been accused of mistreating people; after he was appointed to office, over two dozen community members signed a formal complaint against him, protesting the abuse they received. However, not all community members were opposed to Mamani, which muddied the situation for those who heard the case at the time (and for those trying to understand it later).*

Kurakas *played favorites or had power and support among at least some of the people in the community, but many members of the community argued that Mamani was not really one of them. They argued that he was a* cholo *(an Indian who dressed and acted like a nonindigenous person) whose parents were* forasteros *(not from the community and therefore without the traditional rights and obligations community membership implied). A Spaniard's testimony supported the opinion of the community to a degree, but the Spaniard also stated that Mamani's father had been a* cacique *even though he should not have held the position because he was a* forastero*. The situation became further confused when another witness testified that Mamani's mother had been the daughter of a* cacique*, which could have served as the basis for Mamani's claim to the position.*

Community members also denied Mamani's right to be cacique *on the basis of his not having served in the communal offices that would make him eligible for such a high position. They argued that Mamani never served in the community's forced labor rotation in the Potosí* mita—*this "being a custom among us"—nor did he fulfill other communal obligations. They also complained that Mamani had "done us much harm [and] does not treat us as God orders." However, Mamani had been elevated to the position of* kuraka *by Lima officials when he had presented papers—claimed by the community to be false—that supported his right to be* kuraka *during the absence of the* cacique *principal, Miguel Copa. Copa was in Potosí serving as the* mita *captain. Reparaz, a normally judicious* corregidor *of Canas y Canchis, was in office when Mamani presented his claim. After Mamani's appointment to office, Copa argued that Reparaz favored his rival, whom Copa referred to as "cholo baca (vaca, or cow) Mamani." This dispute continued even after Arriaga became* corregidor.

Lima officials, despite the irregularities and reports of beatings and assaults, upheld Mamani as kuraka*. Arriaga, however, sided with the people of Lurucache against Mamani. Thus, in this case, the* corregidor *who was the enemy of Tupac Amaru supported the community against an abusive* kuraka*. Ironically, less than half a year before Arriaga was hanged, he informed his superiors that it was "necessary to apply opportune measures for the public tranquility because the community resists Mamani." To accomplish this, Arriaga undermined Mamani's power by appointing two* ayllu *members trusted by the people of Lurucache—both from the Copa family—to serve as tax collectors.*

The following account gives a good indication of the degree to which relations between the kuraka *and community broke down during this period.*

He tries to martyr us with whips, rocks, and clubs, beating widows and married women like men. He encourages his wife, mother and son to kill us. To even say *buenos días* to him, it is necessary for one to approach him with *aguardiente*. . . . He takes the bread from out of our mouths. . . . Regarding the distribution of lands, we do not know if we have land to work or not. Whoever has sufficient *aguardiente* is owner of the lands . . . his accountant . . . is a boy who knows nothing . . . and treats older men with disrespect. To remedy this situation, we ask the great favor of Our Majesty that Don Juan Paulino de Andia be our *Casique Y Governador* in order that he put us all in peace and quietude and that we may not be like cats and dogs in one single *ayllu*. [*WOTA*, 231–32]

24. Causes of the Rebellion: Letter from Viceroy Vértiz to Gálvez, April 30, 1781

In the following letter, the viceroy of Río de la Plata, Juan José de Vértiz y Salcedo, sends his thoughts about the uprisings in Peru and Alto Peru to Inspector José María de Gálvez. Although this letter was written during the rebellion, the reflections acknowledge the belief, or at least the suspicion, that great injustices existed in many aspects of colonial life and that these led to the uprisings, especially the "audacious inhumanity that perhaps has no previous example." At the same time, like rulers everywhere, the viceroy is also suspicious of outside influences that might have led to such serious problems for the colonies of Spain in the Andes. The viceroy was well aware of Spain's rivals in Europe, and he was concerned about foreign evildoers who sought to cause problems for the Spanish Crown.

It is certain that Religion, Vassalage, Society, and who knows how many sacred observances we ought to consider to have been trampled on with audacious inhumanity that perhaps has no previous example: for the same reason I have repeated in my strict Orders so that there be inquiries into the cause of each particular action, and of all the rest in common, and with special care if they have root in some foreign influence that caused such disorder.

The innovation of registering *Cholos* y *Zambos* also had its influence: this subject has always caused serious revolutions in the Kingdom. . . . [*RTA*, 719–20]

25. The Rebellious Indians Are of Jewish Ancestry

Spanish feelings of anti-Semitism were nurtured in the long period of the reconquest. The year 1492 not only saw the New World "discovered" and the last Muslim outpost in Iberia defeated, it also saw the forced conversion to Catholicism—or flight—of Jews in Spain. These feelings were all too prominent in the actions of the Inquisition and in the rhetoric of daily life, even in the Americas. Many people saw in the actions and behaviors of the indigenous people characteristics that they attributed to Jews. Others wondered if the Indians were not the lost tribe of Israel. This speculation about the Jewish origins of Indians was ancient, but, as early as the late sixteenth century, Father Acosta—in Book I, Chapter 23 of his Natural and Moral History of the Indies—*argued against this notion of indigenous origins. However, it never fully went away. As European fear of the indigenous people grew, negative comparisons between Jews and Indians came more into the open. Such was the case with the Tupac Amaru rebellion and the Europeans' efforts to understand it, as is made clear by the following document.*

One of the most common and well-founded beliefs is that these *Naturales* [Indians] are descended from the Jews (*Hebreos*), as you can see in the famous work of Father Garcia Dominicano whose title is *Origin of the Indians*. [In that work] he learnedly does away with all objections that might be raised against it. There he makes a very detailed parallel between the customs of these [Indians] and those of them [the Jews]; [such as] the similarity of the uses, tenses, and even the expressions of their language [and then] proceeding ultimately and with detail to the force, ingratitude, brutality and idolatry that was seen in those unhappy ones [Jews], and that the sacred text [Bible] makes clear. [*RTA*, 724]

26. Strict Orders to Prevent
the Introduction of the *History of America*
by Robertson into the Río de la Plata

Officials of the Spanish Crown, disagreeing with and wary of the potential impact of interpretations that differed from the official version of the Spanish "discovery" and colonization of the New World, sought to prohibit the entry of the History of America *by William Robertson into the colonies. The Spanish were not unaware of the impact ideas had in some of the British colonies in North America that were already engaged in a war of independence with their mother country. This was just one of several measures taken prior to the rebellion to control the distribution of ideas and histories that were seen as contrary to the best interests of Spain.*

His Excellency the Viceroy of these Provinces indicates the following in his letter dated 7th of the current month.

His Excellency Don Joseph de Galvez, in a letter dated December 23rd of the current year, indicates the following: Dr. Guillermo Rober[t]son, Provost of the University of Edinburgh and Chronicler of Scotland has written, and published in the English language, the history of the discovery of America; the King having just reasons for not wanting that work to be introduced in Spain nor its Indies, has resolved that, with the utmost rigor and care, the shipment of this work to the Americas and the Philippines should be prevented, as well as any translation already published or published in the future. And that in the event that some copies may have already made it in to some of the ports or other places, or may have already been introduced on land, that they should be stopped and seized. . . . I inform you of this Royal order so that your Excellency can take the necessary, austere, and most convenient provisions in that Jurisdiction so that the order be complied with. This Royal Order is transmitted to Your Excellency in order for you to expedite it in the most efficient and conducive ways for its compliance in the jurisdiction of which you are in charge.

Whose contents I inform you of so that you can help me, with the utmost zeal, comply with . . . the order.

May the Lord protect you. Montevideo, June 18th, 1779.

Joachín del Pino
M.I.C. *Justicia y Regimiento de esta Ciudad.* [*RTA,* 783]

27. Decree by the King of Spain to Prevent a French Book with Ideas Contrary to the Catholic Faith and Good Government

History of America *was not the only book that was banned from the territories of Spain. The prior year, the king banned a French book that was apparently published in England. The king made note of the book's attack on the Catholic faith and the legitimacy of monarchical government and its promotion of freedom and independence. The king ordered that strict measures be taken to prevent the book from entering the dominions of the Spanish monarch. Thus, the king, leery of the ideas of the Enlightenment that had influenced the British North American colonies, sought to prevent such contagion from gaining a foothold in his American colonies.*

Royal Decree of April 20th, 1778, with the order of "publicly burning at the hands of the executioner" all the copies of a book in French that promotes the "freedom and independence of the legitimate subjects from their legitimate Monarchs and Lords."

Having surely and without a doubt understood the reports that a book written in French has been introduced in my Royal Dominions, with the title *The Year Two Thousand, Four Hundred and Forty* [2440] with a date of publication of seventeen seventy six [1776], in London, without an author's name, nor publisher, which not only attacks the Catholic Religion and the most sacred [aspects] of it, but also tries to destroy the order of good Government, the authority of the magistrates, the rights of the sovereign, promoting freedom and independence for the subjects from their legitimate Monarchs and Lords. I have decided that, besides banning this perverse book through the Holy Office [the Inquisition], all copies found should be publicly burned by the hand of the executioner. That very great care be observed to not allow any copies of such pernicious work through any port or most remote confine of my Dominion, and that all measures dictated by moderation and the rule of proper government should be taken to preserve my Catholic States from this pest. For if not stopped in time, it will carry with it the most pitiful detriments. To this end I have ordered my Council of the Indies, through the Royal Order of March 12th of the current year, to issue a circular Order to those Kingdoms so that they can comply with my royal Resolution. It is for this reason that I order my Viceroys, my Presidents of *Audiencias,* the Governors and other Judges and Ministers whom it should concern, that they keep it, guard it, execute it, and comply with it and carry it out punctually in all of their corresponding charge. For which they will issue the necessary orders for its precise and punctual observance. Dated in Aranjuez, April 20th, 1778.

I, the King. [*RTA*, 782–83]

28. Letter Written by the *Hacendados* of the City of Arequipa Complaining about the Administrator of Customs, Sr. Don Juan Baptista Pando

As part of the larger policy of reforms initiated by the Bourbons during the eighteenth century that upset so many indigenous—as well as nonindigenous— peoples, customhouses were established in the Andes to collect more taxes in a more efficient manner. In the process, customs duties were raised not once but twice within a short period prior to the rebellion. In addition, indigenous people were forced to pay duties on items they produced that had long been exempt from taxes, such as the weavings from their small-scale textile production centers (chorillos). *This created a voice of protest that, if not exactly united, came from many different sectors of society. One of the regions in which the protest was greatest and in which violence broke out prior to the Tupac Amaru rebellion was Arequipa. The following document by citizens of Arequipa complains about the policies of the head of the Arequipa customhouse, Juan Baptista Pando.*

Honorable Sir,
Sir,
The involvement of all the principal citizens of this city in the public cause of containing the excesses of the plebeians has delayed this representation, whereby we protest against the Administrator of the Royal Customs. He has imposed an executive order on us, where in addition to the new Tax that your Excellency ordered to help finance the War against Portugal, we have to pay six percent on all the products of the vineyards and sugar cane fields. . . . When asked by the deputies of the open town council meeting [*Cav(b)ildo abierto*] that was organized (of which your Excellency should already have information) for the authorization of the powers he claimed, he indicated that all of them were in accord with the new printed Regulations. But these do not authorize his use of those powers and it is of this excess that we wish to inform

you, and complain about, so that you can impose on said Administrator the punishment that Your Excellency deems appropriate. At the same time, we also beg Your Excellency, with all due respect, that we be considered with respect while taxing our properties. We are loyal Subjects of our Sovereign, we regard him with the law and respect owed to his Sovereignty, and we gladly risk our lives out of love for his name. Moreover, Your Excellency, we, the citizens of this City, are not able, nor does this place permit us, to conduct businesses other than those of our haciendas. These are already loaded down with too many economic burdens (rents, annuities, *censos*). It would be very difficult to find one that does not have an annuity that is over half of its value. The yields [of the haciendas] normally are much smaller than those of Moquegua and Mages; and some years so small that we are forced to raise the rent . . . to satisfy the *censos* and to not lose the land through foreclosure and auction. Our families are larger than in any other regions of this Kingdom. We citizens, for the most part married, normally have some six, ten or twelve children. We leave to the consideration of Your Excellency how much is needed for their precise education and instruction; protesting to Your Excellency only that we are overwhelmed by the weight [of our obligations]. All the clerics and priests of this Kingdom who are Arequipeños are witnesses to the truth of this. . . .

The haciendas, as well as vineyards and cane plantations alike, are in fact small. They are not measured in *fanegas* [land needed to sow 1.5 bushels of seed] as in other areas, but in *topos*. There are only seven cane plantations, the biggest has forty *topos* of [sugar cane] for grinding. . . . These, Sir, are not exaggerations that we are inventing for our King, but realities that we will prove so that Your Excellency may be served. Your Excellency will now contemplate how our spirit is being oppressed by the deeds of this administrator [of the customhouse]. We always maintain hope that, even though our sovereign is far away, his love and pity are close to us . . . that your subjects' just complaints will be heard. And we pray to God that God will protect him for many years. [*CDIP,* 46. 1780-III-31]

29. Ballad That Sings to the Audacious and Inconsiderate Rebellion of Some Indians, and Other Unhappy Individuals in the City of Arequipa

An important form of protest was public songs and verses, including lampoons (pasquines) *that were conducted or placed in public places and that described situations, usually considered unjust by the creator, to win adherents to one side or another of an issue. Although most material was directed against the govern-ment or governmental officials, the colonial regime had its own supporters. Be-cause these materials are directed at a very specific audience during a very specific time in history, their meaning, audience, and impact are sometimes hard to comprehend from the distance of over two centuries. Nonetheless, the document gives a sense of the sentiments and language employed. The following document provides a pro-government view and supports the much-reviled offi-cial Semanat. It castigates the Indians and others in the city of Arequipa who rioted against the collection of customs duties. Verses that rhyme or play with language sounds for effect are even more complicated in translation; it is very difficult to replicate their tone.*

Without even noticing it
and stumbling by yourself
Where do you take yourself
on lost paths?

What is this, you ignorant peoples?
What fantastic frenzy
has tarnished in an instant
the loyalty of so many centuries?

What is this? Towards the royal throne
you insolently approach
so much disobedience
and your untempered whims?

You aim at the Royal Customhouse
through repetitive lampoons
your avaricious passion
your irreverent shots?

The tallest cedar tree
need bow from its highest splendor
as a token of the dominion
of the Customhouse
and its royal ordinance.

Lampoons so criminal that they acclaim
in the one about the Customhouse I have seen
the insolence of Casimiro towards his king?

But, oh! the audacity
associated with iniquity
started the artifice
announced in their writings!

On the 14th of the month of January,
in the year of '80 in which we live
with tumultuous occurrences
of popular uprisings;

At eleven o'clock at night,
with furious and wild shouts
they insulted the entire
respectable Customhouse

Thousands of men with hatchets,
slings and knives broke down the
sturdy door with repeated blows.
Don Fulano, from the guard tower
wanting to blunt their spirited energy,
shot a fusillade at them
with unexpected courage.

But he paid for his imprudence,
for shortly thereafter he was wounded
by a fierce lance thrust to his cheek.

Against such superior forces,
retreat was called for. . . .
If they could settle upon a suitable plan.

The man who held the office of
Administrator of Customs
knew he had to save himself
from this precipice,

And so, jumping from the roof of one
building to another, he was able
to escape death in favor of a different destiny.

[The mob] finally broke through the
sacred façade of the Royal Fortress,

over which the Royal Arms crowned
as a symbol of asylum.

They entered into the interior
with such vengeful furor
that even the rebel himself
was perhaps moved.

All the necessary papers
from the Archives were food for the fire
which burned in their
malignant souls.

Even the delinquents themselves
began to fear such conflict
because in the great uproar
even the wicked became frightened.

Freed now from the prisons,
such a whirlwind of riff-raff
fell on the city, converting their
unexpected joys into threats.

With this infamous recruits
reinforcing their mob, they
wanted to break into the sacred niches.

More than many
intended to carry out this plan. . . .
Could it be that one abyss is always the
consequence of another abyss?

What's more, their fearful intent
hindered the benign resplendence
of the Sun, in its horizon,
starting to shine.

Fearful of the light, the fugitives
dispersed to hide themselves
in the caverns that their meanness
had forewarned them to prepare.

But before this, they made a compact
to suddenly attack the said
Royal Cashiers on the following
Sunday night.

This detestable compact did not
fail to reach a pious ear, and
General Semanat was
loyally warned.

Instantly the banner of our
invincible Carlos was
furled at the site of our
very illustrious City Council.

[The mayor] convoked the chiefs,
giving them their respective orders,
and he also enlisted the foreigners
and principal citizens.

That day in the afternoon
a shining battalion was seen,
of the infantry and cavalry from
the Plaza of the Great Circle.

And even though they were inexpert in firing
and their obedience remiss, [the mayor]
knew how to gain their loyalty from
their fear of the tumult.

Vigilant sentinels surrounded
the entire district of the city,
and complied exactly to
their orders.

Because by ten at night they
detected a growing number of
men on foot, and armed
horsemen.

And shouting "Viva the King!"
but "Death to his Ministers!"

To the sound of harsh voices,
they attacked in unison.

But our brave and noble warriors
met them halfway on the road,
illustrating their heroism
in their resistance to the mob.

For they began to attack
with never-before–seen courage.
They accumulated their trophies
by killing the defeated.

They closely followed those
rebels trying to flee the danger
under fire, trying to find refuge
in their caves.

Of those many on the battlefield
who lost their vital thread, five
were seen as involved in
an unworthy spectacle.

Of the others who were caught on the
18th [of the month] (as I have mentioned),
six were hanged to serve
as a warning.

A blessing that they managed
to enter Paradise, by accepting
the celestial benefit of the
Holy Sacraments.

And although the pity of our one
God is great, it is a painful
travail to die without
this comfort and aid.

The treasure that could satiate
the ruinous appetite inflamed
the cupidity of their villainous
canine hunger.

• • •

Their greed not being satisfied with
their rich spoils, they dreamed
of fatal ideas that were marred by
notions of larceny.

All the city was the bull's–eye
of that pernicious scheme
which announced the death
of all honest citizens.

On the following day many
Indios were convened
with deceitful promises
which gave them a bold beginning.

With a disordered advance,
the daring tumult arrived at the house
of the very pious Dn. Baltazar Semanat.

What's more, later that day, our chief
warned the pious Commander of the
Rendition of Captives.

He took heed of this warning, because
in an unforeseen incident, it is
wise to be respectful of danger.

And thus hidden in the sacristy
He was freed from the steel pikes
that impatiently wanted to stain
themselves with his blood.

What's more, the neighborhood of
men, women, and children sought
refuge in the Religious Hospices.

Where anguish arrived at its final
paroxysm, converting tears
into streams and confusion
into fear.

It was even worse in the Convents
where the least explosion was
stamped onto the hearts of the
Brides of Christ.

But we now return to the thread
of our narration without this
parenthesis causing anyone
to forget what came before.

They broke down the double doors
with the clash of their hammers,
leaving the strength of the hinges
totally weakened.

And forfeit this impediment
they entered, infuriated, where in
their zeal they found the avarice
of a new spell:

Not even a flowering garden
was exempt from their fury,
fattening their wild hatred
even on the plant life.

From a clothing store that was
very well stocked, even the
sack-cloth was used to
cover their wickedness.

Still discontent in a thousand ways
they pursue their destiny,
directing themselves to the stores
of even their relatives and friends!

They all [friends and neighbors] suffered
destruction equal to what I've already
mentioned, so as not to leave anyone
unscathed by their vengeful anger.

From here they make tracks
(although with torpid steps)

to the respective bulwarks
where crimes are expiated.

They approach the Royal Prison
and with the unexpected courage of
their unjust hears, they
form their charity. . . .

To the blows of their axes
that accompany their horrific screams,
they intone a horrific music,
sounding like the songs of the crickets.

And returning now to the cause
of such sudden conflict,
there's no need to wonder
about the motive.

Let us reflect, inside of ourselves,
and we will find that it is a feint
which only seems like punishment.

We render thanks to God with a
contrite heart, our sighs burning
before His Holiness like candles.

And let prosper for many centuries
the life of Sr. Semanat,
whose prudence and steadfastness
cause us to reflect. . . .

He knew how to found this city;
an unbreakable shield under whose
shadow we have achieved the quietude
in which we live.

Let us build a statue of him
with reverend respect,
where appreciation can lend him
his due homage. [*CDIP,* 27. 1780-I]

30. Arequipa *Pasquín* (Lampoon), January 5, 1780

One of the ways that people registered their protests against the increase in customs charges and other changes, such as the expansion of sales taxes, was through printed verse. These lampoons were used to register discontent and were often employed by the more well-to-do, literate citizens who wrote for a literate audience as well. Lampoons could, however, also be read aloud to gatherings that included illiterate people. The following pasquín *was directed at the* corregidor *of Arequipa, Baltasar de Semanat, who had been the target of previous lampoons and even offered a reward for the authors of an earlier* pasquín. *Obviously, the* corregidor *was not pleased with such public protest, especially from the higher social classes. He feared their possible impact, for they called for the death of those who were responsible for collecting customs. The author of the* pasquín *was careful, however, to express loyalty to the Crown while calling for an end to bad government.*

Semanat.
Take care of your head
and also those of your companions;
the *señores* customs officials,
who without charity
have come to this city
from distant and strange lands,
without being moved by pity,
to all see us cry out in mournful tones. . . .

And we also speak here
of those Royal Officials
who with the power to rob want
to increase their fortunes. . . .

Because it is certain and it is true
that if there is no example made by
killing these thieves,
they will leave us naked.
It is in your hands,
noble citizens,
to enjoy all your possessions

without great losses by
taking the lives
of these ruinous, infamous thieves!
[*CDIP,* 26, no. 4. We wish to thank Charles F. Walker
for bringing this lampoon to our attention.]

31. Order Issued by Viceroy Vértiz in View of the Appearance of Lampoons in Buenos Aires

To control information and to limit the criticism and ridicule of individuals, government officials, and governmental policy, efforts were made to control the lampoons that appeared in public places. The anonymity allowed biting words and accusations to be made in public, often to the detriment of the persons or policies against which they were directed. In the following order, the viceroy makes it clear that such public declarations are not to be tolerated. By 1779, the situation was such that Viceroy Vértiz ordered a clampdown on lampoons in Buenos Aires that reflected a growing concern about this form of protest and condemnation.

Buenos Aires, 23rd of August 1779
Being against the law the publication of lampoons, satires, verses, manifests, and other seditious or insulting papers of public Individuals, or anybody else in particular; in contravention of this general prohibition, and against the public tranquility that this City usually enjoys, we have been observing lately that some idle individuals with pernicious intentions have been composing, distributing and copying these seditious papers that are being unwarily read in circles and conversations without realizing the cunningness of their authors, as has been verified in the one addressed to Don Francisco Escalada concentrating on various expressions of mockery and ridicule against several individuals of this town, and among them are some serious and supposed insults. And this Government wanting to apply the required remedy to such a pernicious harm, separating this corrupting vice from the Republic . . . to stop in time such malevolent writings. . . . I order that a thorough investigation be made with the goal of finding out the author or authors of said writings, investigating in first place the aforementioned Don Francisco Escalada so that he can indicate how the mentioned paper attached at the beginning of this, got into his house, who was the individual who delivered, opened, and read it, who was present at the time, giving their first names and last names,

as well as the author of said paper, or whether he knew or thought of who could be the one who, based on the writing or any other assumption, could have written it and this based on prior information, or anything that he legitimately knew or possessed. And let it be known to him that he needs to submit the original that was sent to his houses, as well as the cover or envelope in which it was guarded. And in the case he indicates that he does not have it, he should then indicate who he gave it to and whether the document attached here conforms to the said original: and that all individuals mentioned by said Escalante be searched as well as others that might be deemed necessary to get at the truth. And this is submitted to the First Assistant in Place, Don Josef Borras, Scribe of the Government.

Vértiz Don Manuel de Ortega Before Me Joseph Zenzano
Royal public and government Scribe [*RTA,* 778–79]

32. Account of What Happened in the City of Arequipa with the Uprising of the Indians and Other Discontent Individuals

Spanish officials were often at odds with one another with regard to what course of action to take against the rebels in Arequipa as well as the wisdom of the customhouse existing at all, given the circumstances. The following document not only gives a clear account of the very real danger that many of the leading Spanish officials and others faced, it casts doubt on the wisdom of Areche in forcing people to register with the government. Many people thought that this was done so they would have to pay tribute. Those who had been exempt, such as zambos *and* cholos, *were disturbed at the thought that they too might be subjected to tribute. Thus, in the following document one gets a sense of the growing levels of uncertainty expressed by various segments of society with regard to Spanish policy and to just what this policy actually meant or where it was headed.*

Ever since it was known that the Commission led by Dr. Don Juan Baptista Pando was to impose and administer the Customs: and of his diligence towards getting information from the valleys and coast to ascertain the goods produced by the Haciendas so that the tax-rolls could be made; the good will of people has dwindled and the omen of a fatal ending is looming large. . . . [E]ver since the first of January when the Customs were opened, they have inverted the handling of things that the Royal Officials had instituted and have been charging duties without exempting food nor the goods produced by the Indians' own labor. Things were going in such a way that Pando himself announced publicly that custom duties will go from 80,000 to more than 150,000 pesos.

It is for this reason that on the same day [that the customhouse opened] you could find lampoons that threatened the Administrator and his staff; and even though *Corregidor* Semanat took measures to contain and punish such behavior, every day one could see posses of horsemen from various places, all in disguise. It was believed that they were peoples from the countryside [*chacras*] who without any doubt [felt they] were being harassed or were angry [learning] . . . that they would need to pay taxes on their wheat, corn, potatoes, and fruits. For their part, the muleteers, of which there are plenty in this region, were groaning about having to unload at the customhouse, and then re-pack all their liquors [*aguardientes*] and the rest of their things that came from the valley. In addition to this regulation, they [were upset by the] fact that they could not enter the customs plaza wearing their spurs and hats.

Rumors about [possible action by] the masses in the city, and the peoples from their fields [*chacras*] were being heard. The *Corregidor,* suspicious of any movement, didn't cease sending official letters to the Administrator telling him to take it easy and proceed with fairness, and to not make changes in how the Royal Officials were dealing with things before everything calmed down. The aforementioned Pando, nevertheless, judged [it was] wise to govern everything with despotism. They [Customs Officials] responded shamelessly and with contempt to the latest official letter sent them by the *Corregidor,* which was quite deferential and civil, saying among other things: that they had come to augment the Royal Treasury by virtue of the orders that they possessed to that end, and that they would sacrifice their lives to do that. Ignoring the *Corregidor,* that same day Pando told the city council these formal words: The *Corregidor* is consumed with fear and is trying to make me believe there is a revolt. In my opinion he looks more like a visionary nun than a member of the military.

Thus . . . were things happening when on the night of Thursday the thirteenth, a group of people forced themselves into the Customhouse. They remained there just as a probe, for it seemed they only went with the purpose and will to explore. This was confirmed the following night, when, being informed of the carelessness they had noted in the Customs officials (because the latter thought that nothing so depraved as a tumult could happen) 200 men charged into [the customhouse] with the firm resolution of killing Pando and all the other staff. . . . Pando fled over the walls behind his house, like a frightened cat, when confronted with the possibility of [his death]. . . . God thus allowed me to confirm the bad opinion I had formed about the

Corregidor. The others, among them Torre, stopped awhile to make a fire. But witnessing the destruction of the gates, he got curious to see who was committing such action and when he stuck his head out of a window he was cut with a dagger, miraculously not losing his life right there and being able to escape with the help of his companions who pulled him to safety.

The doors [of the customhouse] being completely broken, the masses rushed into the building, burning some papers and stealing 2,032 pesos that were in the chest. They left everything else that they considered to be from legitimate charges. They left the premises after midnight of the fourteenth, causing some confusion by passing by houses . . . belonging to some of the individuals who had been threatened in the lampoons, especially the Royal Officials who had been . . . carefully searched for but who were able to slip away as best they could.

The *Corregidor* was now totally confused by the causes of the revolt that he could not by himself solve, be it because he felt in obvious danger of losing his life and wealth or for other reasons that are also easy to understand. Immediately he gave orders that such serious circumstances require. He went to the Customhouse on the morning of the fifteenth accompanied by the Town Council members and gathered up all the documents that had not burned and handed them to the Royal Officials who were present. Finishing this task, they left on their own to do whatever they deemed necessary in such circumstances.

Word spread on the fifteenth that Cosío, Goyeneche, and Alvizuri should be killed for having been friends of the *Corregidor* and Pando. With this warning, one could notice the consternation that their hearts were suffering. In fact, they locked themselves in their houses anxiously awaiting the throng. At ten at night of the same day a strange commotion and shouting was heard in the street of San Francisco and then some people threateningly attacked the house of Lastarria. From there they passed by Cosío's house and then went straight to the *Corregidor's* house who had been sentenced to die in the latest lampoons that were circulated. They found the house locked, and setting fire to the windows and doors, they found no living person, for all those who had been hidden there had fled. But, they ransacked it not leaving even a nail in the wall.

They finished their toil at two in the morning of the sixteenth, and after going through the street of Mercaderes, they robbed Candero's store. . . . They then planned to go to the house of Cosío and they were yelling so loud that they could hear them say from the interior of the house: *Let's go to Cosío's house;* but this did not discourage him, although he did keep the door locked so that as soon as the first blow to the door was felt, the entire family could escape to the Bishop's Palace, which had been disposed to receive them: they had previously placed ladders to access that contiguous building. The riches that he kept in the house had already been safely hidden, even though he was not able to gather up things at their store. The mob, leaving this project, decided to continue down Mercaderes street. They went on to the jail, freed the prisoners and wanted to attack the Royal Treasury, but they could not do this due to lack of time for it was already after four-thirty in the morning.

Amidst this confusion and turmoil, the night of the fifteenth and the morning of the sixteenth passed. The *Corregidor* retired to the Municipality where all the noble citizens came to offer their skills and lives in defense of the King and the city. They prepared themselves quickly and organized the best defense possible at the time. Don Mateo Cosío, as Colonel of the Cavalry, gave the order to gather a regiment and . . . most of them were in the plaza by four in the afternoon. It was then that it was learned that it was not the people from the countryside who had participated in last night's uprising, nor had they intervened in the looting. Those who had perpetrated this were the poorest of the city dwellers who were stirred up by the uprising in the Customhouse, even though nobody could tell who gave the order for the mutiny which had been very disorganized due to the numbers involved. The investigation is being conducted with great secrecy in order to punish those responsible.

Once this decision was made, it was ordered that the seven cavalry companies that were gathered on the sixteenth should protect the entrances to the city. The Infantry, which only had two companies armed and ready, stayed in the plaza with orders to go wherever they were needed. The fear was that the people from the *chacras,* especially those from Tiabaya, whose two companies did not want to obey or come, might attack the city. In consequence, they also suspected all the cavalry who were also *chacra* owners. To these concerns were added a rightful suspicion of an uprising by the Indians of the Pampa, so as to warrant a general surveillance from prayer time until nine at night of the area around the city by Cosío and a company of cavalry and accompanied by Pober and two of his friends. All was calm, and there was no movement on the Pampa, but once he came back to the Plaza he was informed at nine that the two companies from Tiabaya were in the outskirts of the city. He went there with his company and convinced them to come to the plaza and serve as good subjects of the King.

They willingly accepted and while they were being separated from the two companies their captains got to know the people, as they all had come together in one platoon, [Cosío] was advised that in the Pampa where Felan and his company were they had been attacked by more than 800 Indians. Cosío immediately left to assist them with the two companies from Tiabaya and the infantry of noblemen. He found them retreating to the small square of Santa

Marta, all the street to the Pampa (more than two blocks long) being occupied by the Indians. Felan resisted the attack with courage and force. He killed two Indians and one of his men was wounded and a horse was dead.

With Cosío's reinforcements the Indians retreated, leaving several dead and wounded in the street. The company of Don Martín Solares of grenadiers . . . arrived. With the help of two more companies that they took from less dangerous locations, the Indians of the Pampas were defeated and they fled to the mountains. That night six dead and four wounded were brought in. With the first sun rays, Cosío left for the Pampas with two of his companies. He caught several wounded Indians who couldn't flee, and found all the *chacras* deserted. He followed the trail of the Indians on the Pampa and captured many that were fleeing with their wives and children.

Dawn broke on the morning of the seventeenth with all those killed in the fighting stacked in the halls of the Municipality, and in the afternoon two cavalry companies with the infantry of the nobility went and burned all of the *ranchos* of the Pampa. At two in the afternoon of the eighteenth another six wounded Indians were hanged, and all the rest are fleeing with their women and children, dead from hunger and need, according to muleteers who have arrived from the Sierra, who also said that there are many who are wounded and some have already died or who are dying in agony from their wounds. The jail is also full of Indians, both men and women, awaiting their fates after charges have been filed.

The defeat of the Indians of the Pampa seems to have mobilized the rest of them [Indians] in the surrounding region. This was supported by a lampoon that was intercepted that indicates that tomorrow, the twentieth, the city would be assaulted during the night. With this warning (that even though it is from the enemy it should not be dismissed) a state of readiness continues with a larger number of cavalry. For this reason the people from the countryside have come to the city, even though they are in the middle of their harvests. The threat has not become a reality so far—seven in the morning of the twenty first—and this is because they are aware that the city is defended by . . . regiments of infantry and cavalry.

Today from nine to eleven in the morning . . . a meeting . . . was held that was attended by several lawyers, royal officials, and some army captains that are here in order to determine the protection that is needed tonight. Two Infantry companies and two more Cavalry companies remain under arms guarding all the entrances to the city. It is hoped that everything will remain quiet, even though it is good to live with precaution for we know the Indians' character which is treasonous.

One of the main . . . concerns that disturbed the people of the countryside and the masses in the city and put them against the *Corregidor* was the order that came from the *Visitador* [Areche] to register as tax-payers not only the Indians—*naturales* and *forasteros*—but also the *Zambos* and *Cholos*. They believed that this was done in order to have them pay tribute. This procedure will need to be suspended for a long time or should not even be considered at all, or the problems that we have seen might be experienced again. Arequipa, January 21st, 1780. [*CDIP,* 40. 1780-I-21]

33. Threat against Bernardo Gallo, Head of La Paz Customs

In most cities in which a customhouse had been established, tensions built up between customs officials and those subject to the duties. La Paz was one of the cities in which criollos, mestizos, *and Indians were raised. The La Paz* aduana *and its head, Bernardo Gallo, came under attack in March 1780. The following lampoon threatened Gallo with death and denounced his actions, claiming that they would surely lead to bloodshed. The author of the document plays with Gallo's name, which means "rooster" or "cock." Gallo was eventually hanged by the rebel leader Andrés Tupac Amaru for his role as the head of the* aduana *and because of the hatred that both* criollos *and Indians had for him.*

This is the third and final announcement, and we will cry with sorrow, because as a result of two or three unworthy thieves, many innocent people will die. And blood will flow in the streets and square on the 13th of March; it will run like water, if the creoles are not defended. And this thieving old cock [Gallo] will be skinned alive, cut into pieces and thrown into the river. He is perfectly aware of what is happening here, and cannot claim that his misfortune is due to unforeseen circumstances, since this is the third announcement. It is only regrettable, that because of this villainous thief, many will pay with their lives. [*RR,* 188. Translated by Scarlett O'Phelan Godoy. This document is also included with the Tupac Catari materials, document 126.]

V. The Rebellion

34. Account of the Most Horrible Crime Committed by José Gabriel Tupac Amaru, *Cacique* of Pampamarca

The following document is an account of the first stages of the rebellion, beginning with the dinner that Tupac Amaru and Corregidor *Antonio de Arriaga shared with others on November 4, 1780. Subsequent to this social gathering, Tupac Amaru took* Corregidor *Arriaga prisoner. The* corregidor *was then sentenced to death, which was carried out on November 10, 1780—the executioner himself was a slave of Arriaga's. The rebel leader Tupac Amaru declared himself the new Inca. The author of the document also refers to Micaela Bastidas, the wife of Tupac Amaru, as no less cruel of a monster than her husband. In this way, the author indirectly attests to the important role Bastidas would have in the rebel leadership.*

The document is most interesting in that so much has been made of the antagonisms between Tupac Amaru and Arriaga. Although this discord is obviously true, they were also united by the bond of fictive kinship. Perhaps this is the reason that the person working for Arriaga did not hesitate to put the corregidor's *wealth in the hands of Tupac Amaru when he received a letter from* the corregidor *asking him to do this.*

One of the first things Tupac Amaru did as the new Inca was to attack textile mills (obrajes). *In doing this, he not only attacked a symbol of oppression, he distributed the cloth—just as the Incas had done to reward people. Thus, he most likely called on this ancient tradition to solidify his claim to the title of Inca.*

On Saturday November 4th of 1780, the day on which our Sovereign Monarch . . . Dn. Carlos the Third (God keep him) is celebrated, a dinner was held at the house of Dr. Carlos Rodriguez, priest of the Doctrine (Parish) of Yanaoca with Crl. Don Antonio Arriaga *Corregidor* of the Province of Tinta, the priest of the Doctrine of Pampamarca, and the *Cacique* of that town José Gabriel Tupac Amaru. Once the banquet was over, the *Corregidor* was pressed to leave early for Tinta where he had some unfinished businesses, but having offered to keep him company, the *Cacique* (who was like his *compadre*) would not hear of it. Instead, José Gabriel left before him so that he could meet with those who were waiting in a ravine ready to ambush the *Corregidor* who had to take that route. Once the *Corregidor* arrived to said site, Tupac Amaru came out and confronted him with all his men. The *Corregidor,* . . . trying to defend himself, grabbed a pistol but he was immediately caught with a rope around his neck and was forced down off his mule before having a chance to shoot. They also wounded the clerk who was accompanying him and captured the rest of his slaves who were following him at a distance. They were all taken to a hidden, secret site off the path and were left there tied up, guarded, and under threat of death if they shouted.

Having done this the traitor promptly went back to a house he owned in the annex [community of a parish] named Tungasuca. And having given his orders, he went back at midnight to bring the prisoners to this house. He put the *Corregidor,* burdened with chains and shackles, in one of the underground cells, and his clerk in another; as well as the other slaves. He made the clerk write several letters of convocation and forced the *corregidor* to sign them and address them to: his principal cashier Dn. Manuel San Roque; to all those who called themselves Spaniards in the region; and to other subjects, from whose persons and resources he desired to take advantage due to being who they were and because of their wealth. In fact, the letter addressed to the Cashier ordered him to come to Tungasuca without delay, bringing all the sealed and minted silver and firearms . . . as these were all necessary to serve the King and to which end he was sending his *compadre* with the necessary mules. In the letters of convocation he threatened, under penalty of death, all those who would not present themselves with their arms in Tungasuca. To Don Bernardo de la Madrid, and the Galician Dn. Juan de Figueroa, the first the overseer of Pomacanchi and the second of Quipococha, he wrote to them in the following manner:

> *Esteemed friend: it is imperative that you put yourself on the road for this pueblo of Tungasuca as soon as you read this, for we have several matters that we need to discuss tonight. And from here I am planning to go to Cuzco where I intend to clear my name. I wish your Honor perfect health and that God keep you for years to come. Tungasuca, November 5th, 1780. Your dear friend—Arriaga.*

After sending these letters of convocation, Tupac Amaru got two strings of mules ready after one in the morning and left immediately carrying the letter to the Cashier himself. The Cashier, recognizing the handwriting and signature of the *Corregidor* and seeing that his *compadre* was in charge, did not hesitate. The traitor carried 22,000 pesos in cash, carved silver, ninety muskets, two boxes containing the sabers of the province, and all the various weapons of said *Corregidor.* And accompanied by the *Corregidor's* family—whom he convinced had also been summoned—he left without delay for Tungasuca. Once there, he put everybody in jail, doing the same thing with Dn. Bernardo de la Madrid and the Galician Dn. Juan de Figueroa.

Such silence was maintained that nobody knew the whereabouts of the *Corregidor*. Some were told that he had left to visit the higher villages of the Province. Others were told that he was attending to very important business in Tungasuca, which did not allow him to attend to anything else. He [Tupac Amaru] put spies in all entrances to Cuzco so that nobody in the Province could go and inform [people there] about what was going on in Tungasuca.

While the armed Indians and *Mestizos* of his faction were arriving, thanks to the Letters of Convocation, he [Tupac Amaru] had a gallows built in the Tungasuca plaza and he sentenced the *Corregidor*, his *compadre*, to die on it. Intimidated by his sentence, the *Corregidor* sent for the priest Dr. Dn. Antonio Lopez, who happened to be in the principal pueblo, a league and a half away, to come and hear the confession of an invalid. The priest walked there and discovered that he had to confess the . . . *Corregidor*. He asked why he was treated in such a way, and he answered that the *Cacique* Tupac Amaru was thinking of killing him. . . . [Tupac Amaru] told the Priest that he had orders from the *General Visitador*, authorized by the Royal *Audiencia* of Lima, and he had had it for twenty-six days. He was worried that he was guilty of taking too much time [to comply with the order]. . . .

The priest then proceeded to assist the unfortunate *Corregidor*, giving him confession and the last *viaticum* [communion] and supporting him during the six days he was given.

On the morning of Friday, November 10th, Tupac Amaru ordered that three columns . . . be organized from all the people from his Province that were already there. Two were composed of Spaniards and *Mestizos* armed with muskets, sabers, and sticks; and one of Indians with slings. In the middle of this, he brought out the *Corregidor*, dressed in his military uniform, and publicly started taking his uniform off, stripping him of his rank following the rituals he had understood and seen in other occasions, until he was left in his shirt. He then put a shroud on him . . . that had the title of *La Caridad* on it. He then gave the order to take him to the gallows, accompanied by the Priest and two other clergymen, where he went with a resignation and patience worthy of somebody who was already touching the portals of eternity.

Once on the gallows the *Corregidor* was forced by the tyrant to publicly declare that he deserved to die in that way. A black slave of the *Corregidor* served as his executioner, but the ropes snapped and both fell to the ground. But they suspended them again with a lariat around their necks, and thus they completed the execution in clear sight and tolerance of all his Province. Not one voice was raised that would disturb the operation. And most surprising of all was that those same Collectors and those close to the *Corregidor* were the ones who (oh, what an awful spectacle of perfidy!) sped his way to the ignominious place of execution, and who pulled on his feet so he could die even more violently.

While all this was happening, the *Cacique* [Tupac Amaru] circled the village and its entrances on his horse. The troops were surprised at an action so unimaginably cruel as . . . that of a *Corregidor* being executed by one of his subjects. . . . They were all so intimidated by these events that nobody dared to complain or contradict what was being carried out. And everything was done with such secretiveness and care that even though the execution took place six days after his arrest, the news was not known in Cuzco until after the death of the *Corregidor* was confirmed by those closest to him. Two days later the body was buried with the regular pomp in the church of the same town. The *Cacique* was not present at the function as he was occupied on other expeditions.

With this first coup the tyrant was getting ready for even more audacious deeds, showing himself capable and willing to do whatever it took. Several years before he had gone to Lima and appeared before the Royal *Audiencia* to determine the legitimate quality of his descendancy from Dn. Felipe Tupac Amaru, the last of the Incas. It is there where he gladly started down a path filled with contradictory judgment. . . . The papers that were approved through the recklessness of those who handled the documents of his lineage gave him the chance to form a high idea of his own lineage, a fact that took him where he should have never gone.

Returning from Lima with even more presumption than when he had left, he knew how to hide his intentions under a facade of moderation, general affability, and generosity . . . tricks used by those who try to command the affection of all only to despotically dominate them later on. Nothing of his plans was discovered until the very insolent act of publicly killing the *Corregidor*. More than six thousand men, Indians and *Mestizos* from surrounding villages, assisted him. And having called upon those in the surrounding area, he intimated in the tongue that the Incas used [Quechua]: *That the time had come when they must shake off the heavy burden under which they had been suffering for many long years at the hands of the Spaniards. . . . The* Corregidores *of the Kingdom would be punished in equal measure for all the taxes they had imposed. . . . They would exterminate all Europeans and terminate the* repartimientos, *customs, and other similar burdens that were only devastating the kingdom. He added that this in no way went against the obedience due to the King and . . . the Catholic Faith. The . . . [Catholic Church] had all his veneration, and . . . respect. Once all injustices were removed, his only goal was to bring the infidel Indians to the faith and retire to enjoy the fruits of his expeditions. They should not despair at the beginning and they would attain their freedom. They should rest assured that the love that he expressed through all this would probably cost him his life in a similar torment as they had just witnessed, but that he would do it with happiness if it meant giving his nation glory and restoring its ancient state.* He then put a rope around his neck as used in the previous execution, so as to move the Indians, who . . . cried out offering to follow him and to lose their lives before withdrawing their support.

He then proceeded to issue a proclamation with this beginning: Don José Gabriel Tupac Amaru, Inca, of royal blood and main lineage. In it, he called on all his beloved American *Criollos* of all classes, as well as Spaniards, *Mestizos,* and Indians . . . to follow him. He made it clear that he was a Christian Catholic and that he would never violate the Church's immunities. His only objective was to abolish the introduction of *Corregidores,* free the Kingdom of customs, monopolies and other taxes, and to do away with everything that was European and responsible for such institutions. Those who would oppose and resist his plans would suffer . . . the full weight of his anger. Copies of this proclamation and other edicts were distributed through people of trust so that they would be posted in public places in the Provinces and cities close to Cuzco and Arequipa. . . . He wrote . . . to the priests so that they would not influence the believers of their parishes and prevent their following his precepts. He did the same with other private individuals, even those who he did not know and whose trust he assumed, even though in reality he did not have it.

It was mentioned that the traitor Tupac Amaru did not attend the burial of the *Corregidor* for he was busy with other expeditions. These were reduced to him going personally to Tinta, to the said *Corregidor's* house, and ransacking it of what he had not had the chance to get when he went there with the Cashier. He took everything of taste and value that had been left, leaving not a mule nor food, of which he took plenty. Then he went to the *obrajes* of Parupuquio and Pomacanchi. He demolished the first and looted all the fine clothes he found and which he used as the first demonstrations of his generosity to all those who were helping him with the rebellion. In the second, we were assured, he took even more loot. . . . [H]e took over twenty mules loaded with clothes, lots of provisions, and 13,000 pesos in cash.

He then proceeded to go to the neighboring province of Quispicanchis to conquer it and surprise its *Corregidor* Dn. Fernando Cabrera, who . . . was in the town of Quiquijana some eight leagues from Tungasuca. He had arrived from Lima not even one month before but had the fortune of being able to flee to Cuzco, hidden by the dark of the night and riding bareback on a mule or mare that he managed to get. He was forced to leave 2,000 pesos in . . . silver and all his jewelry, which the rebel confiscated. This Province (Quispicanchis) declared itself in support of the rebel, and the Indians kissed his feet and hands as if he were their lord. He distributed the clothes that the *Corregidor* had for the *reparto* among the Indians and went back to his pueblo of Tungasuca where he established his royal throne with great ostentation and with guards who were named chiefs so as to better rule their people.

Then he went to hang those Europeans that he had taken prisoners when he arrested *Corregidor* Arriaga, but his wife, the *Cacica* Micaela Bastidas (she is as cruel a monster as he is), convinced him not to kill them for they could be of help in fixing arms, casting cannons and bullets, especially the Galician Figueroa whose skills in these matters were well known. And, in fact, after securing them with shackles and guards, he put them to work on those tasks. Tinta, November 10th, 1780. [*CDIP,* 60. 1780-XI-10]

35. Death Certificate of
Corregidor Antonio de Arriaga

The priest Antonio Lopez de Sosa was almost like a father to Tupac Amaru. He was probably the person responsible for getting the future kuraka *into the* kuraka *school in Cuzco after Tupac Amaru's father died. He also performed the marriage ceremony for the rebel leader to Micaela Bastidas. He was asked by Tupac Amaru to hear the confession of* Corregidor *Arriaga, and the priest was then present during Arriaga's execution. In the following document, Lopez de Sosa presents Arriaga's death certificate in a very matter-of-fact way, giving no indication of his personal relationship to the rebel leader nor the momentous implications of this death (one would not necessarily expect him to say such things), but briefly mentioning his role in the events surrounding the execution.*

Don Antonio de Arriaga, *Corregidor* of this Province.
In the Pueblo of San Felipe de Tungasuca, annex of the Doctrine (Parish) of Pampamarca, Province of Tinta, on the thirteenth day of the month of November of 1780. I, Dr. Don Antonio Lopez de Sosa, Priest and Vicar of this Doctrine, buried the body of Don Antonio de Arriaga, *Corregidor* of this province, whom I assisted [with his confession] at his request and after seeing that all my efforts to save his life were in vain due to the resistance and disturbances of those [who were] accomplices in his imprisonment. And it was not registered then due to the rebellions, loss of the [register] book, and being late so that I forgot to register it, so I am doing it now, and signing it.
Doctor Don Antonio Lopez de Sosa [*CDIP,* 64. 1780-XI-13]

36. Tupac Amaru Declares Himself Inca and Ruler

Tupac Amaru most often argued that he was acting on behalf of the Spanish monarchs to create good government, but in the following selection he declares himself the Inca and ruler of his Andean territories and people. He also discusses how the Spanish rulers have usurped his legitimate position and exploited his people. The document was undated and unsigned. For this reason, and because other documents do not declare a break from the Spanish Crown, the possibility that it could be a forgery has been suggested.

Don José I by the grace of God, Inca king of Peru, Santa Fe, Quito, Chile, Buenos Aires, and the continents of the seas of the south, highest duke and lord of the Césars and Amazonians, with dominion in the Gran Paititi, commissary and distributor of divine piety . . . decided in my council . . . on repeated and secret occasions, already made public, that the Kings of Castile usurped the throne and dominion of my people three centuries ago, making them vassals with unbearable services, tributes, money, custom dues, *alcabalas,* monopolies . . . tenths, and fifths. The viceroys, *audiencias, corregidores,* and other ministers [are] all equally tyrannous, selling justice at auction; and to him who bids most, most is given. Ecclesiastical and secular officials enter into [administering justice] without fear of God, trample upon the natives of this kingdom as beasts, and take away the lives of all those who do not wish to rob. . . . In the name of God, all powerful, we order and command that none of the said pensions shall be paid to the intrusive European ministers of bad faith or shall they be obeyed in anything. Respect shall only be held for the priesthood. We shall pay the tenth and first fruits [*primicia*], which are given to God and the tribute and fifth [*quinto*] for the King as the natural Lord; and this with the moderation which shall be made known with other laws to be observed and kept. . . . I command . . . an oath to be taken to my royal crown in all the cities, towns, and places of my dominions; and [I wish] to be informed briefly of the ready and faithful vassals, for rewards, and those who rebel, for imposing fitting penalties. [*LIR,* 134–35. Translated by L. E. Fisher.]

37. Tupac Amaru's Proclamation of Freedom for Slaves

One of Tupac Amaru's first actions was to try to gain support for the rebellion and to undermine the strength of the Spanish. One of the ways he attempted to accomplish this was by stirring up the fears of the Spanish and by creating doubts about the loyalty of those around them, especially the people who worked in their households and served them. In the following proclamation, he asks all Peruvians to join him in the rebellion, and he calls not only for the freeing of the slaves but for the slaves to leave their masters. He offers the slaves their freedom if they comply with his orders, and he makes it clear that those who do not accept his offer will suffer his wrath for their disobedience.

Don José Gabriel Tupac Amaru Indian of noble-blood of the Incas and royal family (*Tronco Principal*).

Proclamation of November 16, 1780 to the citizens of Cuzco so that they desert the Spaniards [*chapetones*] and free the slaves.

Through this proclamation let it be known to all Peruvians who live and inhabit the City of Cuzco who are friends of Spaniards and *Mestizos,* religious men that are in the city, priests and other distinguished persons who might have developed friendships with the Peruvian people and those who participate in my efforts to benefit this Kingdom: let it be perfectly understood: the hostilities and ill-treatment caused by all European people, who without fear of the Divine Majesty nor abiding by the Royal Orders of our natural Lord, have pushed to the limit the peace and tranquility of these lands by their ill-treatments and affronts, their taking advantage of the common good, even letting the natives die. And as everybody has experienced rough treatment from the Europeans they should all come, without exception, and support my position by totally deserting the Spaniards, even if they were slaves to their masters with the added benefit that they will be freed of the servitude and slavery to which they were subjected. And if they do not abide by this proclamation they will experience the most severe punishment that I can impose, regardless of whether they are Priests, Friars or of any other quality or character. And so that nobody can allege ignorance, I order that this proclamation be posted in all public places of the city. This was done in the Sanctuary of Tungasuca[1] Province of Tinta the 16th of November of 1780.

> *Joph.* Gb. Thupa Amaro Inca [*sic*] [*CDIP,* 69. 1780-XI-16]

---

1. One of the four annexes of the parish of Pampamarca.

38. Rebel Views on the Illegitimacy of Spanish Rule

In the period leading up to the rebellion, and even after it began, rebels sent mixed messages concerning the role of the Spanish king, the Spaniards, and their right to govern. Some argued that the Spanish king was sovereign, and that the local government and Spaniards needed to be removed. This was often Tupac Amaru's position, but it was not always his sentiment. Others, however, argued that Spanish rule was illegitimate. The conquest by the Spanish did not give them a right to the territory or to rule. The following are three brief passages that point to the illegitimacy of Spanish rule and, by implication, the legitimacy of indigenous actions. The first is from the province of Huarochirí, not far from Lima. The second is from Tupac Amaru. The third is from indigenous testimony in the region of La Paz. The prophecies referred to are unclear, but they could relate to the notion of Inkarrí, in which the Inca or the Inca Empire would be reborn and legitimate Andean rule reestablished.

1. Huarochirí
The prophecies of Santa Rosa and Santo Toribio would be fulfilled, meaning that the territory would return to its former owners since the Spaniards had conquered it wrongfully [*la habían ganado mal*] and through a war brought unjustly against the natives who had lived in peace and quiet.

2. Tupac Amaru
The kings of Castile have usurped the crown and dominions of my people for close to three centuries.

3. La Paz
[The king of Spain] had conquered the kingdom wrongfully, and that the time had come for the fulfillment of the prophecies.
[*WAWR*, 164. Translated by Sinclair Thomson]

39. Tupac Amaru Orders
Corregidor's Goods Embargoed

Tupac Amaru frequently claimed to be acting on royal orders that he had received from the king. In the following document, he orders another kuraka *to take* corregidores *prisoner and to embargo their goods to compensate the indigenous*

*people from whom the wealth had been extracted in the first place. This was a
very public way to demonstrate the vulnerability of Spanish officials. It is hard
to determine to what degree others believed that Tupac Amaru actually had
royal orders for his actions. In this case, the* kuraka *to whom the command was
issued, Sucacagua, did not prove to be a willing follower of the Inca, but instead ended up favoring the loyalists.*

In as much as the King has ordered me to proceed in an extraordinary manner against several *corregidores* and their lieutenants, based on legitimate reasons that cannot be disclosed at the moment; and the *corregidor* of the
province of Lampa and his lieutenant general being included in the royal order, and being unable to follow the judicial orders myself as I am attending
to other more immediate concerns that require my assistance for their resolution; I authorize Governor D. Bernardo Sucacagua to do it in my place. He
will, with the utmost care and reserve, apprehend the *corregidor* and his lieutenant for which he will call upon the soldiers and Indians of said province,
keeping the prisoners in the most secure of prisons with guards to watch them
and prevent them from communicating with anybody until decided otherwise; he will produce legal inventories of all the goods and papers that might
be found without leaving anything out, making sure that I am informed with
great care. All these goods belong to the royal patrimony and the good administration of justice in order to make amends for the wrongdoings perpetrated against Indians and other individuals up until now. Done in the pueblo
of Tungasuca, on November 15th, 1780.

José Gabriel Tupac Amaru, Inca [CDIP, 71. 1780-XI-15]

40. Letter from the Rebellious Tupac Amaru to the *Cacique* D. Diego Chuquiguanca (*sic*)

*Even though he had great power as Inca and leader of the rebellion, Tupac
Amaru had not been among the upper-echelon elite of either the indigenous or
Spanish* kurakas *before the rebellion. He hoped to convince other* kurakas *to
follow him, especially powerful ones like Choquehuanca, who controlled strategic territory and people along the route from Cuzco to Lake Titicaca. In the
following letter, the rebel leader—writing as though he is acting in the name
of royal authority—seeks to enlist the support of Choquehuanca.*

Sir Governor D. Diego Chuquiguanca [*sic*]:
Honorable Sir and esteemed relative:—Following higher orders I inform you
that you should extirpate all *corregidores* on behalf of the public good; in this
way, there should be no more *corregidores* and all *mitas* to Potosí should be
extinguished, as well as taxes, customs [duties], and other pernicious burdens.
It is for this reason that I inform you of my authority as a loyal subject of the
King, Our Lord, so that you can carry out these orders with the greatest of
care, by—if I were you—first and foremost taking the *corregidor* prisoner and
seizing all his property. To this effect you should rally the whole province
around the King without explaining the precise orders, but at the same time
be alert to any resistance from either Indians or Spaniards, and have gallows
placed in the pueblos of this province, advising that they are only for those
who do not obey. This is all. I count on your skills and discretion to execute
these orders. In the meantime, I remain all yours praying that God keeps you
safe for many years to come. Tungasuca, November 15th, 1780. I kiss your
hand, your very passionate relative.

José Gabriel Tupac Amaru, *Inca*
Copies of the original proclamation should be made and distributed throughout all the pueblos of the province and [on the] doors of churches. If help is
needed you can call on a relative of mine by the name of D. Estevan de
Zuñiga, who is in the Province and who will behave as if he were of your
household. . . .

José Gabriel Tupac Amaru, *Inca* [*CDIP,* 67. 1780-XI-15]

41. Brief Submitted to the *Corregidor* of Azangaro
by D. Diego Chuquiguanca (*sic*),
Cacique and Governor of Said Province

Despite the efforts of Tupac Amaru to recruit the kuraka *Choquehuanca to his
cause, Choquehuanca wanted nothing to do with the rebel leader and immediately sent the following letter to Spanish authorities to make sure they were
clear about his loyalty and that of his family, especially his son. Choquehuanca
was fully aware of the seriousness of the situation and probably had little doubt
about the severe retribution by the Spanish against those who challenged the
legitimacy and authority of the colonial state. However, he also must have
understood what would happen to him if the forces of Tupac Amaru captured
him after he refused to join the insurrection.*

Dear *Corregidor:*

Crl. D. Diego Chuquiguanca [*sic*], *Cacique* and Governor of this pueblo of Azangaro. Following procedures, I come before you and state: That a subject by the name of Pedro Tito, from the pueblo of Pampamarca, sent by the rebellious Indian José Tupac Amaru has just arrived with a closed letter addressed to me, and as soon as I received it, I informed everyone about it in the correct manner . . . so that it be opened with everybody present, so that my loyalty to the Sovereign, Don Carlos III, King of Spain and these lands, my natural Lord, be public and well-known. Under his banner I give my life, I sacrifice my children and all my descendants to his service, as well as all the investments that I might have in haciendas, lands and other [goods]. Additionally, I and my son, Sergeant Major D. José Chuquiquanca, also submit three letters written by Crl. D. Pedro de la Vellina dated Tungasuca, November 15th of the current year of 1780: one for me, one for my daughter Doña Teresa Chuquiguanca and another one for my aforementioned son D. José Chuquiguanca in which the before named Vallina [*sic*] claims he has been taken prisoner by order of the rebellious Tupac Amaru, and that the sealed envelopes contain communication to alert the *corregidores* from Azangaro and Carabaya; thus says Vallina, and apparently all this has happened. I am submitting this to you, so that you can, without delay, have the Spanish regiment ready to protect you and this province of Azangaro as well as the surrounding provinces. I, for my part, have just written to the *corregidores* of Lampa y Carabaya informing them of what is going on. I call on your well-known devotion and ask you to certify my loyalty, that of my household, and that of my son D. José Chuquiguanca who is here with me denouncing these facts, so that you would kindly inform the Court, the Viceroys, the *Audiencia,* and the *Visitador General* of our solid loyalty and good behavior toward our Catholic King. . . . Therefore, I ask and beg you to please attest of my presence and give the necessary orders, without any further delay, so as to prevent the rebellious Indian José Tupac Amaru from entering these provinces. And if possible to raise soldiers from peoples of Lampa, Carabaya and Azangaro in order to destroy the rebellious Indian and all his supporters, which would be a good service to our royal Majesty (God save him). Moreover, I hope that this denunciation will be used by you as the proof of my loyalty, in all tribunals, and in front of the nearby . . . *Corregidores.*

Diego Chuquiguanca [*sic*]
José Chuquiguanga [*sic*] [*CDIP,* 70. 1780-XI-16]

42. Tupac Amaru's Edict to the Province of Chichas

The following edict was one of several issued by Tupac Amaru that was designed to win support from criollos *and others in the province. He states his purpose as ending the oppression and tyranny of the Spanish. At the same time, his edict carries with it a threat; he expects people to join his side and to support his proclamation. Those who don't will be punished. He also makes a special effort to clarify that he wishes no harm to, nor does he disrespect, the Catholic faith. Given his actions and statements toward the Church, there is no reason to doubt his sincerity. However, these assurances were also meant to calm fears or doubts among the majority of his followers who saw themselves as Christian believers.*

Don José Gabriel Tupac Amaru, Indian of the royal blood and principal line of descent (*tronco principal*): "Let it be known to the *criollo* countrymen, *moradores* [residents] of the province of Chichas and its vicinity, that seeing the strong yoke that oppresses us with such force (*pecho*), and the tyranny that those in charge bring to this task without taking consideration of our misfortunes, and exasperated by them and their impiety, I have determined to shake off this unbearable yoke, and contain the evil government that we experience from the leaders. . . . [It was for this reason] that the *corregidor* of the province of Tinta died on the public gallows, and to whose defense came a group of Spaniards (*chapetones*) from the city of Cuzco, dragging with them my beloved *criollos,* whose audacity and daring was paid for with their lives. I only feel for the *criollo* countrymen who have been a source of my courage. I do not wish them any harm, but [desire] that we live together as brothers and, joined together in one body, destroy the Europeans. . . . [T]his effort does not oppose in the slightest way our sacred Catholic religion, but is only to suppress disorder. . . . I have taken only those measures that have been necessary for the support, protection, tranquility, and conservation of the Spanish *criollos,* of the *mestizos, zambos* and Indians. For all of them being countrymen and compatriots born in our land . . . and all having suffered equally the oppressions and tyranny of the Europeans, it has been expedient to make known to them—said *criollos* and countrymen—that if they choose [to follow] my counsel harm will not follow them, not in their lives nor on their haciendas. But if my warning is rejected they will find the opposite. They will experience ruin, my meekness converting to rage and fury, reducing this province to ashes; and . . . I have the forces, money, and all the surrounding provinces at my disposition, in union with *criollos* and *naturales,* not to mention the rest of the provinces that also are under my orders. . . . Thus do not underestimate my warning that is born of my love and clemency and which promotes the common good of our kingdom, and that ends in re-moving all the *criollos* and *naturales* from the unjust servitude that they have suffered. . . . At the same time, the principal goal is to end the offenses to God our Lord, whose ministers, the priests (*Señores sacerdotes*), will have the right-ful regard and veneration of their positions, and so will have the clerics and monasteries, by whose pious and just intentions with which I proceed, I hope for Divine Clemency, as one destined for it, so it will enlighten and govern me for this undertaking (*negocio*) in which I need all his assistance for its joy-ous success.

And thus so that you have understood, copies of this proclamation will be put up in prominent places in said provinces . . . [so that] I will know who follows this edict, rewarding the loyal and punishing the rebels, that they may know our rule of law, and afterwards may not allege ignorance. . . . Lampa, December 23, 1780.

Don José Gabriel Tupac Amaru, *Inca* [*CDIP,* 112. 1780-XII-23]

43. Excommunication of Tupac Amaru and His Followers

Tupac Amaru had been close to the Church and particularly close—or so he thought—to the bishop of Cuzco, Juan Manuel de Moscoso. Although Tupac Amaru continued to demonstrate respect for the Catholic Church and its reli-gious members (priests, nuns, and so forth), church officials were not about to reciprocate his loyalty. Once the rebellion began and churches—normally places of refuge—were attacked, the bishop quickly excommunicated the rebels. It is difficult to determine the impact of this on the rebellious movement. Some In-dians who fought against the rebels were aware of, and respected, the excommu-nication. However, some rebels who fought with Tupac Amaru were glad to be rid of Christianity's hold, and others, though they maintained basic Christian beliefs, were not bothered by the act of the bishop. The following is the notice of excommunication for Tupac Amaru and his followers.

Be it publicly known that José Tupac Amaru, *cacique* of the town of Tunga-suca, has been excommunicated, through high excommunication, due to having set fire to public chapels and the church of Sangarará . . . for being a rebellious traitor of the King, Our Lord, for seditiously working against peace and being a usurper of Royal Rights. If, after receiving this ban, all those who have supported him, helped him, and those who accompany him, continue to communicate with him and help him in his depraved intentions; and under the same penalty, any who dares to remove this notice [*cédula*] from where it was fixed in the church, reserving the right to absolve them from everything, this which was done in the city of Cuzco.

—Juan Manuel, Bishop of Cuzco—By mandate
of His Holiness the Bishop, my Lord.
—Dr. José Domingo de Frías, Secretary. [*CDIP,* 73. 1780-XI-17]

44. Letter from José Gabriel Tupac Amaru to the Honorable Bishop of Cuzco

As a result of some of the early actions of the rebels that involved attacks on churches where loyalists gathered—which normally were considered sacred sites and places of refuge—the bishop of Cuzco, Moscoso, was especially adamant in his condemnation of the rebels. Part of this zeal may have come from his rather close association with Tupac Amaru before the rebellion; both shared a strong dislike of Corregidor Arriaga. This association even included shared social occasions. In the following letter, Tupac Amaru tries to assure the bishop that he is a good Christian and does not wish to do harm to the Church or to its religious personnel.

Honorable Sir,
[Due to] the Catholic zeal to which I abide and which as a child of the church as I profess, and being a Christian believer by the power of saintly baptism, I cannot ever profane the sacred tabernacle of God . . . nor can I offend His priests, unless it were necessary to renounce the faith and embrace the extreme and torpid vices of licentiousness, with the abuse of renovating the heavy burdens of some phenomena, titled *corregidores,* and the increased taxes they have been introducing with the creation of a general Customhouse and even more taxes imposed at the miserable doors of loyal subjects of my nation. [These taxes are] being spread inexorably by a second Pizarro in tyranny who not only exacts them from my nation, but from many other nations. And while hoping that somebody would liberate us from this pharaoh's yoke, I came out to defend and speak for the whole kingdom, to prevent even greater inconveniences, robberies, and murders along with other abuses and other unusual actions. . . . Even though they currently see me as a traitor and

rebel, disloyal and despotic towards our Monarch, Carlos, time will tell that I am his vassal and that I have never knowingly denied my Holy church and Catholic Monarch. I only want to liberate my people from tyranny and make sure that the holy Catholic law be respected, so that we can live quietly and in peace. It is for this reason that I am sending my envoys to that Cabildo, so that the city [Cuzco] be rendered to me without any quarrel so that I am not forced to use violence, because then I will enter with fire and blood.

Your Honor, do not be discomfited with this news, nor perturb your Christian fervor, nor the peace of the monasteries, whose sacred virgins and sacred others will not be desecrated in any way, nor the priests exposed to any offensive acts from those who follow me. The goals of my intentions are clear, that of attaining for my nation the absolute freedom from all types of taxation, complete pardon for what appears as the lapse in the servitude that I owe, and the total abolishment of all customs. . . . I will retire to Tebayda [?] where I will ask for mercy, and your Excellency will send me all the documentation needed to these glorious ends, for which I hope through Divine Mercy, to Whom I cry out, with the greatest devotion of my soul, for your Excellency's important life. Tungasuca, December 12, 1780.

José Gabriel Tupac Amaru, *Inca* [*CDIP,* 101. 1780-XII-12]

45. Letter from Bishop Moscoso to the Royal War Council over the Threat of Tupac Amaru Taking the Apurímac Bridge and Isolating Cuzco

The residents of Cuzco, including the bishop, realized that they were in great peril from the superiority in numbers of the insurrectionary forces. The rebels had control of the roads or passages to and from the Lake Titicaca region and beyond. In the following letter, Bishop Moscoso clearly spells out the fear the residents of Cuzco had of being cut off from Lima if the vital bridge over the Apurímac River were taken or destroyed, and the grave situation this would create for those loyal to the Spanish Crown in Cuzco. It also demonstrates the active role the bishop took in military affairs to defend the city and defeat the rebels.

We have many reasons to believe that the main project of the rebellious Indian José Tupac Amaru is to cut the Apurímac bridge to prevent the resources sent from the capital of Lima from reaching us, or to intercept any essential communication which is the foundation of our subsistence. . . .

This is also confirmed by the report presented to you by the priest of Colcha, Don Feliciano Paz. It is also expressed in the edict included in the canvas sent by the *cacica,* wife of the Rebel [Micaela Bastidas], to Maras. . . . You well know how much damage will occur if this hellish plan comes to be, so this is the only way that we have left to save ourselves from it. . . . Under these circumstances, I want to inform you of the importance of guarding this bridge with a respectable garrison and with an experienced and honorable officer who could assure us that the rebel will not succeed with his hideous intentions; and if possible to get a couple of mortars [could be cannons] that fire stones, one on each side of the gorge, something that I have also mentioned to the Viceroy. I hope that you will immediately provide for this to be accomplished, as any omission might give an opportunity to the rebel to circle us and conquer us through siege, as he is planning to do. May our Lord protect you for many years.—Cuzco, December 16th, 1780.

Juan Manuel, Bishop of Cuzco.
Mssrs. of the Royal War Council. [*CDIP,* 106. 1780-XII-16]

46. Account of the Deplorable Defeat That the Traitor Tupac Amaru Inflicted on the Military Expedition

One of the first major encounters between rebels and loyalists took place in Sangarará. The following document is a description of this encounter and the events leading up to it, including misgivings on the part of some loyalists about the capabilities of the expedition. The church in Sangarará, normally a place of sanctuary, was burned with people inside it. Tupac Amaru offered to let the creoles leave, but they apparently did not trust him or preferred to take their chances with the Spaniards, and so they too perished in the flames. The document gives a sense of the brutality of conflict, and of the actions Tupac Amaru was willing to take to bring victory to his cause.

Once the news of the rebellion of Tupac Amaru reached Cuzco on November 17th of said year of 1780, and having Dn. Fernando Cabrera, *Corregidor* of Quispicanchi, arrived [in Cuzco] it was judged that it [the rebellion] was too potent to easily be dissipated by them. The War Council of *Junta de Guerra* (that exists for these type of issues in the said city) ordered that an army of over 800 men be organized, including Spaniards, *mestizos,* and some

Indians of the Pueblo of Oropesa led by their Cacique Dn. Pedro Ximenes de Saguaraura who had assured them of his loyalty. They were to measure and test the forces of this rebel, and invade him there where he exercised his tyrannies. To this end *Cacique* Pacheco wrote a letter to the *Corregidor* of Cuzco asking him to send men to help him apprehend the Rebel and that he would deliver him into their hands. As Pacheco did not receive a prompt answer, he assumed that his letter had not been given to the *Corregidor,* and decided to write another one which was intercepted by José Gabriel's scouts. They took the messenger prisoner, and him and the letter were taken and presented to Tupac Amaru.

The troops armed with muskets, sabers, and lances left Cuzco under the command of Dn. Fernando Cabrera as he was the *Corregidor* of the Province where the rebel was at the moment. The troops included some European officers like Dn. Tiburcio Landa, a former *corregidor* of Paucartambo, and Dn. Francisco Escajadillo who are mentioned due to their being known by many. This expedition was not known for being prudent: it was lacking in good judgment, and even some members of the Council tried to delay it for a better opportunity. But the judgment of the great majority of the officers of that battalion prevailed, whether due to the passion of their characters or their desires for glory, or better yet due to the outrage caused by the never before seen insolence of that Indian. . . . [T]hey pressed their march and posted their soldiers in the pueblo of Sangarará, five leagues from Tungasuca and around twenty leagues from Cuzco, with the intent of engaging in battle with the Rebel the following day. They say that the Rebel had detailed information of the movements of our people, their number, their arms, their intentions, and everything else that pertained to them. And taking advantage of the darkness of the night which preceded November 18, he set off to encounter those who were looking for him. The Indian advised his people not to let them be seen by the troops, and to stay away from the road they were supposed to take, and so it was thought that the rebels had retreated in fear. . . .

With this vain confidence, and against all good judgment, they carelessly did not take [up a position on] either an available mountain or hill. Believing it advantageous for the coming battle, the Spaniards and *Mestizos* quartered themselves in the church and surrounded its exterior with the Indians they brought from Cuzco. Before the next day began, a tremor of the earth was felt, which was from the many enemies approaching. Some precautions were taken to engage in the battle that started at dawn, and when they were ready to come out they found themselves under a heavy, nonstop shower of rocks that forced them to stay inside the church, preventing them from using their muskets, sabers, and stone-firing cannons. Tupac Amaru ordered the Priest to remove the Holy Sacrament from the church as he was going to set the church on fire. He then proceeded to offer to let every Spanish creole who was a member of the Expedition and who would distance themselves from the Europeans to go free. . . . They [the *criollos*] decided to stay, and once the temple was on fire they all found themselves in peril of dying by being burned, of smoke inhalation, or due to a beam, statue or altar piece that was being consumed by the fire falling on them: or going out and facing the inevitable death at the hands of those who were forcing them to go through blows, contusions, or being wounded by knives, sticks, rocks, or clubs and cudgels. Many confessed but none received communion, as they could not find the key to where the ciborium [vessel containing the consecrated bread for the Eucharist] . . . was deposited which also burned without mercy. Such was the destruction that with the exception of some Indians and *Mestizos* who crossed to the contrary party, and one Spaniard, who dressed as a priest and was able to escape, all the rest were sacrificed to the ravages of the wrath of those barbarians. After Tupac Amaru gave the order, the bodies were buried with a priest being paid one peso per body. One cannot omit what the Rebel executed against the deceased Cabrera. Finding Cabrera's body lying on the ground, he kicked it in the head expressing that . . . due to his thick-headedness he finds himself here; and he [Tupac Amaru] continued to recognize other dead officials.

This sad event gave the rebels sufficient wings to speed ahead with their exploits. They lost the horror and natural compassion that humanity requires after they saw such a runaway spectacle, to which they had not been accustomed for years. Their losses were no more than twenty men and some others wounded. The guns and stone mortars that our miserable dead carried only augmented their strength, and their arrogance grew to such levels that after having executed this destruction, the Rebel dispatched his people against the *Cacique* Pacheco who, after having fought with valor and loyalty and having killed many Indian enemies, died on the gallows together with his family. Quispicanchi, November 20th, 1780. [*CDIP* 76. 1780-XI-20]

47. Bishop Moscoso of Cuzco Writes to Antonio de Areche about Tupac Amaru Threatening Cuzco

In the following document, Bishop Moscoso reports to Visitor General Antonio de Areche about some of the early fighting between rebels and loyalists. He makes reference to the strategic acts of burning bridges and refers to the Indians as inhuman for killing Spaniards, when, of course, the Spaniards and others did the same or worse to the rebels. He makes it clear that the fact that the rebels have intelligent leadership and organization makes them more dangerous

than he would normally perceive them to be, not to mention more difficult to de-
feat. He also points to ways in which the clergy, who are his responsibility, have
served the loyalist cause. Even in these desperate times, the formulaic recognition
of status and honor that begins most official documents was maintained.

"Honorable Sir, Don José Antonio de Areche, *Visitador General.*—My Most
Venerable Lord.—On the 20th I wrote to your illustrious Honor, informing
you about the status of the rebellion and of the measures that have been taken
to contain it. And I am sending separately, for better security, the same duplicate documents so that if the documents are intercepted by any chance, Your
Illustrious Honor will still be able to inform yourself and act accordingly.

Even though the principal leader [Tupac Amaru] of the rebellion is still
alive, we have not been able to gain any advantage over him nor [has there
been] decisive action in the frontier (La Raya) of Vilcanota, where people
say the rebel Tupac Amaru is staying with the intention of facing the five
Corregidores who, acting together, have been able to prevent his march to
this City. However, some satisfaction resulted when our soldiers punished
the neighboring Indians on the twentieth and twenty-first. Encouraged by
the incitements so cruelly lodged in these pueblos, they had become so bold
and insolent as to cause those in the City to fear this was the day of their final extermination.

The unrest first took hold in the town of Ocongate, an annex of the Doctrina [Parish] of Catca in the province of Quispicanchi. From there some Indians descended to the neighboring ravine stirring up those they found from
Caycay to Calca, laying waste to these places and increasing their numbers
and their force in each of them due to the resolution they inspired and the
poor conditions of the Indians they were encountering.

Once together, they burned the bridges of Caycay, Sierra Bella, San Salvador, Pisac, Coya and Lamay one after the other; they killed all the Spaniards
they ran into without distinction of sex or age, and hanged, on the same gallows that the *Corregidor* of Calca and Lares had built, several unfortunate citizens whose bodies can be seen from this side of the river.

The furor of these inhuman *naturales,* besides freeing themselves from the
reparto which they knew they were responsible for, was fueled by their generalized robbing and looting to which they had delivered themselves for some
time; but with such iniquity that they were throwing the furniture they could
not carry into the river. The tumult didn't stop there because the cancer
spread as far as the town of Taray where, mixed with some individuals who
were able to cross the river, or were moved by the bad example they had before them, also placed themselves in action, joining together with all the Indians of the surrounding area. And stirred up to the point of rebellion, with

flags, drums and trumpets, as a war battalion, they marched to a plain known as Pampa Chica which is located less than two leagues from this city.

There the enemy divided into two columns; and in an effort to provoke them, or at least disperse this mob who were trying to test the city at several of the entrances, the corresponding measures were taken in the various sections of the city. On the other side of the river where it begins to enter the pueblo of Huayllabamba, Don Juan Nicolas Lobatón, *corregidor* of that district, positioned himself. Don Francisco Laysequilla, who was commissioned by the *Junta* for the expedition, positioned himself in Taray and he was dispatched with a small party of soldiers which almost immediately was reinforced with another one. The same was also done to help the *Corregidor* of Urubamba. The latter, noticing that the Indians who were coming down through the narrow passages of Calca between the mountains and the river were putting up resistance, did his job and with his soldiers killed at least one hundred Indians, besides those who in their dejection threw themselves into the river and those who were wounded. Some counted at least 400, others a thousand, something that we have not been able to confirm yet due to lack of more specific information, and because the troops have not come back yet. For it is very opportune for them to survey the invaded pueblos and warn everybody in them of the damages incurred, and take information about the accomplices in the insurrection.

It seems that in the *pampa* of Chita, which is the jurisdiction of three parishes of this Capital, there were less people to defeat. But the more than 600 Indians that were there were very loyal to the rebellion, and being defeated they fled through the surrounding hills. Some of the dead remained on the ground and their heads were taken and put on the lances and displayed on the streets and squares, a ceremony that was judged as very appropriate to warn the masses and to try to redress the bad disposition in which they might find themselves [and be tempted] to take part at the first opportunity in some domestic movement of their own.

There is no doubt that the victory has not been complete, as what I say indicates that the main conspiracy of Tupac Amaru has not been dissipated. [I]t is difficult to instantly defeat a considerable number of Indians because these, especially when they find themselves without a leader as in this case, rarely are able to sustain an organized attack, as has happened in other shorter confrontations. They usually attack en masse and at the first setback they disperse into the mountains, in order to join together again like a cloud of flies shooed away from a plate of sweets.

The soldiers who came back recounting their glories find themselves very encouraged and serve as an example for the rest; and when I am walking down the streets they introduce themselves to me indicating that they are from the group that took part in the combat and ask to be blessed, something that I do with goodwill as this means a great deal to those poor people who have not been raised in the clamor of arms.

For another thing the masses find themselves perplexed with the public declarations of victory and full of fear at the sight of the hanging heads, a very useful spectacle to contain the boldness of the masses and prevent its spreading. Our suspicions about the *caciques* of the suburban parishes have also been confirmed. It was only natural that the fliers that Tupac Amaru distributed to these pueblos arrived in our hands. Thanks to the diligence of the Priests, the *caciques* have been informed that they will be called in our defense in this and other cases. The Indian *principales* who have not responded to this request are being considered as accomplices and supporters, a crime already accredited by the priest from San Sebastian, one of the parishes, whose case I include here and in which the interest of a *Cacique* in a future conspiracy is demonstrated. As it is something that others might be interested in doing, I have warned the *Junta,* even before the appearance of any of the signs we have previously seen.

My clergy have fulfilled their obligation in this occasion, giving proof that the units your armies and their respective officials formed under the orders of the Dean are very useful. At the first news of the past insurrection, the Inspector demanded they come. And they appeared marching through the Plaza and the barracks with all the necessary weapons and assorted banners with sacred images (worthy of pride) and hieroglyphs which give the idea of the inclusion which the Church has in this war, as much through faith and morality as through the rights of our Sovereign. . . .

This all being so pleasing to God and the world, it provoked abundant tears and tenderness from the public. So much so that even the soldiers who have served in formal expeditions of Europe could not stop themselves from crying, as their hearts were moved by impressions as holy as they were unusual to behold. I have already previously expressed to your Illustrious Majesty that the ostentatious practices of our clergymen in showing their love of the King, without sparing any comfort or even their lives, is one of the anchors that secures the ship of this Dominion which has seen itself at the verge of sinking. . . . [F]inding myself totally convinced that this is true and supported by the evidence, I will not cease to concentrate all of my efforts on the continuation of this action, so necessary and edifying, without forgiving those elements that work against God's will.

Besides the sermon which I have happily concluded, I have also prepared another one to the Indians and *Mestizos* in their own language and this should begin either today or tomorrow. Due to previous diligence I have already instructed the preachers about the points they need to address, especially emphasizing the fidelity and subordination that our Sovereign requires of them for being Christians, and that they will stop being one [Christian] as soon as they ignore the requirements of obedience. If we cannot heal the spiritual damage, I will be able to say to the City: we have cured Babylon, but it has not healed, even though this will not be enough reason for me to abandon it or desert it. And I will console it up to the last of my breath in the event that the Heavens do not incline themselves benignly towards our wishes.

I have disclosed more than I planned, and more than what trying times permit, with the wish of informing Your Illustrious Honor of the latest events, considering that Your Illustrious Honor is the convergent point from where all the strings are pulled in the effort to put order into the operations that will lead to success.

Our God the Lord guard Your Illustrious Honor for many years to come. Cuzco, December 22nd, 1780.

Juan Manuel, Obispo del Cuzco. [*CDIP,* 111. 1780-XII-22]

48. Unfriendly Description of Bishop Moscoso

The bishop of Cuzco was a political as well as religious figure. He brought his ongoing feud with Corregidor *Arriaga with him when both were transferred to Cuzco. Both developed friends and enemies in their new positions, and their dislike of each other continued. One of those who sympathized with the bishop in his feelings toward Arriaga was Tupac Amaru. In the following selection, a resident of Cuzco—who obviously did not like the bishop—reflects on the impact the bishop had on local society and his attitude toward Spaniards.*

As soon as Señor Moscoso arrived in this neighborhood the tranquility and peace, which it enjoyed, perished, because under the hypocritical zeal of discharging his duties he has not done another thing but clink chains and draw blood on account of his passions. . . . He abhorrs [*sic*] the Europeans extremely, takes vengeance upon various inhabitants for despicable motives, and maintains relations with persons of the other sex, not of good fame, causing serious scandal to the city. The first high office he obtained was in Arequipa and in that city he began to show insubordination. . . . He says he has no superior in the land but the Pope. [*LIR,* 43. Translated by L. E. Fisher]

49. Letter of Don Bernardo Gonzalez de La Madrid That Relates the Travails That He Suffered while a Prisoner of the Rebel Tupac Amaru in the Pueblo of Tungasuca

In the following document, an obraje *owner—who apparently believed he had a reasonably good relationship with Tupac Amaru because of past dealings of a positive nature with the Inca—gives an account of how he was tricked into coming to Tungasuca by the Inca and then taken prisoner in the earliest stages of the insurrection. He was held with* Corregidor *Arriaga until the* corregidor *was executed. The* obraje *owner was quite understandably terrified of what might happen to him, and he was kept in irons to prevent his escape. He tried his best to win over his captors so they would not kill him, and he managed to get close to Micaela Bastidas. Eventually he was used as a messenger to carry Tupac Amaru's wishes to authorities in Cuzco, where he was very warmly received because most people thought he had been killed. The document conveys a sense of the fear that any person in such a situation would feel, and how he used all means possible to spare his life and win back his freedom from the clutches of death.*

Dear Sir: On November 5, 1780 I received in my *obraje* of Pomacanchi, situated four leagues from the Pueblo of Tungasuca, a letter that seemed to me to be signed by my friend Colonel Sr. Antonio Arriaga, the past *Corregidor* of the Province of Tinta, with the following content: *Dear Friend, it is of the utmost importance that Your Honor come to this town of Tungasuca as soon as you read this, as we have several issues that we need to talk about tonight. From here I am planning to go to Cuzco to vindicate my honor. I wish Your Honor perfect health and may God keep it for you. Tungasuca, November 5th, 1780. Your Honor's beloved friend, Arriaga.*

Having received said letter, I left for the above-mentioned pueblo in a hurry after having attended mass at around ten A.M. And after arriving at the House of the Rebel Tupac Amaru, I found him eating in the company of his infamous relatives and, coming to the door, he took me by the hand offering me the chair where he had been sitting and asked me whether I wanted to eat. To which I answered that I had already done so [eaten] in my *obraje*, and that I had only come in response to the *Corregidor's* call, for whom I asked. He answered that they were expecting him [and that he should arrive] at any moment, which I thought was strange as I saw that the letter I received had come from this very pueblo. Seeing that the *Corregidor* was not showing up after an hour of having arrived, I told him [Tupac Amaru] that I wanted to return to Pomacanchi as I had to give Don Diego Castillo (clerk of the *Corregidor* of Quispicanchi, Don Fernando Cabrera) 40,000 *varas* [each *vara* equals 33 inches] of clothing the next day for the *repartimiento* that he was going to distribute in his Province. Seeing my intention, the Rebel called me to the Patio and whispered into my ear that the *Corregidor* was hiding in his House as it was very convenient for him to do so because of some inquiries that he was conducting. Guiding me to the room he said the *Corregidor* was in, he left while at the same time telling me to go in which I promptly did. I was surprised by twenty-five Servants who had been forewarned against my arrival. Using great force, they tried to tie me up. But they were not able to do so as I defended myself (even though without any arms) from that evil knavery. Asking about the *Corregidor,* I was told that he was in one of the rooms destined to be used to keep those who were being caught. When I entered the room where the *Corregidor* was being kept, I found him a prisoner in stocks. I asked him why he found himself in that situation and he responded that he did not know. At that very moment the twenty-five corpulent fellows charged me and tied me up with ropes that they had for this purpose and put me in the same stock where the *Corregidor* was held. . . . I asked him, even though I was amazed by the events, whether he had written me a letter asking me to come to see him. He said no, which put me beside myself with foreboding of what had happened to me.

After two hours in this fatal prison, I received a note from the Rebel in which he told me that it would be convenient to write a letter to Don Fernando Cabrera asking him to come and help me, and if I refused I would pay notable consequences. I, blinded by rage at seeing myself the prisoner of a servant of mine who served me as a muleteer taking my cargo to Potosí, answered that once I was freed from this oppression, he would suffer worse consequences than those inflicted on me. After a while the Rebel ordered them to put me in shackles, which the guards promptly did.

That night around twelve I heard a tumult in the Plaza of beasts and people screaming which made me think my final hour had arrived, because the soldiers who were guarding me came into the cell where they kept their arms and got lances, rifles, and pistols, threatening to kill me as well as the *Corregidor.* And I, asking for mercy, and making loving gestures, spent the rest of the night with this fear, and very uncomfortable with no more cover than a riding cloak of hide. Even though I asked the rebel for some blankets he did not send any, [which he would] have done if he had had any good blood. . . . He should have treated me well considering that he owed me 1,500 pesos, money that I had supplied him on various occasions for his expenses and many other favors that I have done for him and all his infamous relatives.

The next day he wrote me another letter telling me that he was very angry with me. . . . Once again he was asking me to [write to] the *Corregidor* of

Quispicanchi or his Lieutenant: and I, who already knew his depraved thoughts, responded with the utmost submission and rendition, telling him that it was impossible for me to obey his orders as I was not a friend with said *Corregidor.* . . . [It was then that] I learned that the Rebel's clear intention was to declare himself King.

Up until the 9th I suffered much fright just by observing the care with which the guards were doing their job, preventing me from talking to the *Corregidor* and treating me with such contempt that I was losing my patience. But it was important to keep my patience because otherwise they would have taken my life.

During these nights there were frequent disturbances in the Plaza by the soldiers who were keeping guard of the house as they had several spies throughout the region and all the way to Cuzco. [These spies were] saying that the soldiers were going to come and get me out, and with this . . . the guards would insult me and say they wanted to shorten my life. On one of those days on which I saw myself in peril, I wrote a letter to the Indian wife of the Rebel, begging her with utmost submission and love, to remember the favors that I had done for her as well as her Husband and family. Her answer was that she was waiting for a letter from Cuzco to put me in the place I deserved, which according to what I later experienced, was to send me to the gallows.

On the 9th I endured a lot of disrespect from the Guards and the relatives of the Rebel with the announcement of what he intended to do with me. At five in the afternoon Antonio Bastidas, the brother of the wife of the Rebel, came into the room where I was being held prisoner with two handcuffs, one each for the *Corregidor* and myself. He put them on with such cruelty that, due to their tightness, the skin on my wrists was cut. This despicable one called the Guards and told them to take up arms. Amidst this conflict I begged all of those who were present for whom I had done much good to ask the Rebel on my behalf to disclose the motive behind making me suffer so much. At this time I spotted one of the Rebel's sons and I asked him with great humility to beg his father, in my name, to keep in mind all the favors I had done for him since I had met him. And if that was not enough, I asked if he could bring me a Confessor so that I could prepare myself, something that they did immediately. [The Confessor] made an altar where an image of the crucified Jesus was put, and another of the Virgin of Dolores with a candleholder and candles that were brought from the Church. Having all this in order, the Rebel came in. I begged him again to spare my life as it was in his hands, reminding him of how much appreciation I had shown while serving him with my person and my silver on all the occasions when he had asked me to. The Rebel, intent in not caving in to my supplications, told me that this was an order from the King our Lord . . . so he could not agree to my request.

[K]nowing very well that it was in his hands to give me or take my life away, [I told him] that if he was doing this to take the wealth and property that I owned, he could take everything, as I only wanted my life. He responded condescendingly to this last petition and ordered the Indian soldiers to take me to another room where his older son took off my handcuffs, but I was still being secured with a pair of shackles that weighed more than thirty pounds and were welded very well, which they took off after four days.

Coming back from such a horrible lethargy, I started to thank God for having spared me from such disastrous luck, when another cleric appeared telling me that he had orders from the Rebel to give me confession. With this news my sorrows increased until the wife of the Rebel came in and consoled me, telling me that I should not worry as I had been forgiven with the condition that I would enter a religious order as soon as they took power in Cuzco and that I would have their protection while they would be alive. Despite all these promises, I spent that night in continual fear, hearing the noise the soldiers guarding the *Corregidor* were making.

The next day in the morning from dawn until ten A.M. the Rebel gathered in the Plaza people from the outlying districts . . . of Tinta, both Spaniards and Indians who . . . numbered between 8,000 to 10,000 men. They had been summoned to the town through fake letters that he had written them in the name of the *Corregidor.* In the meantime he proclaimed in the Plaza so everyone could understand, how the King Our Lord had given him an order to end the *repartimientos, obrajes,* taxes, customs, the Potosí *mita,* and the Tobacco Monopoly. Having finished with the proclamations, they brought out *Corregidor* Arriaga and had him executed. I then learned that the Rebel and his evil relatives, as well as those who attended the deplorable event and spectacle, were rejoicing. And I, who did not find myself nor consider myself free of the risk; I who had witnessed the death of my friend. . . . Your Honor can imagine the state of my heart.

From said 10th to the 27th of December I did not have one minute of rest. In the interim, two friends of mine arrived at the Rebel's house and ardently begged him not to kill Don Juan Antonio Figueroa, Don Manuel San Roque, Don Juan Martinez, Don Francisco Zisneros, Don Yldefonso Mendieta and myself. But God wished that their desires should not be fulfilled as neither the Rebel nor his wife or family agreed. . . . The Rebel's wife continued to visit with me, offering the ownership of whatever she should come to own, and afterwards I would be ordained and I would become the Bishop of her dominions. I agreed to everything as it suited my intentions of winning her goodwill as well as that of her family and saving my life.

In this predicament, a *Cholo* from the family filed a complaint and told an Indian that I wanted to kill her [Micaela Bastidas] as well as her oldest son. Due to this I lost all the ground that I had gained, and wanting to know whether this was true, they offered silver to the Guards that were on duty, so that if they would corroborate [the accusation], I would be executed. But God who always protects his cause, did not allow those depraved ones to testify against me as I was innocent.

An Indian spy came back with news that the soldiers from Cuzco were close to town and that they were coming with the intention of freeing us, the poor prisoners who were being held. There was such an outcry that it looked as if the day of final judgment had arrived. Taking up their arms, they spent two hours raising such continuous alarms and voices that even the heart of the hardest soul was constrained. Thinking this news was true, I showed myself to be happy and the guards, having noticed this, told the Rebel and he immediately ordered that I be put in very secure shackles in which I remained for eight very uncomfortable days as they were very heavy. They were so tight that my legs started to swell so badly that I could not walk at all.

On the 19th, around prayer time, a brother-in-law of the Rebel came to let me know that my comrade Don Josef Antonio Urizar and my nephew had died in a battle in the pueblo of Sangarará along with some Spaniards, and *criollos* who had come with the intention of freeing me from prison. His happiness, as well as that of others in the house (of having been successful when least expected), was such that they spent that day and the following shouting their victory. I despised all that, while feigning happiness as it would help my being set free. A few days after this misfortune, the Indian [Micaela Bastidas] informed me that when we approached Cuzco her husband had decided to send me as an ambassador to ask those compatriots who were left [in Cuzco] to surrender. Otherwise they would be speared, as well as any *criollo* who would oppose his orders. I was eager to obey everything they told me to so that they would not suspect me, nor have any suspicion.

After being freed from prison, I accommodated myself to serve the Rebel and his wife with humility and zeal, behaving as the most humble of blacks. When the Indian [Micaela Bastidas] would go to mass I would take her by the hand holding the umbrella in the other so that she would not be offended by the sun's rays or harsh weather. I occupied myself in these tasks, as well as others that I found beneficial, until January 3rd, 1781, trying by these methods to win their approval. On this day they decided to send me, carrying the documents of an Ambassador, from the Pampa de Ocoroc which is three leagues away from the city to visit the Honorable Ecclesiastical Mayors and secular authorities in the company of two priests. Recognizing that I had finally attained my goal of being set free, I sped up the pace of the beast I was riding before the Rebel could change his mind. Arriving around five in the afternoon at the Barracks of La Compañía, we caused such a commotion and happiness among the residents of Cuzco that it took me more than two hours to be able to see the Commander, spending all this time hugging and receiving all sorts of congratulations from my friends as well as from people I had never met, as everybody in this City thought I was dead and were praying to God to take me to his kingdom. . . .

Having given the *Junta de Guerra* the documents of Ambassador, they asked me whether I would like to go back with their answer. I responded angrily that I would not go back under any circumstances because the treatment they had given me was not desirable, and that in retribution for what they had done to me I offered to sacrifice myself to defend the King from the Rebel, as I did on January 8th when said Rebel attacked half a league from this City, and I, who had been wronged, got closer than anybody else, and shot at them thirty-five times in less than an hour. This is all I can say for the time being to Your Honor, may God protect you for many years. Cuzco, January 9th, 1781.

Don Bernardo Gonzalez de la Madrid [*CDIP,* 125. 1781-I-9]

50. Female *Kuraka* Tomasa Titu Condemayta to Tupac Amaru

In the following letter, one of the few female kurakas, *Tomasa Titu Condemayta, writes to Tupac Amaru concerning an incident in which a person was killed and his goods embargoed. Apparently there was also some degree of mischief behind the situation that involved the potential disappearance of silver; Tomasa asks Tupac Amaru to use his good judgment to evaluate the situation. She also informs him of loyalist troop movements. Titu Condemayta was a trusted rebel who maintained fairly constant contact with both the rebel leader and his wife, Micaela Bastidas. Despite these close associations, her concern suggests that rebel leaders were held accountable for their actions by Tupac Amaru.*

Honorable Governor Don José Gabriel Tupac Amaru:
My most beloved brother and Lord.—I again received Your Grace's [letter] with much pleasure and, having understood its content, I inform you that concerning the silver you've requested (with which undoubtedly the false bearer and his uncles will come with their lies, as I did not name him as [the official] bearer, but [instead] Tomás Farfán): Your Grace does not know what type of an individual he [the false bearer] is; if he saw the silver why didn't he

tell me, for the people dismantled [the equipment and luggage] from his [the person who was killed] horses and the saddle was taken away from someone [named] Villena by the *alcalde* of Chalco, who will keep it for when Your Mercy may ask for it. . . . He had two mules and that horse. One mule was shot by accident, the other one is still here. I took its pack saddle (*gurupanda*) from the *alcalde* of Colque. It contained odds and ends, socks and such unimportant things that I can have at your disposal whenever your Honor feels like asking for them.

It also carried the note that the deceased Don Andrés wrote to you, with which Your Mercy will know best what to do.

The bodies have already been buried, his hacienda consists of no more than his cornfields, his small orchard, a house of little worth which they burned down but perhaps already mortgaged. The entire estate was in bad condition. . . . I told the Priest that he should bury the man and compensate himself with the harvest of the dead man's hacienda because he had been very corrupt. Your Grace will do what you deem necessary. I have been told that in Cuzco as well as in Chumbivilcas—even though I do not know whether this is true or not as they are just rumors floating around—that they [the loyalists] have garrisoned many soldiers [in the province].

The servants of the defunct *Corregidor* say that they saw them [the soldiers] on the outskirts of Saint Tomas and they are falling back toward Cuzco and that a Torre from Acomayo could give you more news if Your Grace so chooses . . . his name being José Torre.

I beg Your Grace, as a man who handles mules, they tell me that they (the mules) are in that Sanctuary and the branding marks will identify them. . . . There is one that they brought on Saturday, the brown mule with his saddle, and a black mule, one of mixed colors, a bay which had no branding mark because I had just recently bought it, but which did have a completely new leather saddle, which the soldiers know very well. With the two [mules] that they took to Quiquijana that makes six standing, and here we stay without having any reason to move them. The branding marks are a *D* and an *A* interlaced. The aforementioned [mule] of mixed colors did not have branding marks as I had borrowed her.

In the other letter I wrote to Your Mercy in which I warned you that the people with little [provocation] wanted to move forward, and so that they would be reprimanded in these pueblos it was necessary that Your Mercy order someone, under your signature and with your authority, to notify them that they should not harm anyone, because they have been destroying the *obrajes* and have been tempted to go astray and commit other excesses against the creoles. For all this, I await orders from Your Mercy and pray to God to shower Your Grace with health, and all the sympathy and grace of God as well as Your Grace's wife, to whose authority I offer my humble services for you to command and beg the Lord to keep you safe for many years to come. Acos, November 21st, 1780.—I kiss Your Grace's hands, yours very truly.

—Tomasa. . . . [*CDIP*, 80. 1780-XI-21]

51. Continuation of the Account of the Sad Acts Carried Out by the Traitor, José Gabriel Tupac Amaru

This document, the longest in this collection, is remarkable for the frankness with which it discusses some of the bloodiest fighting and most horrendous acts that occurred during the rebellion. As the author notes in the conclusion, "These are the consequences of the war and of the fires of Mars." The author records a narrative of the fighting that stretched from the region near the north end of Lake Titicaca at the beginning of the document to the battles in the siege of Cuzco that conclude this piece. The author notes that the Spaniards sometimes killed women, not just rebel troops. The following document addresses the atrocities committed by the rebels, including the killing of children, rape, and murders committed in a church as the rebels sought to kill and desecrate not only the Spaniards but their God as well. It addresses the rough justice and revenge handed out by both loyalists (such as Pumacahua, the kuraka *from Chinchero who killed troops who had left the rebels and gone over to the Spanish side) and Tupac Amaru (who killed family members of the influential* kuraka, *Diego Choquehuanca, because of his opposition to the Inca-led rebellion) as they sought to win people over to their respective sides through persuasion and intimidation.*

In the document, the bishop of Cuzco and the actions of the loyalist priests are praised, including their decision to take up arms to protect Cuzco in the most desperate moments for the loyalist resistance. Attention is also given to the respect many of the loyalist Indians demonstrated for the act of excommunication—so much so that they did not seek the spoils of war from their fallen rebel enemies, as was normally the case. The praise of the priests and the bishop probably was meant to counter suspicions about the previously close relationship between Tupac Amaru and the bishop, and to put aside the fact that the bishop and his priests had also been enemies of Corregidor *Arriaga.*

The effort of priests to convince rebels to accept Jesus as they lay dying on the battlefield, and the rebels' rejection of this deathbed conversion, attests to the role of religion in everyday life, as did the Spanish demonstrations of thanks to —and supplication for help from—God for their survival and victories.

Although the author (apparently a member of the Junta de Guerra *of Cuzco) is firmly on the side of the Spanish, a grudging respect for the capabilities of the rebels and their leader comes through even in the midst of the condemnatory language. Amid the discussion of strategies, deceit, and the horrors of the conflict, the author discusses the beauty and benign climate of the Yucay (Sacred) Valley. In the end, however, it is the suffering, the loss of life, and the viciousness of war that come through the strongest.*

Despite the considerable effort that went into translating this document, it is still difficult to follow at times. This is due in part to the nature of the document, for it jumps from place to place and topic to topic, but it is also a result of the exceedingly complex structure of the language and punctuation employed by the author and the need to remove less significant sections of the document.

Full of defiance and emboldened with the victory that he had just attained by destroying our troops in the town of Sangarará in the Province of Quispicanchi, the rebel Tupac Amaru retired to Tungasuca with the depraved goal of invading the immediate pueblos and provinces. Indeed he went to that [the province] of Chumbivilcas and tried to remove the current . . . *Corregidor,* Don Josef Campino, from power. And he would have been able to accomplish his hideous plan if he had not been prevented from doing this by the priest of Velille, Don Francisco Arata, who through a ruse he devised . . . helped him (the *Corregidor*) to flee. [The *corregidor*] . . . left by foot and in a disguise, at a speed that can only be imagined. He encountered an Indian woman whom he asked what road he should take, with the resolution of not taking the one she would indicate. She willingly told him how to go, and once he lost sight of her, he took the opposite path. Soon after the Indian woman encountered the troops that had left to find the *Corregidor* and having been asked if she had seen him on the road, she indicated what had happened. The troops hastily took the direction the Indian woman had indicated, and the more they walked the farther they got from the *Corregidor* who was able, in this way, to get to Majes. With these events, the Province was subject to the Rebel and the people were forced to surrender their homes and all properties owned, with the pillage of the royal tributes and other valuables ensuing. Finding himself later in the parish of Livitaca in the same province, he [the *Corregidor*] encountered the wife of Tupac Amaru, who appeared with reinforcements of more than 5,000 men, as she had learned that that town had not surrendered. And those who know both of them attest that this *Cacica* has a more daring and bloody character than her husband. She was the one who had the greatest hand in the torture of *Corregidor* Arriaga, and despite the weakness of her sex, she promoted the unjust act of that homicide, even carrying bullets needed by the guards in her own scarf. She replaced her husband when he was away, directing and planning expeditions, and even riding a horse with her weapons in order to recruit people in the Provinces, to whose pueblos she directed repeated orders with an audacity and boldness that is rare, even authorizing edicts with her signature.

José Gabriel had written beforehand to his cousin Engenio [*sic,* Eugenio] Canantupa, *Cacique* of Coporaque in the . . . mining center of Caylloma, asking him to put aside the caution and concern the death of the *Corregidor* of Tinta had caused him and ordering him [Canantupa] to rally all his people and to wait for him in his house in Tungasuca where he would attend to him. His Cousin, the *Cacique,* delivered [Tupac Amaru's] . . . letter to the *Justicia Mayor* of Caylloma asking him for help so he could be protected from the effects of the declaration, and his people defended and prevented from being infected [by the rebellion]. The Rebel, learning that his Cousin had taken refuge in Caylloma and that he had not provided the help he had asked for, decided to dispatch troops against Caylloma in order to bring that Province under his control and to apprehend his Cousin.

The *Justicia Mayor* speedily communicated a warning to the Governor of Caylloma, Don Domingo Guerrero y Marnara, who was living in the city of Arequipa due to an illness. [The Governor] immediately asked for help to leave for his Province, but they [*Arequipeños*] were not able to give him even one-sixth of the troops he was asking for. So with very few men and thirty muskets he left without delay. Near Caylloma he ran into the Royal Accountant who was bringing money from the strongboxes for safe keeping in . . . Arequipa. Marnara then returned [to Arequipa] in order to provide more guards for the Royal Treasury, for based on the reports by said Accountant it was impossible to defend Caylloma.

Three days later it was learned in Arequipa that the troops of the traitor Tupac Amaru had gone into the mining center and demanded that the *Justicia Mayor* surrender his Cousin Eugenio so that he could be under the orders of José Gabriel. The *Justicia* succeeded in putting the Cousin in the hands of the Priest who thought it best to allow him to escape on the back of a mule. But in the very act of fleeing he was taken prisoner by the enemy Indians who brought him before Tupac Amaru. In view of these events, the mining center was delivered to Tupac Amaru, and in a moment it was abandoned by the Spaniards, who could not expect good treatment from the barbarous Indians. Some were walking, some were riding their animals bareback, and those who were better off took the road to Arequipa, among them the *Justicia Mayor* and the Royal Treasurer. The latter left more than 60,000 pesos in quicksilver [mercury] in the royal treasury, and knowing for certain that José Gabriel had left orders in Caylloma to the rest of his people to go and take possession of other Provinces, it was decided to send the Royal officer, Don Luis Baron, who left on December 10th with twenty men and sixty mules to see whether he could bring the quicksilver to Arequipa using whatever artifice and taking all risks necessary, which he was able to accomplish as desired.

. . . On December 4th a Cousin of José Gabriel, who had been sent [by the rebel leader] with Letters of Convocation to be distributed all over Collao, was hanged in Lampa, having been recognized by the *mayordomo* [foreman] of an *estancia* [rural estate, in this region most likely engaged in stock raising] named Queque. He was denounced to the Justice of the pueblo of Santa Rosa where he was arrested and taken to Lampa, whose *Corregidor* restated the charges. He not only confessed to having distributed and posted the proclamations, but to having participated in the uprising of his cousin and in the death of Arriaga, for which he was sentenced and suffered the above cited punishment.

The Rebel Tupac Amaru was not intimidated by the battalion of the five *Corregidores* [sent against him], nor did he consider retreating to his stronghold in Tungasuca. Instead, he took advantage of the brief moments good fortune provided him and went after them (the *corregidores*) in order to attack them. He arrived in the town of Macari, in the jurisdiction of Lampa, that same day of December 4th, where he distributed his troops composed of 3,000 Indians and *Mestizos* into three divisions. The first moved to the right to destroy the properties and cattle of the *Cacique* of Umachiri . . . for having revealed the information that he [Tupac Amaru] was going to apprehend the Gentleman Parada and the *Corregidor* of Lampa. The second division was detached against the said *Mayordomo* of the *Estancia* of Queque, whom Tupac Amaru detested for having caught his cousin Noguera, who was hanged in Lampa as mentioned. At this point he [Tupac Amaru] was informed that *Corregidor* Urbiola from Carabaya was in Santa Rosa and had tried to flee to the town of Ayaviri on a pack mule while Tupac Amaru was going to the *Estancia* of Chiquibamba where he had detached his third division. There he reunited with the three of them and on the 6th, between nine and ten in the morning, he entered Ayaviri, but he could not find Urbiola as he had taken care to hurriedly leave the Pueblo before the assault. . . .

The *Corregidor* of Lampa arrived in Arequipa, defeated, malnourished, half naked, sick, and with the look of someone who hadn't slept in over forty hours. The *Corregidor* from Carabaylla [*sic*, Carabaya] arrived in the same condition along with some Europeans and *Criollos* of distinction. The ones from Chucuyto and Puno went to their Provinces, as they feared they were going to be attacked by the Indians. This was the goal of the militia headed by the said *Corregidores;* but, even though it will appear to be a digression, the favorable success achieved by the *Corregidor* of Puno, Don Joaquin de Orellana, must be mentioned, and his later return to Puno, which is related in the following pages.

Account of the Success That the Corregidor of Puno Had with His Expedition and Sortie from His Province to That of Lampa with the Goal of Containing the Injuries That Those Commissioned by Tupac Amaru Were Committing There, Not Without the Risk of Suffering Equal Damage in [the Town of] Paucarcolla, and Along the Border of Chucuyto at His Return

. . . [D]espite the discomforts that the harsh rainy season presented, the party left on November 27, 1780, without being deterred by the heavy rains that were falling and which posed serious hardships and effort the following day in crossing the turbulent rivers and rapids between the towns of Paucarcolla of the Puno jurisdiction and of Caracoto of Lampa the day after. There they received trustworthy news that the Indian rebels, ordered by their Inca King Tupac Amaru (that is how they called him), were traveling in three different groups or parties carrying out their forays and that the first one of them was very close to Saman, Taraco, and Pusi burning the jails, killing the Spaniards, and enlisting people through violence to fulfill the perverse plans of their infamous Chief. . . . In view of this, they [the loyalists] continued their march until they got to a river that supposedly comes from Juliaca and the cavalry was ordered to cross it with the intent of surprising [the rebels]. . . . At this moment a letter was received from the priest of Taraca in which the priest assured him [*Corregidor* Orellana of Puno, leader of the royal forces in this engagement] that the Indians were crossing . . . the river at Saman. With this news in hand, he ordered twenty-four musketeers to cross and he incorporated them into sixty-two others from the cavalry and, leading his forces, he marched towards those pueblos. But when he arrived in Saman, which was six leagues away, they [the rebels] had already crossed the river due to the news that he, *Corregidor* Orellana, was in Juliaca.

Without stopping, not even for an instant, he ordered the few soldiers that were with him to get on the rafts and by two in the morning he had been able to cross the high water of that river and march in search of the Indians who, protected by the shadows of the night, had marched ahead. . . . He . . . caught up with some of [the enemy] at five-thirty or six in the morning. He carefully asked for the person of that bloodthirsty Indian Nicolas Sanca who, having sung in a church, had crossed sides to serve Tupac Amaru with the title of Colonel. . . . [His] troops had carried out the most horrible destruction everywhere. They [the rebels] obstinately refused to answer those questions; and after having irritated the troops by calling them rebels and rabble, they [the enemy] intended and began an attack with their slings and sticks. He then ordered the thirty men that happened to be next to him to open fire, and in an instant all who had been there lay dead.

Among the papers that they found on them [the dead rebels], and among the original documents used by the traitor to recruit people and oppose the clerics who were against him, there was a letter from an *alcalde* who . . . along with Andrés Yngaricona, was also commissioned to recruit people in the towns of Achiya, Nicasia, and Calapuja, and to assault *Corregidor* Orellana with said Sanca in the *Estancia* of Chingora which was only two leagues away from Juliaca. . . .

On the 14th an order from the Indian Sanca was presented to the *Corregidor* by the *Cacique* of Caracoto to enlist people from the said pueblo to destroy the rafts from Juliaca and Suches, sentencing anyone who opposed them to death, in the name of their Inca King and Lord of Peru. Conjecturing that the plan was to evade the *Corregidor* and, leaving him behind, attack the City of Puno and Chucuyto and move forward to Pacajes and the City of La Paz, the *Corregidor* directed his march to the vicinity of Coata where he camped next to the river. He had already ordered twenty-five rafts from Capachica to be brought as soon as possible. He stayed there on the 15th to rest and inspect his troops and their arms, in which he spent the majority of the day. But on the 16th, anxious to know for sure . . . the intentions of . . . [the rebels], the *Corregidor* ordered 200 men to cross [the river] and find out whether in fact [the rebels] . . . had done what was expected of them in the pueblo of Juliaca as he had been assured.

Regarding this, an Indian who lived nearby informed them that the enemy was already coming after them. . . . The *Corregidor* immediately believed him because already they had begun to discover rebels in the hills, and he ordered his 200 men to retreat. At midday they [the rebels] were already down the mountains and were advancing with the intention of attacking our camp as [their position] . . . looked advantageous. . . .

It was learned that the two enemy Indian commanders, Yngaricona and Sanca, were having a heated debate that lasted until after three P.M. as to whether or not it would be advisable to start the combat, the second resisting the wishes and efforts of the first who anxiously wanted to risk it, considering the small number of our troops, which although actually quite small compared to the multitude commanded by both of them, seemed to them even smaller because the *Corregidor* had ordered the infantry to rest as they had fought a battle earlier that morning. His intention may have also been to muster them and have them attack vigorously in case the rebel Indians approached. . . . This maneuver . . . caused the rebels to believe, from a distance, that they faced no more than the handful of cavalry they could see, and to persuade themselves that the [loyalist] infantry at rest were no more than bundles of clothes and beds that had been set in such fashion to act as a wall against their slings.

Convinced by this deception, and helped by a *Cacique* from the Province of Carabaya who joined them with auxiliary troops . . . which were received [by the rebels] with notable joy . . . they decided to attack our forces that same

afternoon with great confidence of victory and with the opportunity to take possession of all our weapons so that they could send them to Tupac Amaru.
. . . Around three in the afternoon the cleric . . . Don Manuel de Salazar and the priest's assistant from the town of Usiacio and several others who accompanied [the loyalist forces] approached . . . [the rebels] . . . to exhort and persuade them to surrender their arms, and to humbly take advantage of the offer of a pardon that long ago the *Corregidor* had made public in the name of His Majesty, granted to all those who, knowing the serious crime of having followed the rebel's party, would abandon it immediately and come and submit themselves again to obedience and subordination to our legitimate Sovereign. An Indian with a staff in hand came forward to answer in the name of all others and, with scandalous and sacrilegious audacity, resolutely declared that they did not need such a pardon nor did they recognize the King of Spain as their sovereign, but only their Inca Tupac Amaru. They added taunting threats in which that same night they were going to finish with our troops, freeing only this priest, to take him as their chaplain.

In view of such blind obstinacy from this scoundrel, and based on the movements they were engaged in, it appeared they were getting ready to attack our troops. The *Corregidor* ordered the infantry to remain quiet, allowing them [the rebels] to get closer. Indeed at four P.M. they were charging in a semicircle, whose right wing was led by Sanca and the left one by Yngaricona, and the center (or so it seemed) by the . . . *Cacique* of Carabaya. . . .

In this situation, appearing to be surrounded, the *Corregidor* formed his troops in battle order; the muskets in the center, spears, sabers and sticks divided in half on the two sides, and the same with the cavalry. He ordered one-fourth of each [flank] . . . to attack, one side engaging Yngaricona and the other Sanca. The attack was lively and impetuous, and both sides fought with ardor and care. Colonel Sanca and his troops suffered little, and once some [of their forces] had been killed they fled crossing a deep estuary where some drowned, the rest fleeing chaotically to the neighboring mountains whose splendor paid witness to the bloody theater where their comrades died. Then the *Corregidor* ordered the conquering left wing to reinforce the right that was fighting with the center and left of the enemy troops led by Yngaricona. And even though they [the rebels] were fighting with courage, the order and perseverance of our troops prevailed. Consumed with fervor they killed many Indians who, facing the continuous attack and fire from our musketeers, fled in confusion and disarray to the hills and mountains which the unhappy rebels attempted to reach to avoid certain death. They were followed closely by our troops who thereby procured a glorious victory. The Lic. Salazar, chaplain of our troops, was running back and forth moved by his zeal and piety, asking those who were struggling with death to call on God to this conflict; *but his charity was thwarted by the stubbornness and indolence with which they*

die without ever passing through their lips the sweet Name of the Lord that he
had so earnestly dictated to them.

This is the memorable day's work [battle] that can be named after Man-
anchili, as it happened very close to that place. More than 370 Indians died
there, among them many women who came as assistants to their husbands
or relatives, helping them with stones that they carried in great quantity to
be given to those with slings. In order to reach those rebels with slings, the
women also brought with them, as their own weapons, some animal bones
with the tips well-sharpened and filed in order to defend themselves; some of
them attempted to use these against our troops, who punished their audacity and stubbornness. It is known that the number of Indians who engaged
in this battle climbed to 5,000, this based on a statement made by one of
them who was gravely injured but lasted until the next day when he died after having gone through confession and having declared what was just said.
That same night of the 16th the *Corregidor* provided the troops with ammunition and spears to replace those that had broken or bent while fighting the
Indians who protected their bodies with some kind of hard and thick skin so
that they could resist these weapons.

The flight of this rabble must have continued during the night as the next
day, the 17th, while the *Corregidor* maintained [his position] on the battlefield, not one of them showed up. Reconnoitering personally the places where
they had been the day before, he knew that they had retreated to the mountains of the previously mentioned *Estancia* of Chingora. With this in mind,
the *Corregidor* ordered [his troops] to cross to this side of the river with the
intention of attacking on the 18th any rebels who might have fled toward Juliaca; but there remained little desire among the rebels to confront our troops
after the latest combat. Some Indians from the little town of Huaca and its
surroundings, having learned a lesson from what the others had suffered, even
presented themselves [to the *Corregidor*] that day humbly asking for pardon
and forgiveness, which was granted to them in the name of His Majesty following what had been announced and published in regards to being granted
protection from the infamous traitor Tupac Amaru. After this, the *Corregi-*
dor of Puno was reinstated, and he solemnly thanked the Sovereign Queen
of Heaven for the continuous help that she showered on our troops in the expedition that was undertaken and which had been successfully concluded
under her tutelage and patronage.

. . . Following the thread of the narration about the exploits of the traitor
José Gabriel in the Province of Lampa, it is said that before entering Ayaviri
on December 6th he had the animosity to write to the Priest in the Capital,
warning him to not allow our allies to take refuge and shelter in the church
or the cemetery. . . . He ordered that he preach to everybody that they should

follow his side (*partido*) if they did not want to see themselves destroyed and devastated, for which he had 60,000 men under his command. And . . . [the priest] should wait for him at the door of the church with cloak, chorus cape, incense, and holy water as corresponds to his persona, and he should be received in other settlements in this manner. The Priest only thought of fleeing and left for Lampa, from which he then went to Arequipa.

As soon as the traitor was in Ayaviri, he set the jail on fire, destroyed some neighboring *estancias,* killing all the cattle and laying waste to the fields, and then directing his march towards the pueblo of Pucara, next to Lampa, he carried out the same atrocities there.

On the 9th he entered Lampa, capital of the Province of that name, where many illustrious and wealthy people lived. He destroyed the jail and City Council building, ransacked all the others, and sent his people to the haciendas and mines of Europeans such as Barrios, Cosio, Goyeneche, Alvizuri, and those of the *criollo* Tobar, which were ruined by destroying their grinding mills and warehouses and taking all the amalgamated ore [most likely partially refined silver] and goods they found.

The residents of Lampa had hidden their riches—currency, silverware and jewelry—in the church; but all was appropriated by him, as certain people would tell him where to look and he would then go directly to the exact place and get what had been hidden. With such [action], he laid waste to the town. He named as his *Justicia Mayor* the *Cacique* Pacoricona and ordered him to kill every *Chapetón* [Spaniard] he could find and attempt to arrest every *Criollo* who had fled and send them to appear before him in whichever place he might be found.

From Lampa the traitor continued on to the Province of Azangaro, feeling at home with all towns receiving him as their Sovereign. He arrived in the Capital of this Province and committed the same ravages as in Lampa, destroying on the 13th all the livestock from the *estancias,* but particularly those belonging to the *Cacique* Don Diego Chuquiguanca [*sic*] and his son Don Josef and his brothers who were the wealthiest people in the Province. This was in revenge for having turned the letter [Tupac Amaru had sent him] over to the *Corregidor* in which he was ordered to apprehend [the *Corregidor*]. . . . The traitor made . . . [Choquehuanca] pay dearly for his loyalty, as there was no relative of his who was not put to the knife. In all these parishes and pueblos the Rebel imposed the same order of setting the jail on fire, naming a *cacique* and a *Justicia Mayor,* and representing his acts as only an effort to abolish the *repartimientos,* the *mitas* for the mines, and the customs duties so as to hide his ambitions from those unwary Indians with this pretense. [These Indians], through their native propensity for robbery, allowed themselves to be seduced, seeing how easily they could now sack *Estancias* and Haciendas.

This they had already done in many of the ruined [properties] in the Collao, where in a single day 4,000 head of sheep were killed, and even these did not suffice to satiate the rebel troops.

While the Rebel was in Azangaro perpetrating these cruelties, he received some letters from his Court in Tungasuca where he returned in a hurry. . . . [F]ueled by his daring ideas he passed through the pueblos like lightning, committing unbelievable atrocities and killing every European he ran into. . . . With these barbarous cruelties all the Provinces were left so scared that they just awaited the Rebel's entry so that they could pledge their obedience: so much so that . . . *they acclaimed him as their King, Redeemer, and Lord and Owner of the Kingdoms of Peru.*

These acclamations emboldened him so much that he wrote several letters to the Bishop of Cuzco, to its General Vicar, and the Municipal Council. In one he advised them, with affected hypocrisy, of the motives of his rebellion and in another that was dispatched to the priests in their respective parishes, [he ordered them] to remove the just obstacles they had placed against the acceptance of his doctrines, and if they did not do so he would take other measures. He added that he came only with the intention of remedying the harm that was being suffered due to the abuses and unfair introductions [of demands such as taxes]. His [action] was not against God, nor against Religion; and finally if the City would not receive him in peace, and with demonstrations of joy before their Restorer, he would punish their audacity with a quick fire.

The Bishop received these letters (brought by a prisoner whose life the Rebel spared just to do so), but he had already excommunicated [Tupac Amaru] at the beginning of his rebellion in all the churches of the City and the allied Provinces, as well as all those militants who were following his banners, or who assisted or helped him. He also ordered that these proclamations be affixed in the Churches of the seditious Province of Tinta, due to the fact that he was . . . a tyrannical usurper of the King's dominions; and finally, for having committed the sacrilege of attempting to burn the public chapels in the *obrajes* of Pomacanchi and Parapuquio and having reduced a temple to ashes.

Those proclamations [of excommunication] lasted just a short time on the doors of the Churches, for the Rebel ordered them taken down and he wrote a letter to the Bishop trying to prove to him that he did not understand his excommunication based on several reasons that he presented without support. The style of said letters was not the same as the others . . . nor did they correspond to an Indian muleteer whose profession was that of a traitor, even though it is claimed that he had studied theology in the School of San Bernardo in Cuzco; but, be it as it may, the letters were not fake for they were indeed addressed by him and he dispatched the originals to the Viceroy of

Peru, regardless of whether they were his or not or from some of the Spaniards who we knew for sure were forced to stay with him in order to save their lives. . . .

The worst fear was that the traitor could reach Cuzco and fortify himself there due to the great numbers of Indians there are inside the walls [of Cuzco]. If he was able to do this, it would be much more difficult to oust him than it had been to conquer the whole Kingdom. However, since God, through His mercy, denied him the assistance needed to accomplish this at the beginning of the rebellion, and again after the defeat at Sangarará (which without resistance he would have been able to manage, because the inhabitants there, overcome by a fearful panic and without arms, without ammunition and without troops, did not plan to defend themselves, but instead many of both sexes intended to flee to save their lives, fearful of the threatened attack), He will not permit it today, now that some precautions have been taken for their defense, not the least of which are the steady flow of tears that the afflicted virgin wives of Jesu [*sic*] Christ shed in their enclosed monasteries.

. . . His Very Illustrious Bishop also organized a company of priests who went out to the public plaza armed and with their purple banner. And even though this action was censured by critics who considered it irregular and not appropriate except in the most extreme circumstances, nevertheless there are histories where this last recourse became indispensable: many secular and regular priests taking up arms without embarrassing the dignity proper to their status . . . or going against the prohibitions of church law to not shed the blood of others from those who ought to be disposed to spill their own.

. . . The right of our Spanish Monarchs to these Americas is without doubt, and the wisest are seen working to ensure it. The miracles that opened the path to this conquest show that the heavens justified their possession and that the Arbiter of Kingdoms [the Pope, through the Treaty of Tordesillas] adjudicated them to Spain. . . . It is true that sins and injustices force the transfer of Kingdoms, and the subtraction of His benefits, transforming the beneficial touch of God into an avenging hand. But the present anguish may have touched our citizens' hearts and converted them to God, Who alone should dominate them. A fervent Mission has been observed that, at the request of the Bishop, was carried out by the reverend fathers of the order of San Francisco in the Cathedral. Perhaps their desires have borne fruit, because the entire City has come to purify themselves in the Fountain of Penitence and they have offered before God's eyes a spectacle that is sure to placate His ire. A fast that was ordered by the Prelate for the days of November 27th, 28th, and 29th has brought the city down to the humility God expects from people whose excesses moved Him to just indignation.

Of course we cannot assure that these public demonstrations have already placed our citizens under cover from the blows and effects of His ire; but His magnanimity and mercy are the assurance that this will happen, as it is steady and true that in other times lesser indications of conversions have placated the ire with which He punishes. . . . It is an extremely powerful consideration that [the people in] these Regions, in their pure although not always living faith, offer a belief of God worthy of His approval and worthy of the sincerity of these inhabitants, among whom the ferment of extravagant and foreign Doctrines have never been perceived. This encourages *Jesu-Christo,* moved by such acts of purification, to cleanse our minds more and more and to esteem with singularity a captivity of understanding [of Catholic doctrine] that there is given as tribute [to God] in a greater degree than in other places. . . . Here one does not hear those absurdities based on incredulities that seem a fashion in other lands. Here is unknown the audacity of licentiousness, brought about by ideas that limit hope to the material and physical [world] that surrounds us. It is true that we sin, and that we sin with dissolution and without restraint: but the pure and sincere light of a faith without limits calls and reduces us to implore the aid of God, in Whom we believe without any more than is proposed to us by a Teacher whom we know does not and cannot ever mislead us: that is to say by the Church of a God Who, deep in our minds, never loses His ascendancy based on the state of our faith despite so many iniquities that stain us. It cannot be true that the Señor would abandon the faithful of this type unto the hands of someone [Tupac Amaru] who gives us no more assurance of his faith than some fantastic protestations which disappear as soon as they're found to not fit into his ambitious interests.

Once Tupac Amaru returned . . . to his house in Tungasuca with the increase in the troops he acquired from the places he had fleeced, he urged the Indians and *Mestizos* to join him and appear at his stronghold on December 19th. He decided that on this day he was to march on the City of Cuzco, a fact that was communicated by some prominent men through letters received on the 23rd of said month. With this news, and that concerning the retreat of the *Corregidor's* troops that came from Lampa, terror and horror spread throughout the region and prayers to God and His Saints multiplied. His Excellency the Bishop ordered the churches of the secular and regular clergy to stop the celebration of midnight Christmas Mass . . . in order that the Mass correspond with dawn. This was done to prevent the temples from being open at night so no uprisings could be staged by taking advantage of the situation. But before we engage in full detail of the primary intention of Tupac Amaru, it would be advisable to first refer to the commotions in the surrounding ravines, which at firsthand looked as if they were feeding the [Tupac Amaru] rebellion.

Account of the Commotions in the Pueblos of the Ravines Surrounding the City of Cuzco

Seeing that several towns near Cuzco did not want to obey them, the tyrant Tupac Amaru and his wife Micaela Bastidas tried to destroy them in an effort to later intimidate and besiege the City. To this effect, some . . . uprisings took place continually in the intermediate [between Cuzco and the forces of Tupac Amaru] populations, which were very close to . . . Chita. This is a prairie [*pampa*] located two leagues from the city, comprising the annexes of the three parishes of San Sebastian, San Blas, and San Christobal. The movement of December 21st was felt with such alarm here in Cuzco that . . . even the clergymen took up arms. Afterwards, a military detachment was sent out on the 22nd at nine A.M. under the command of Dn. Francisco Laysequilla and in the space of an hour the enemy was defeated, with between twenty-five and thirty killed and many more wounded. During the time that the combat lasted, word spread that our soldiers were asking for help, to which end Don Simon Gutierrez was immediately sent with the Company of Comercio; but they did not arrive in time because they encountered the return of Laysequilla's men carrying four heads belonging to the Indian rebels and twenty-five prisoners, two of which were hanged and the rest are being interrogated.

The decision to come into the City with the heads on their spikes was a very opportune one, as it sealed the victory throughout the main Plaza in the eyes of the masses who had never seen such a demonstration; the City caught its breath, and the soldiers from the expeditions felt gratified by the public applause, gaining a different and superior feeling than they had experienced before. . . .

This revolution [in the pueblos close to Cuzco] originated in the higher towns of Catca and Ocongate which felt the ferment of Tupac Amaru through the emissaries he had sent to them. These emissaries carried his written demands that justice be done, which have been distributed since the beginning of his rebellion. Once convinced, the Indians of those two parishes, which are the worst of this diocese, descended impetuously into the pueblo of Caycay where the ravine starts and goes as far as the pueblo of Urubamba and ending in the towns of Tambo and Lares, which is on the other side of the river that runs through the mountains creating the most beautiful and delicious landscape of all the Kingdom; because both banks of the river, besides being beautiful due to the trees and forests that harmoniously cover the populated area . . . have the most beautiful climate and benign sky so that at least in Yucay and Urubamba, springlike weather can be observed throughout the year.

This location, most delightful to the Bishop, was assailed by the furious troops of Indians who came down from said pueblo of Caycay robbing haciendas and stealing cattle, cutting bridges all the way to Guayllabamba, in defense of which the military command in Cuzco sent a force commanded by Dn. Juan Nicolas Lobaton, *Corregidor* of the Province of Urubamba. The Indians were attacked from the other side of the river in Guayllabamba with such fortunate success that more than 200 died, with many more wounded. A large part of this victory was due to the loyal and noble *Cacique* of Chinchero, Pumacahua. With the readiness by which he is known, he was able to attack the enemy from the rear, and coming over the hills with his people, he permitted the enemy to see a white flag waving. Under this banner of a truce, those of the contrary faction who were occupying the lower slopes of the mountain invited him to come down. And descending to a distance that was calculated to allow him to take the offensive, he drove the enemies [from their position] with boulders forcing some of them to throw themselves into the river where the number two colonel of Tupac Amaru drowned, and others were forced to take the narrow passages where the sabers, rifles, and spears of our own forces could be successfully employed.

This victory was also celebrated in Cuzco with the same demonstrations used in the first one, and the soldiers came back with some prisoners. Somewhat later the triumph was repeated in the Plaza of Yucay between Urubamba and Guayllabamba. In this battle over 300 Indians died out of more than 3,000. . . . In this fighting the forces of the *Cacique* of Chinchero, and the *Cacique* himself, participated with equal effort and activity as did all the parishioners of Urubamba, Maras, and Yucay, following the industriousness of their priests—Dn. Manuel Gayoso from the first, Dn. Manuel Castillo from the second, and Dn. Manuel Alzamora from the third, and these were joined by Dn. Antonio Valdez, the priest of Cotoata who at the time was in the town of Urubamba. These good clergymen were offering their best to their highest Father who . . . guided . . . the priests and the defense of their respective parishes. They led their Indian troops and other soldiers, through spiritual and material means, to success in the battle that they fought to the satisfaction of everybody, having managed the [additional] benefit of inducing more than thirty Indians to voluntarily come to fight under our banner at the urging of the Priest of Urubamba. And in their behalf, the guardian of the Monastery of San Francisco of said town wrote a letter of recommendation to the Bishop so that he could intercede in front of the Royal *Junta* . . . [to spare their lives].

With these defeats, it seemed the Indian rebels should have been humiliated, but far from becoming more moderate they retreated to carry out in the pueblo of Calca the greatest atrocities that can be felt in a tragedy. They cruelly killed every single Spaniard—man or woman—that they encountered, taking for Spaniards or *Mestizos* anybody wearing a shirt. What is even more awful, they physically enjoyed those women who looked pleasing to them before killing them, even having sex with them on top of the cadavers. They profaned the Church with homicides without respecting the asylum of that sacred tabernacle. They killed with impunity a poor Spaniard who had dedicated his life to the Lord. Their infernal cruelty did not stop there as these rebels repeated on the children the cruelty of Herod. Many of these innocents died, some of them torn apart, others smothered, and others thrown against the ground and rocks. Some were left without a mother or a father and just like little lambs bleating pitifully, begging for some tenderness without finding any relief under the Heavens except the ground on which they walked, stained with the blood of those who had been granted the perhaps better fortune of being killed. . . . To describe with detail this painful event would be to revive the sharp pain that afflicts our hearts and if we do so it is to pass it down to posterity so that in the future the actions of Tupac Amaru will be remembered and hated.

The Indians who perpetrated such atrocities were punished with the appropriate sentences, even though these did not match such a gigantic crime. Once they learned about what happened in Calca, the Priests of said towns and our soldiers went there, accompanied by the *Cacique* of Chinchero, and surprised the delinquents who were celebrating their preceding triumph over women, elderly, and defenseless children with a very festive banquet in the Plaza. They [the rebels] left more than fifty dead and the rest escaped to the hills. Among them [there was] a very ugly *Mestizo* whose lip was divided into three parts making him look like a dragon and who both before and after killing a poor white woman used her carnally in the church of said Calca, also killing her husband and children. But he was taken prisoner and sent to the jail in Cuzco where he will pay for his crimes. Here [in Cuzco], the torment left in our hearts by the news of the described fatalities was increased by the presence of several children who had been made orphan and who cried sorrowfully to the priests who had accompanied the troops, who felt obliged to take them to Guayllabamba without knowing what they needed to do in the face of so many children who asked them with tearful voices with whom they were going to be left, as Dr. Valdez who participated in the events with sympathy and merit in this occasion could attest.

It is worth mentioning the attitude of the loyal Indians in these victories. In the midst of many of them finding themselves naked and hungry, they did not want to handle the food and clothes that the vanquished had left, indicating that those were the remains of men who had been excommunicated. Such was the effect of this news published by our Lord the Bishop that its effects had been felt in Saylla, near a place that they call La Angostura. These people were commanded by Dn. Joaquin Balcarta [or Balcarcel], and nearly 400 Indians died, our people resisting in the same way taking the Spoils of War as they [the dead] were included in the order of Excommunication.

In San Geronimo, according to the Priest Dn. Juan de Dios Pereyra, an Indian of that locality was named *Justicia Mayor* by a representative of Tupac Amaru, but having been forced to receive the staff he gave it to another Indian supporter of the Rebel excusing himself from the office as he was contaminated due to his having been censured (excommunicated) by the Government. . . . This ecclesiastical decision [the Excommunication] has attained such esteem that thirty Indians who deserted from Tupac Amaru's forces to those of Chincheros, who is on our side, were not forgiven by the famous *cacique* Pumacahua who had them killed the night of the last uprising, justifying his decision based on the fact that they were part of those who had been separated from the Church, and that his people would be infected by the unhappiness and lack of atonement that these brought with them. It cannot be denied that this generous Indian, who had been honored by the *Junta* with a rich sash and a golden Royal Medal, proceeded in this action [going] against the Rights of War and the Peoples' Rights that have been observed by our Spaniards who have spared the lives of those who voluntarily defected. But ignorance of the law, and this *cacique's* good intentions, have made his actions praiseworthy omitting what other reasons he might have had to kill those fugitives who were planning to join his forces, as many other *Mestizos* from the Province of Chumbivilcas have done, terrified of censure [excommunication].

The sound judgment of the Señor Bishop in promulgating these excommunications has been so thoroughly demonstrated that they should be given greater regard and recognition if at its base one considers the utility to our war effort that results, and always result, from news concerning the designs, forces, and path of the Enemy. Those of this *Junta* have been the beneficiaries of the vigilance of many priests and other clerics who, having been encouraged by their Prelate, have informed us . . . of the most needed information without which the defense would not have been able to advance. No Priest hesitated in front of the fearful threats of Tupac Amaru; and that of Quiquijana went as far as to take down the gallows which the Rebel had placed with the intention of executing the *Corregidor* of the Province of Quispicanchi in an effort to intimidate the neighbors of that pueblo that he wished to join his faction. . . .

Finding the city of Cuzco in the midst of organizing the final details of its defense, Tupac Amaru, impelled by his obstinacy to act upon his disparate ideas, finally left his pueblo of Tungasuca with the bulk of his army of over 4,000 Indians. His march lasted several days during which some battalions of 400 to 1,000 Indians would descend into the intermediate pueblos of Urubamba, Guarax(o), Andaguailillas, Oropesa and San Geronimo. In order to contain them the *Junta* sent some of its infantry and cavalry and in all the engagements they succeeded in defeating the Enemy who suffered more than 1,200 deaths, and many others wounded. On January 3rd, 1781, he arrived in the highlands of Ocororo three leagues away from Cuzco. And even though his army suffered the mentioned casualties while getting to Cuzco, they were inspired by the hope that they would win the support of the masses [of indigenous people] and the parishes. They advanced along the same highlands until they positioned themselves on a pass between the mountains of Picchu and Puquin one-fourth of a league away from the City. There he waited until the day of the Wise Men, the 6th, showing all his Indians in a line with all their livestock and equipment. Some artillery shots were heard as they had brought four campaign cannons with them, among them one of good caliber. And based on the testimony of some prisoners who fled to the City which was so near, this was done in order to persuade the masses that Tupac Amaru thought were with him, but he was not able to move them. On the contrary, far from being moved [to fight] against the "Patria," they served as an impregnable wall: Indian residents, *mestizos,* and *cholos* all volunteered to fight with rocks and clubs in hands. . . . [W]hat is even more praiseworthy is that women showed even more rancor. These [women] have occupied the base of the mountain that the enemy had taken, providing beverages to our Soldiers so that they could be refreshed, as well as lots of rocks for those armed with slings. Those who did the least still provided ashes to blind the enemy Indians. While they maintained the siege, all those who lived in those barrios stayed in their houses and streets close to the entrance to those barrios, and fear was observed only among those of noble descent who fled to the Churches, Monasteries, and Convents, all with just cause and due license.

. . . The second battle, which was waged between Picchu and Puquin, lasted more than four hours. At two in the afternoon of said day the Indian set his two cannons in front of the bluff where our forces also had two [cannons] and he started to fire them with a vigor that might have been executed by the most well trained in Europe. The same was done from our side . . . although with more of an advantage to the rebel than to us, until four in the afternoon when Don Simon Gutierrez arrived with his Comercio Company. And with their first volley they forced the Enemy to retreat two blocks up the hill, as there was another mountain higher than Picchu where the two sides fired canons at each other until the time for prayers.

Even though this battle was not decisive, nor very bloody, as both armies had fought at a distance and at different elevations as there was a ravine between them that neither party wanted to descend as this would give the enemy a superior position. Nevertheless, Tupac Amaru was disabused of the favorable thoughts [of gaining support from the city residents] that had possessed him. Despite his deception, he recognized that the entire City, without exception of nobles or plebeians, great and humble, men and women, were resolved to spill their last drop of blood defending their liberty and their King. He was confronted with a force he never thought we had, as our troops were comprised of over 2,000 men, in addition to many Indians from Anta, Chinchero, and Maras. And at the same time, from his elevated position, he could see the 5,000 Indian and *mestizo* troops who came to help this city from the Province of Paruro, captained by the priest of Colcha, Don Feliciano Paz.

The exact number of enemy casualties is not known for they took care that if one of them fell they would pull the body away and replace them with another [Indian]. Very few of ours were left on the field. Well into the night the Rebel kept on fighting, while at the same time retreating little by little. The Company of Comercio, along with the rest, stayed in the field that night even though there was a terrible fog and rain. The Indians were also yelling and howling for most of the night, and the day dawned with the same fog. It was hard to see the enemy until ten in the morning when the fog broke and we could see the enemy retreating along the same high ground by which they had come. That night the Rebel suffered a great desertion of his troops as they saw what little effect their war effort had accomplished; and as they were in disarray they disposed of some equipment like a big cannon, a powder chest, another made out of silver, many mules, donkeys, and cows all of which were taken by our people. A *mestizo* was lucky enough to pillage Tupac Amaru's bed right when they were moving it, discovering that the silk pavilion and the golden mattress had once belonged to the *Corregidor* Arriaga.

Afterward the Rebel stayed put on the hills of Puquin and Cruz de Picchu during the 6th, 8th, and 9th, he retreated further with more than 30,000 Indians and his retreat was caused by a heavy downpour. . . . Let us allow him to ponder over what he needs to do next, while we make known far and wide the exemplary merit due to our Very Illustrious Bishop in the resolve he had, with great personal risk, on that afternoon in which our Battalion fought against the forces of Tupac Amaru engaged in combat, gets to be known.

. . . With the great number of troops that have filled the City, and the extortions that Tupac Amaru and his commissioners have forced on the haciendas of the Provinces of Tinta, Quispicanchi, Lampa, Azangaro, Carabaya, Paucartambo, Paruro, Calca and Lares, and Chumbivilcas—stealing grain, sheep, cows, lard, and dried meat—leaving only hunger in his wake. Making the calamity even more dire is the fact that there is little hope of a harvest as the enemy troops have laid waist to the field and trampled the seedlings. . . . These are the consequences of the war and of the fires of Mars. Cuzco, January 10th, 1781. [*CDIP,* 126. 1781-I-10]

52. Micaela Bastidas Admonishes Her Husband, Tupac Amaru

Micaela Bastidas, Tupac Amaru's wife, proved to be a very capable leader and an important influence on her husband during the insurrection. She understood, perhaps better than her husband, the importance of not losing momentum by taking too much time to achieve goals or allowing the troops to become demoralized. In the following letter, she takes her husband to task and tells him to take action. She, in a wifely tone, warns Tupac Amaru—whom she refers to as "Chepe"—about protecting his image, about the tenuous commitment of their troops, and about the very real danger that existed for all of them.

Chepe: you will kill me with grief for you slowly go through the villages, especially Yauri, taking two days with great disregard for soldiers who have reason to get bored and who want to go back to their villages.

I do not have any more patience to face any of this, as I myself am capable of surrendering to the enemy so that they take my life. I see you with very little eagerness in confronting this very serious issue that might take our lives. We are in the middle of enemies and we do not have our lives secured. And it is because of you that the lives of my children are also in danger, and the lives of those who are with us [supporting our cause].

I am tired of telling you not to dally in those pueblos where there is nothing for us to do. But you occupy yourself passing through them without any consideration that our soldiers need to be fed even if one gives them money and this will also run out in due time. Then everybody will leave, abandoning us, so that we pay with our lives. For they—as you might have figured out—are only here seeking their own interests and to get as much as they can from us. . . . The soldiers are deserting us after having heard what Vargas and Oré are saying about the provinces of Lampa and Arequipa getting together to ambush you. They are terrified and trying to flee the punishments to which they might be subjected. We will also lose all those who I had rallied for our taking of Cuzco and they will unite with the soldiers sent from Lima who already have been on the road for days.

I have been warning you of all this, and it hurts me. But if what you want is our ruin, you can go to sleep in the same way that you thought you could wander alone through the streets of the village of Yauri, even going to the extreme of climbing the church tower, when you should not have committed these excesses, given the present situation. These actions do not correspond to your honor, but can be used to discredit you and make people think very little of you.

I thought you would understand these issues and would not show so much carelessness that it is taking my breath away and I do not have any to waste! So I beg you to go forward with these particulars.

You promised that you would honor your word, but from now on I will not believe in your promises, because you have betrayed your word.

I do not mind losing my life, but I do mind losing that of this poor family who needs your help. And thus, if the forces from Paruro come here, as I insinuated in my last letter, I will soon be on the march with our people, leaving Fernando [their youngest son] in a designated spot, as the Indians are not able to mobilize themselves now with so many threats.

I warned you many times to go immediately to Cuzco, but you have not paid any attention. This has given them time to prepare themselves, as they have done, placing cannons on the Picc[h]u Hill and other such dangerous machinery, so you no longer hold the advantage. May God keep you safe for many years. Tungasuca, December 6th, 1780.

I also want to inform you that the Indians of Quispicanchi are already tired and bored of serving as guards for so long; I guess God wants me to suffer for my sins.—Your Wife.

After finishing this [note] I have been given true information that those from Paruro are in Acos; so I will begin my march, even though I know I will lose my life. [*CDIP,* 95. 1780-XIII-6, 7]

53. Letters to and from Micaela Bastidas

The following series of letters written to and from Micaela Bastidas offer different insights into her power, character, and how she was perceived by others. In Letter 1, she is the local leader of the rebellion—in Tupac Amaru's absence —to whom one of the few female caciques writes to warn her of the dangers surrounding her. In Letter 2, this same female cacique (cacica), Tomasa Titu Condemayta, complains of some of her problems with maintaining authority because, as she sees it, she is a woman and therefore not as respected as she should be. In Letter 3, Bastidas writes to her husband ("Chepe") and tells him that he needs to hurry because her life is in danger. Thus, she is really telling him what he should be doing. In Letter 4, she orders the arrest of a cacique who has sided with loyalist forces. Finally, in Letter 5, two officials of the community of Santa Lucía de Pichigua inform Bastidas that they are trying to comply with her orders and that they will take advantage of the day of Santa Lucía (December 13) to try to recruit more people for the cause.

1. Letter from *Cacica* Tomasa Titu Condemayta to Micaela Bastidas about Fears of Capture and Tupac Amaru's Absence

Señora Doña Micaela Bastidas.—Tungasuca.—My very dear Lady.—I hereby inform you as I have been surely informed, that those from Cuzco are determined to get out to the provinces and Chumbivilcas this Monday.

That individual who you left or put in place as *Justicia Mayor* in Livitaca, Juan Zubizarreta, left with all his people for Cuzco, but was apprehended in Paruro. And in this manner they [loyalists] have come from Quiquijana from the ravines, from everywhere to surround us. They know that the Inca is far away and with this lack of protection they want to ambush us. I do not know what we can do. Be mindful so that they do not descend on your Mercy.

I have been very worried by Don José's (Tupac Amaru's) tardiness; I hope God will bring him back safe as soon as possible.

In Corma, 500 sheep and some cows have been seized from Bedoya, who has been against us, for which Pedro Antonio will account, and in this I suppose Your Mercy will give me counsel and advise me when you arrive. May God conserve the health that Your Mercy desires, and I beg that you will keep and protect us with your power. Acos, December 9th, 1780.—I kiss your hand—Your humble vassal.

—Tomasa (Titu Condemayta)

2. Letter from *Cacica* Tomasa Titu Condemayta to Micaela Bastidas on the Difficulties of the Situation and Being a Woman

Señora Doña Micaela Bastidas.—My most beloved lady. I received yours [letter] and have taken due notice of its content. I have to say that here among our Band we are so close [intimate] that just for being a woman, I have done much to defend my position; that Don Marcos (de la Torre) is so fresh that he presumes I go about putting on airs.

And under these circumstances I do not know what to do; I am so at a disadvantage just by being a woman, and despite this I did what was needed and all I could in Los Altos, and thus you can see my situation. Also, I warn Your Mercy that you will not be able to get out of Acos or Acomayo, as we are in a bad spot. I warn you so that you can choose a better leader like Don Julián Escalante, who is young and more educated than Marcos . . . so that we have somebody who can motivate us, and you can name Marcos as a sergeant.

And please, Your Mercy, will not permit us to be ruined; already two people have not returned, and I am being very careful; and I do not know when you will be coming here. . . . Your humble.

—Tomasa (Titu Condemayta).

3. Letter from Bastidas to Tupac Amaru about Problems and Betrayal

Chepe: I just received information as to how those [loyalists] from Cuzco departed for three different places, and one of them is Catca, whose people (based on trusted information) have been wiped out. Sucacagua and the others have betrayed us, as indicated in the attachment; and thus I am not myself, because we have very few people. You have ignored my letters, trying to deliver me to the bulls' horns, but do not allow them to take my life, for your absence has been the reason for all this. On Monday, which is tomorrow, they will enter in Quiquijana and then Acos and the surrounding villages on the same day; so, speed up your march.

May God keep you for many years.—Tungasuca, December 10th, 1780.

—Your *Mica*

4. Bastidas Gives Orders to Apprehend a *Cacique* Who Betrayed Them

COMMISSION.—Don Diego Berdejo is commissioned to go to Quiquijana as soon as possible, and with the help of the people and their *alcaldes,* apprehend Francisco Sucacahua for contradicting the orders of my husband, Don José Gabriel Tupac Amaru, and bring him to this town of Tungasuca, well guarded and protected; preventing him from asking the *caciques* of Combapata and Checacupi for help, who will also be dealt with, under the threat that if they do not carry them out [the orders] they will severely be punished.—Tungasuca, December 10th, 1780.

—Doña Micaela Bastidas

5. Letter from the *Caciques* of Santa Lucía de Pichigua to Micaela Bastidas about Sending Reinforcements

Our Lady Doña Micaela Bastidas. Revered Mother. We received your letter today the 12th, on which [day] all the people should go. But the *caciques* have not arrived, nor any more people than those who were with the Governor, your husband.

Tomorrow, we will celebrate Santa Lucía's day, patron of this village, and we will gather all the people who have not yet gone and are able to arrive. The *caciques* will send them as you have ordered, and if not, we, the two *Alcaldes,* will go with the people [on the following] Saturday; and we are always ready to obey and comply with your orders; May our Lord keep your life safe.— Pichigua, December 12th, 1780.—Your servant *Alcaldes* kiss the hand of Our Lady.

—Andrés Cotates.
—Marcos Chasares.

[*CDIP,* 100. 1780-XII-9, 10, 12]

54. Letter from Her Brother to Micaela Bastidas

The following letter is from Antonio Bastidas, the brother of Micaela Bastidas, and contains the warmth and concern of a brother for his sister. As part of the insurgency, Antonio is also informing his sister about having received the food so necessary to maintain forces. Without rations, the army would quickly disintegrate. He also asks for more munitions for his forces.

Sra. Doña Micaela Bastidas.—My most beloved, sister of my heart.—I received Your Honor's [letter] dated 28th of the current month, where you warn me to be careful of my enemies; I do not relent, I am always very careful and always successful.

I received six blocks of cheese, sugar, rice and tea *yerba* for which I am most grateful. I am not sending the bread, as we do not seem to find any. I am keeping the four *reales* with me, so I can order it to be kneaded and will send it soon.

Please ask Your Honor the Inca to send us *piedra de fusil* [rocks specially rounded for the mortar or cannon] which we are badly missing, and to God, whom I beg to protect Your Mercy for many years.—Quiquijana, March 29th, 1781. Your Honor's brother.

—Antonio Bastidas. [*CDIP,* 171]

VI. Capture, Confession, Execution, Retribution, and the Instilling of Fear

55. Edict Published to Exhort the Indians of All Provinces of This Viceroyalty Not to Help the Rebel José Tupac Amaru

In the following document, Viceroy Agustin de Jauregui gives his view of the way the rebel leader has managed to deceive his followers, and the measures he will take—when and if necessary—against those who follow Tupac Amaru. At the same time, he makes it clear that the indigenous peoples have been freed from the reparto *and that those who abandon the rebel's cause will be pardoned. If they refuse, however, the punishments will be severe. This "carrot and stick" approach was designed to encourage rebels to give up the struggle.*

One of the interesting things about the following document is the way it runs on, without a period. We have inserted and altered some punctuation; however, because this document is reasonably understandable in this form, we have left much of it close to the original so one can get a sense of the complex writing style.

Don Agustin de Jauregui. . . . Based on the present news and authentic documents that I possess that have informed me and made me sure of the insidious tricks that José Gabriel Tupac Amaru, Indian of the Pueblo of Tungasuca, has used for his crazy and extravagant presumptions that led him to his atrocious, scandalous, and sacrilegious operations, and to be able to stop these and other practices that inspire his torpid, coarse, and imprudent ways of thinking; for which purpose he offers huge promises through which he has seduced many of his nation (the Indians), and even some of other castes who he has managed to convince to help him in his vain ideas of a subject unworthy of the title of *Cacique* and that should only be used by those who have gloriously maintained themselves loyal; he a true forsaker of the Holy Catholic Faith, which he professed in his baptism, and in whom evil suggestions made by our common enemy [the devil?] have made an impression so that he could ruin many innocent souls, whose candor is confirmed by the mere act that of following orders of a Rebel who, agitated to particular ends, plans to tempts (at the cost of their blood and lives) the unhappy *Naturales,* who lend credence to his falsehoods and chimerical dreams and to the methods he has used to further his malicious and vain plans, faking humanity, compassion and love in order to attract those who would abandon Divine and human Laws, investing himself with an authority that he does not have and lying in regards to the seemingly broad support that he has in order to inspire fear and respect so that they would follow him, so that they would involve themselves in the ugly, hateful and grave crimes of infidelity and insurrection against the obedience due to our benign Sovereign, and depriving them of the known spiritual and temporal benefits that all those who have the honor and glory of living subject to his gentle dominion enjoy, and of the great protection that he dispenses through his Laws and his ministers who supervise them, and that in a series of Royal *Cédulas* [documents] and Orders, breathing in all [of them] his Majesty's Royal clemency and generosity, stressing the gentleness with which they should be dealt, and without having any other objective in the immense cost that it incurs on the Royal Treasury than that they be instructed in the dogmas of our Holy Religion in order that they live in civil and Christianly manner separated from any type of superstition and deceit for their own good, his pity overflowing handsomely through the many great privileges that he has conceded them, always ahead of them attending to their miserable conditions; all of which is being taken away by the tyrant [Tupac Amaru] who knows them well and takes advantage of them while at the same time separating them from their wives, children, and families, exposing them to suffer the heaviest work and hardships, without being able to face the forces that will be directed against them for they find themselves few and far between, insisting, nevertheless, in the delirium of persuading them not to obey the *Corregidores* and the Justices, making everybody a delinquent, and complicit fugitives of his serious crimes, and even claiming to have orders from his Royal Majesty for his great excesses. It is for these reasons that they heed the barren statements [of the rebel leader] and that I attest that the followers of this perverse Tupac Amaru continue to be deceived by his lies, and due to the fact that his Majesty (may God keep you) has put me in this place to act in his name so that I maintain peace and justice among all and severely punish those who have broken your just and wise laws and have remained obstinate and in rebellion. [I am] hopeful that other unwary ones do not catch the contagion of Rebellion, and so that the time will not come when those who have declared themselves in support of he who rose up, giving favor to his audacity and resolution, will need to experience the rigor of my just indignation. To this end I have readied more officers, soldiers, arms, ammunition and supplies to act against such mentioned rebel and supporters in the case that it is necessary. I have required and begged them to abandon him and go back to their Pueblos and Homes, with the understanding that if they do not comply in separating themselves [from Tupac Amaru] when the publication of this proclamation is certified and placed close to their whereabouts, they will be treated as Apostates and Rebels and they will suffer the most severe and unpardonable sentences established for such criminals, while at the same time being informed that the *Repartimien tos* have been totally banned in all provinces of this Kingdom with severe penalties to those *Corregidores* who would impose them again, so that they will not be able, under any pretexts, to distribute anything to the Indians. [The *Corregidores*] have been assigned salaries and wages congruent with their work and survival, allowing only those who currently have them [*repartos*], complete, or partially complete, to continue with them, being subject precisely to the terms and ways that are equitable and just, and to which effect several judges have been dispatched to protect and work towards the Indians' benefit preventing any *Corregidor* from taxing or bothering the Indians, and this as a continuation of what has been bestowed through my office in this Kingdom and based on the rectitude that I maintain in their protection, vindication, and administration of justice. And so that everybody is informed, this will be published as a proclamation in all cities, Villas, and Pueblos of this Kingdom, to this end copies of this are being sent to all corresponding *Corregidores* and Justices so that they make sure they are affixed in public and customary places. Done in the City of the Kings of Perú on December 12th, 1780.

—Dn. Agustin de Jauregui
By order of His Excellency Simón de Dolarca [*CDIP,* 102. 1780-XII-12]

56. Account of the Progress Made by the Military Expedition That Left the City of Cuzco against the Rebel José Gabriel Tupac Amaru

As the Spanish forces grew in number, the chances of victory for the rebel forces diminished. Any defeat against the insurgents could leave them in a precarious position. The following very dramatic document gives an account of the final moments of freedom and resistance for the Inca and many of his family. It first deals with conflicts that lead up to the death and defeat of important rebel leaders and forces, and then turns to the betrayal and capture of Tupac Amaru. In the end, it was two women who had lost family members in the fighting against the rebel forces who grabbed the Inca and kept him from trying to resist or escape. At the same time, many others members of the extended Tupac Amaru family were also taken prisoner. Amid widespread celebration on the part of loyalists, the prisoners were brought into Cuzco on the day before Easter. The city was bedecked for the religious celebration, but the decorations instead became part of the festivities that surrounded the capture of Tupac Amaru. The prisoners' future was made clear when they were forced to dismount in front of the gallows.

It is a known problem among secular writers as to whether good luck is more important than prudence and courage in War, or whether one should favor luck over military virtue. But as good Christians, we say that our good fortune is sent to us from above. . . . And that the means that the Lord of Battles has used to concede us this victory, for which we congratulate ourselves today, has been the courage and hard work which have distinguished the Spanish nation throughout the centuries. For our compatriots and Europeans do not lack the two principles: that of the divine protection and innate courage. The miserable José Gabriel Tupac Amaru has also experienced this despite his insolence, and masses of Indian soldiers and *mestizos* who have not been able to resist the omnipotent virtue that the *Junta de Guerra* has demonstrated through . . . [our soldiers] who in collaboration with the *Visitador* who was in charge of the Field Marshal and Inspector General of Arms, left Cuzco on March 9th of this year. They successfully attained their goals, with the exception of the painful eventuality that those under the command of the *Corregidor* of Aymaraes, Don Josef Cavero, suffered the loss, inadvertently, of nearly eighty soldiers and fifty muskets.

The troops from Cotabambas came back from those towns full of trophies and glory after having attained four full victories in which the priests handled themselves with the . . . pastoral zeal so proper of the State they exercised. These most loyal ecclesiastics did not spare their own health, not even their own lives and faculties, exposing themselves to the worst dangers and rigors of the rainy season. They paid wages to their parishioners and walked in front of them, causing much confusion . . . among the enemy. And what was most praiseworthy was their submission to, and agreement with, the officers. In this way, the troops became respected and stronger, increasing the unity with those who commanded them, so that over half of the success we celebrate today could be attributed to them. For it is to them that the imprisonment and death of those famous generals of Tupac Amaru, Tomas Parvina and Felipe Miguel Bermúdez, Captain General of said rebel, is due. They maintained the siege with incredible strength . . . [even though it] . . . snowed heavily on them and they had to crawl over very rugged ground, a situation that helped to distract and defeat the Indians. . . .

Not being able to sustain the fire from the Spaniards any longer, the Indians fled leaving behind more than 800 [dead or wounded] on the battlefield, after which our troops were able to penetrate the enemy camp, taking advantage of many of the provisions, ammunition, and one piece of artillery that was left behind by the vanquished. The cadavers were inspected . . . and those of Parvina and Bermúdez were found. Their heads were sent to Cuzco where they were certified as being those of the aforementioned.

Besides the Column containing the contagion and misery [of the rebels] to the Pueblos of Cotabambas, it also recovered those who had been lost in Chumbivilcas through . . . pardoning those who would surrender and punishing the stubborn, until they were able to pacify that territory which used to be the most loyal to the orders of Tupac Amaru. They were joined in Livitaca by those from Paruro who were led by the *corregidor* of that Province, Don Manuel Castilla, who has behaved like a hero. He was invincible in the job and he took the Enemy by surprise, weakening their forces in the pueblos of Acha, Pilpinto, and Quisguares. . . . [T]he troops were strengthened and they were better able to enter the towns of Acos and Acomayo, where they killed many as an exemplary punishment to other rebels of said District. And they managed to capture Francisco Tupac Amaru, uncle of José Gabriel, and Francisco Torres, a *Cacique* fighting on the side of the Rebel. . . . [T]hrough those actions they exterminated the worst poison of that *Doctrina* which, being so close to Tinta, was very firm in its sedition.

In the meantime, the troops from Paruro and Cotabambas were also fulfilling their duty. They marched so as to unite up with the force that went through the ravines of Urcos under the leadership of Don Miguel Campero, and the force from El Alto that accompanied the Inspector. They spent some days in the siege of Yanacocha, where they overcame some minor difficulties of little consideration, later advancing five leagues to a place called Altos de Pucacasa. Here they were forced to suffer through a rough storm, and some of the rebel troops who crowned the hills were setting snares at each step and movement of our troops. If the hand of God had not been in our favor, we would have lamented a defeat like that [we suffered] at Sangarará, because in the darkest of night, in which the snow obliged our troops to seek shelter in their tents, Tupac Amaru was marching rapidly to attack us by surprise, something that would have happened if it were not for a traitor, Yanuario Castro, who deserted the royal enemy and broke the news to us just in time. Having been put on alert, our troops took their arms and resisted the rebels' advance, losing only one mulatto drummer who, out of laziness, decided not to move to a better place: also some were wounded, and of the contrary Indians, their numbers were unknown.

The Dragoons from Lima missed their temperate weather and started to get sick, so that because of this, and the difficulties they had passing from Tinta through the highlands of Pucacasa, it was decided to have the troops descend to the town of Andaguailillas where the weather was better. And from then on the route [along the river] was followed, which was the decision behind our good luck. But before taking this narration to its main objective, it is worth taking note of the audacity that the Rebel demonstrated in the letter he wrote to the Inspector . . . while he was still camping in the highlands of Pucacasa. On this occasion he repeated what he had already written to the *Visitador,* where he declared that our troops did not deserve peace, nor the Sovereign respect. He even added that he would continue with his operations if his family was not given clemency and his demands granted. The one who delivered this letter was Father Ramon de Salazar from the order of St. Domingo, who was taken prisoner by some Indians when he had gone to explore a cave. He was brought before the Rebel who treated him with kindness, offering him his bed so that he could rest better. Perhaps the Rebel would not have received the priest so favorably if he had been informed of the damage that priest had done to him in the battle of Piccho, where the priest had killed many [rebel] soldiers. But God erased this incident from his memory, or perhaps prevented the priest from suffering the same fate [being killed in the battle].

Agitated by the zeal with which he had watched the pacification of the Uprising, the Señor *Visitador* traveled personally to the bridge at Urcos some eight leagues away from Cuzco. The Indians had the courage to shoot three cannon shots, even though without damage as the shots were truly off mark. It is then that this gentleman was disabused of the idea he had about the docility of these people who are uneducated, tough, unfaithful, bloody, and ungrateful of character. In this occasion he was also able to encourage the morale [of our forces], especially when he saw the troops of Antonio Bastidas that were located not too far away. He then extended his march, and, after having agreed with the Inspector about the best way to attack Tupac Amaru in his own trenches in Tinta, he returned to Cuzco.

Having taken the appropriate measures, the Inspector started moving his troops, considerable by the numbers it encompassed. Having crossed the narrow passage of Quiquijana he proceeded to the vicinity of Combapata without any opposition, because the intermediate pueblos had been subjected easily, managing to gain amnesty and pardon; or perhaps they recognized our [superior] force; or, most likely of all, because they had only lightly supported the seditious partisans, and that only through fear of violence. It was believed that Tupac Amaru was expecting the troops in the security . . . of Tinta, but he was found on this side of the River Combapata with his campaign tents, and all the rest of his people disposed on some hilltops, which [the rebel] eventually abandoned, for our musketeers had climbed up one side, and the Indians from Chinchero with their *Cacique* had climbed the other; and even though the [rebel] Indians on the high ground defended themselves with slings and boulders, the forces from Chinchero nevertheless gained ground by hiding or throwing themselves to the ground while the musketeers were shooting. With all this, the hill was taken and direct combat ensued. Just one solid discharge of our well-governed Artillery (which killed an infinity of Indians) was enough to defeat Tupac Amaru and for his Indians to flee. He crossed the river at once and warned his family to follow him as soon as possible. His wife carried out his order, but her interest in taking with her all that had been stolen, delayed her departure until six in the afternoon, when she left with a herd of mules that made their way very slowly, being so weighed down with their cargos.

The Rebel Tupac Amaru arrived in Langui trusting the loyalty of Colonel Ventura Landaeta, whom he informed of his travails and his resolve to carry on. The friend rejected the [Rebel's] judgment and very well inspired by God as to what needed to be done with the tyrant, he convinced him with kindness to rest a while, persuading him that what was needed was not a retreat, but firm resistance, which he, the Colonel, could ensure due to a large number of reinforcements which he had under his command. Tupac Amaru was convinced, and while they were fixing him lunch, the good Colonel left in search of people who would fulfill his intentions, and then came back. The Rebel became aware of this ruse and tried to leave the house; but as the hour had arrived for him to pay for his crimes, the Colonel disclosed his intentions and clearly told him: how could he want to save his own life after having lost so many? After charging him with this, he took him prisoner, and two women, one who had lost her husband to the rebellion and the other two sons, with an insolent animosity embraced the rebel from behind impeding him from any action. He was ultimately secured by the people that the priest of that parish, Don Fernando Gamarra, had gathered for that purpose. The Colonel asked for help through a letter and then went to Sicuani where fifty dragoons were stationed under whose protection the prisoner was placed in the hands of the Señor Inspector, along with the greater part of the rebel's family. Among those taken was the famous Antonio Bastidas, brother of the Rebel's wife, along with two of his sons, Ypolito and Fernando. The only ones to escape, by misfortune, were Diego Tupac Amaru, and his nephew Mariano. The first is the brother of José Gabriel, and the second his son.

When the Inspector and all his soldiers arrived in the pueblo of Tinta, he found hung on the gallows a portrait of Tupac Amaru on a horse with the royal insignias he had brought as trophies from [our] very painful defeat at Sangarará, where he had burnt the Church and taken prisoners—ecclesiastical as well as lay—among them three priests who had been sentenced to be burned by this infamous character. Relief was awakened in everyone [by the capture] and they received the Inspector full of happiness. He was moved . . . by the tears and clamor of all the people who gathered there to lament their oppression and past sorrows. The news was sent to Cuzco where it was received with general glee and a tolling of bells that lasted for several hours. The Very Illustrious Bishop gave thanks to heaven with a solemn mass where the Te Deum was sung, recognizing that the hard work of his Church and priests had paid off through great vigilance to restore peace. . . .

After several days, the group of prisoners was conducted [to Cuzco] by the Inspector who had decided that they should enter the city on Holy Saturday, which was the most solemn that it had ever been seen, and is how Tupac Amaru would have desired his organization, and this was done on that appointed day. The *Visitador* went out of the city to the town of Urcos, eight leagues away, to receive the prisoners and entered with them in triumph, savoring the public acclamation. The troops were distributed into two contingents [stretching] from the square of Santo Domingo also known as Limapampa to the barrack doors, giving the whole city the satisfaction of witnessing the defeated Tupac Amaru, his wife, children, and other allies who came in without hats on their heads by order of the *Visitador*. The first object that appeared in front of the prisoners' eyes, at which they were forced to stare for a long while, was the gallows which reminded them of their wickedness and their well-deserved deaths. And thus, they were dismounted from their mules in front of the doors of the barracks. The *Visitador* separated them that night, preventing Tupac Amaru, his wife, and children from saying good-bye to each other forever, as they would not see one another nor would they be together before eternity, except on the day of their execution, to their very great sorrow. Cuzco, April 16th, 1781. [*CDIP,* 184. 1781-IV-16]

57. Edict That Was Found in the Rebel Tupac Amaru's Pocket When He Was Captured

This edict was in Tupac Amaru's pocket when he was captured. It demonstrates that he had clearly committed himself to being the Inca king of the lands in South America that were under the Spanish Crown, and that he had also given himself the power to distribute divine piety. In the edict, he seeks to cripple the colonial economy by relieving people of the burdens imposed by unjust officials and leaving in place only those taxes that he, as king, would need to run his kingdom. It is interesting that, although some people connected with the church are mentioned among the evildoers, religion is still respected.

Don José the first, by the grace of God Inga [*sic*] King of Peru, Santa Fe, Quito, Chile, Buenos Ayres [*sic*] and Continents of the Seas of the South, Duke of la *Superlativa,* Lord of the Caesars and Amazons, with dominion over the Great Paititi, Commissary distributor of Divine Piety. . . .

As it was agreed by my Council in several careful meetings, both publicly and privately, that the Kings of Castile usurped the Crown and dominion over my people for almost three centuries, taxing vassals to pay unbearable service, tribute, excises, duties, customs, mercantile taxes, monopolies, land taxes, tithes, and fifths (*quintos*), and the Viceroys, *Audiencias, Corregidores* and other ministries all sharing in the same tyranny, selling justice in public auctions . . . Ecclesiastical and Secular people who, without fear of God, harmed the *naturales* of this Kingdom like they were beasts. . . . For all this, and for their just clamors that have regularly reached the heavens, in the name of God Almighty we order that the aforementioned peoples, and intrusive European ministers, should not receive any payment nor be obeyed in anything. Full respect being shown only to the clergy, paying them their tithe and offering them the first fruits as it were given directly to God: and the tribute and fifth to their King and Natural Lord [Tupac Amaru], and this with the moderation that will be known, along with the other Laws that will need to be obeyed and respected. And so that everything mentioned here is promptly enacted, we order that the declaration of my Royal Coronation be disseminated and published throughout the cities, villages and places of my dominions and I should be informed as soon as possible of those willing and loyal subjects so that they may be rewarded. And those who may not follow the order will be given the sentence that suits them in reference to this Declaration. . . . Done in Tungasuca, March 18th, 1781.

Don José Gabriel Tupac Amaru Inga [*sic*] King of Peru.
[*CDIP,* 165. 1781-III-18]

58. Confession of Micaela Bastidas

After her capture, Micaela Bastidas was interrogated. In her confession, Bastidas very cleverly attempted to use the Spanish paternalistic system to her advantage. She denied having power, or having exercised power, on her own. She claimed to have done only what her husband ordered and not to have had access to many of his decisions. She contended that she remained ignorant of most of what was happening and only acted on direct orders she received from her husband. She also stated that Tupac Amaru was strict or stern with her, indicating a proper husband–wife model that was designed to make her claims more believable. The Spanish did not believe any of this, but nonetheless she attempted to use the language, culture, and paternalistic-sexism of the colonial world to give credence to her claims of innocence. Thus, she mocked the Spanish until the very end.

In the city of Cuzco, on April 22nd, 1781, before Señor Don Benito de Mata Linares, of His Majesty's Council, *Oidor* [Judge] of the Royal *Audiencia* of Lima appeared a woman, who is held prisoner . . . from whom the Judge received an oath which she swore by God, and having made the sign of the cross, as it is her right, and having done all that was required, she promised to tell the truth.

And having been asked her name, where is she from, her age, marital status, quality, and whether she knows the reasons for her imprisonment, she said: that her name was Micaela Bastidas, originally from Pampamarca, that she is over twenty-five years old, married to José Gabriel Tupac Amaru, *Cacique* of Pampamarca, Tungasuca, and Surimana, and that she is in jail because her husband killed the *Corregidor* [Arriaga].

She was asked whether she was in jail for other reasons, and she answered no. She was asked how could she not know that she was in prison for other reasons, when it was clear she had taken up arms jointly with her husband; she responded: that it had not been against the King or against the Crown.

She was asked what the reason was for her husband to kill the *Corregidor,* being their superior; she responded: that her husband told her that the *Corregidor* wanted to hang Pedro Mandigure and her husband (José Gabriel Tupac Amaru).

She was asked since when was she informed by her husband of what he was thinking of doing: she responded that she did not know, nor did her husband tell her, anything until after the *Corregidor* was in jail; even though based on her husband's declarations and that of others she knew that this was not so and that she knew of this long before [the events occurred]; and even when her husband wanted to start the uprising on October 2nd, she told him to wait; she said: her husband only told her when he went to see *Corregidor* Arriaga, and it was then when he revealed that he had a Royal Edict to apprehend the *corregidores.*

She was asked, whether this same intention that her husband shared with her, she shared with others, and she said: she never said anything, and that she only discussed it with Diego Tupac Amaru, and that her husband always treated her sternly.

She was asked exactly what her husband had communicated to her, and she said: that he only wanted to abolish the *repartimientos, corregidores,* taxes, customs and other taxations; but that he never went against the King, nor had he ever thought of such a thing.

She was then asked why did she not dissuade him from these thoughts and, seeing his obstinacy, why did she not flee and retreat, and she said: that even though she tried to dissuade him, he would dismiss her, and sometimes he had even wanted to beat her because of it; she did not flee because she couldn't; that she has relatives here [in Cuzco] and she had wanted to come [and stay] with them. She was reminded of her previous answer where it is clear that she, in the absence of her husband, remained in charge, giving orders to rally people, even leaving with some in some instances, and she said: it is true that she stayed giving orders, but it was because her husband ordered her to do so; and that it was the scribes who wrote those orders and that she only went as far as three or four leagues, and that she could not come [to Cuzco] due to the number of people who were keeping guard.

She was asked, how in light of wanting so much to come back she did not flee when she went to Picchu, as some others had done; and said: that by then she was practically dead with fear and that just seeing her they would know she was José Gabriel Tupac Amaru's wife and she would be killed.

Asked how her husband mobilized the *caciques* and Indians, whether it was by telling them that he was of royal blood or other means; and she said: that he gathered them in the name of the *Corregidor* [Arriaga], and then later it was they who called her husband Inca.

She was then asked with whom her husband had communicated in regards to gathering the *corregidores,* who had advised him to do so, who had helped him, with whom he had corresponded, who would come from Cuzco, what type of letters did her husband receive, with whom had he written these things; and she said: she does not know whether her husband shared this [information] with anyone, nor does she know whether somebody had advised him, nor who could have helped him, nor to whom he might have written, or who would go to Cuzco, nor had she seen any Indian disseminating the news, nor did she know whether her husband ever received letters in regards to this issue; only his agent wrote to him from Lima regarding his suit, and that was Mariano Barrera. Asked how could she not know, when her husband and others had confessed that they had received letters and others had helped them; and that it is quite incredible that she would not know all this as his wife; and she said: I never knew anything, nor did her husband ever communicate any of it to her.

She was asked whether it was true that her husband had hanged the *Corregidor* Arriaga, why he had done so, and who had helped him to do so; and she said: that it is true that her husband ordered *Corregidor* Arriaga to be hanged, and he had been hanged by a *zambo* named Antonio, who had been with Noguera before, and he had offered to do it; and that he hanged him to abolish the *repartimientos* and that those who had helped him in the execution were the Priest of Pampamarca, Don Antonio Lopez de Sosa, Don Ildefonso Bejarano, Don Jacinto Castañeda, and Don Clemente.

She was asked whether her husband had a good friendship with these priests, or with some of them; and whether he consulted with them about his business, or with some of them; and she answered: he did not have any friendship in particular nor did he consult on anything with them.

She was asked whether these priests admonished him and asked him why he was attempting this crime; and she said: that the Priest from Pampamarca asked why he was doing this and whether he had a wife and children; and he responded that he knew what he was doing, and that the other priests did not say a word.

She was asked whether after Arriaga's death her husband wrote letters to some people or whether he received letters from others, and she said: that she knows her husband wrote to several *caciques,* asking them to take their *corregidores* prisoner, and that he had also written to the *caciques* in Cuzco; and she knows that among them were Chillitupa and Sahuaraura, but that she does not know of others nor whether others wrote to him.

She was asked whether she knew if the scribe José Palacios wrote to her husband, or any other important person; and she said: she does not know anything, that if Palacios had written to him, she would have been told.

Asked whether she had any knowledge of correspondence between her husband and the Ugartes of this town, she responded: she does not know anything.

She was asked about who were the persons her husband trusted the most; and she said: everybody was his friend, and those who he associated with were his relatives.

She was asked who, among all the scribes he hired, was the one he trusted the most, and she said: Mariano Banda and Felipe Bermúdez; and later when he came to Cuzco, it was Manuel Galleguillos and Francisco Cisneros who handled all his papers.

She was asked who among those scribes was the one who incited him the most to pursue this enterprise and whether Molina and Cisneros were on his side with enthusiasm; and she answered: all of them were united, and some would say that it would be good to gather all the *corregidores* together, although she does not remember who they were. She was then asked for a second time, how can you not remember when those were people . . . who were customarily more esteemed and distinguished; she responded: I do not remember.

When asked who were the main leaders of this expedition, she said: remit this to her husband, that he should know.

She was asked whether those captains obeyed orders that she would give in the absence of her husband; and she said: yes, they did.

Asked who the most trusted of the scribes was, and she said: Mariano Banda.

She was then asked whether she had not tried to rise in arms against the Crown in the belief that her husband would be successful and that he would rule; and she said she never thought of anything like that. This charge was made against her: how could she claim that she never thought about it, when in the orders she gave, which accompany these indictments and are signed, it appeared that she was in fact interested in the victory of her husband; and she said that it is true that she gave orders, following her husband's orders, and that those were written by the scribe Mariano Banda, and that she cannot say what they are as she does not read or write. She was asked one more time how can she insist in denying that she did not think of ordering anybody, and that she would only order when she was told to do so, when it is obvious that she called him, without a doubt, Inca, assuming he was of royal blood; and she says: that she called him that because she heard him call himself that and he also said that he was going to be taken to Spain and that the King would make him Captain General; and everything included in those orders were included there by the scribes.

She was asked whether she knew that her husband had been excommunicated, as well as all those who followed him; and if she knew this, how was she not fearful of that and why had she not abandoned her husband; and she said that her husband told her that they could not be excommunicated, that God knew his intentions, and that they should not fear.

Asked whether she knew of a draft that discussed her husband's coronation and swearing in as José I; who had brought it; to what letter had it been attached to; who had sent it; and she said she knows about the draft, that an Indian from Marcapata brought it, that he gave it to her telling her that he had grabbed it from the pocket of the *alcalde* of Marcapata who had been killed on the road, they hadn't given her any letter, nor did she know who sent all this.

She was asked whether she was hiding documents, silver, gold, jewelry; and she said that she is not keeping anything, and that everything she had she gave to the Inspector [General José del Valle].

She was asked whether she or her husband had a hidden mine; she said: no.

She was asked from where did her husband get all that silver, gold, and jewelry; and she said that all of it was from what they had confiscated from Arriega [*sic*], plus a few more things that the Indians had brought.

Asked whether the Indians brought her husband silver or gold as tribute, and she said: yes, they indeed brought him that, but not as tribute.

She was asked what belongings, gold, silver and jewelry, she had when she was apprehended; whether she gave some away; she said that she had three pairs of earrings, eleven rings, golden buckles, a golden choke, four golden weavings, and some small bundles of gold dust, part of which she had bought from the Indians and part from what they had brought to her; 600 pesos in stamped silver, four boxes of gold, much engraved silver, some clothing from Castille and from the region, all that was taken by the men from Langui, and that they gave it to the Inspector; that the *Yaya* [priest] of Langui asked her for a silver trunk and that she gave it to him; and that she knows that a certain Landaeta distributed what he grabbed, and that his wife took some clothing.

She was asked whether any Indian from Cuzco would bring them news . . . how could she not know, when it was obvious that an Indian Pedro Sotelo, had come and gone [with news] of what was happening in Cuzco; she said she didn't know. She was asked again if he continually came to her house; she said she does not know him.

She was asked whether she knew of any priest who might have helped her husband; and she said she does not know. She was asked again, how could she claim she didn't know when the case documents made it clear that the priest Maruri, under orders from her husband, had sent people to him; and she said that she does not know anything.

They showed her a canvas on which a portrait of her husband had been painted, mounted on his horse with royal insignias showing, so that they could ask her who had painted it, who had given them the idea, and to what end had it been painted; she said it is true that it is her husband's portrait, with the royal banners, that it was painted by a *zambo* Antonio [Oblitas?] who was in prison and was ordered to paint her husband; saying that if they killed him, this portrait would remain so the family of Tupac Amaro [*sic*] would remember him; that the idea was her husband's, and was made with the intention of showing it in the provinces and later on in Spain.

She was asked whether all their relatives, both his and hers, participated in this; defended the effort, under oath or otherwise; and she said everybody was helping together, but that she does not know whether under oath.

She was then asked and asked again; and she said that she did not know anything else, and that was the truth under the oath that she had sworn; and she ratified and affirmed all said, and her confession having been read to her, it will remain open for any convenient issue; she did not sign it as she did not know how, Don José Brito and your Honor signed for her; which I certify.

—[Signature of Mata Linares].—For the accused,
José Brito.—Manuel Espinarete Lopez.
Cuzco, May 1st, 1781.—In respect to Micaela Bastidas who finds herself under many charges that are part of this trial and the witnesses who made their depositions.

—[Signature of Mata Linares].—*Manuel Espinarete Lopez.*
[*CDIP,* 192. 1781-IV-V]

59. Three Lists of Rebel Prisoners and Executed Rebels

The following lists contain the names of rebels held, killed in battle, or executed by royalist forces in the Cuzco region. Among them are not only many of the principal rebels but also some creoles *(Spaniards), slaves, and* mestizos. *Some were officers; others had skills that were useful to the rebel forces. The list includes many family members as they became a focal point of repression. One list also includes the name of Pomainca, a* cacique *from the Quiquijana region of Quispicanchis who was nearly beaten to death by a tax collector in the years preceding the rebellion despite having a solid reputation for working with the state. To save his life, the people of his community rose up and freed him, killing the tax collector. Given this history, it is hardly surprising that Pomainca joined the rebel forces, even though the colonial state did not punish him or his people for their action. The comments about the prisoners and what happened to them are especially interesting.*

List 1: List of the Principal Rebels That Are Held in This Jail [Barracks] of Cuzco, and of Those Who Have Died in the Fighting That Has Taken Place between the Sacrilegious Troops of the Traitor and Our Forces

José Gabriel Tupac Amaru, principal leader

Michaela [*sic*] Bastidas, his wife, from Abancay

Two of his children, one eleven years of age, the other twenty

Francisco Tupac Amaru, uncle of José

Marcos Torres, *cacique* of Acomayo

José Mamani, Indian of Tinta, his colonel

Diego Berdejo, Spaniard of Macari, son-in-law of Francisco Noguera, his commander

Tomasa Titu Condemayta, *cacica* [female *cacique*] of the pueblo of Acos

Melchor Arteaga, Spaniard, from Layo, overseer and cattle guard

Ramon Ponce, Spaniard, from Livitaca, commander and guard of powder and bullets

José Hunda, Spaniard, from Cuzco

Manuel Galleguillos, Spaniard, from Oruro, scribe

Diego Ortigosa, Spaniard, from Arequipa, advisor

Patricio Noguera, Spaniard, from Surimana, cousin of the rebel

Estevan Vaca, Spaniard, from Cuzco, founder [metal caster]

Blas Quiñones, *mestizo,* from Tinta, confidant

Mariano Cataño, Spaniard, from Huancavelica, sergeant major

Andrés Castelo, captain

Felipe Menizabal, captain

Isidro Poma, commander and *cacique*

Ursula Pereda, maid of the rebel

Miguel Zamalloa, captain

Pedro Mendigure, *capitan*

Cecilia Tupac Amaru, half-sister of the traitor

Manuel Quiñones, captain

Pacual Mancilla, same

Manuel Ferrer, same

Rafael Guerra, same

Antonio Valdes, same

Lucas Herrera, same

Francsico Herrera, same

Mateo Avellaneda, same

Gerónimo Andia, porter
Lucas Colqui, *cacique* of Pomacanche, commissary and *alcalde*
Francisco Torres, confidant, and commissioned in various jobs (*asuntos*)
José Manel Yepes, slave of the priest of Pomacanche
Antonio Oblitas, slave, and the one that hanged Arriaga
Pedro Pablo, slave of D. Manuel Tagle
Miguel Landa, slave of Tiburcio Landa.

List 2: The Following Have Been Prisoners in This Jail (*Cuartel*) for Some Time

Mariano Banda, Spaniard from Cuzco, scribe of the deceased Arriaga, and
    afterward of the rebel
José Estevan de Escarbena y Villanueva, from Arequipa, also a scribe of the
    rebel
Francisco Castellanos, he brought the edicts and letters of convocation
    [summons] of the rebel to Cuzco
Dionisio Medrano
Jacinto Inquillitupa, *cacique,* of the parish of Hospital, accused of being a
    follower of the rebel

List 3: Killed in Battle or Hanged

Juan de Dios Valencia from Velille, captain
Tomas Parbina from Colquemarca, famous captain and *Justicia Mayor* of
    the rebel, in the province of Chumbivilcas
Felipe Bermúdez, Spaniard of Cuzco, treasurer of Arriaga: afterward
    secretary, principal commander, and one of the five who composed the
    private *Junta* of the rebel

. . . These three led the rebellion in Chumbivilcas, and commanded the
troops the rebel had there. They were killed by a column from
Cotabambas in the four battles that took place from the 19 to 22 of
March; the heads . . . were brought to Cuzco . . . [and] displayed on the
gallows two days and afterward they were placed on the main roads at
the entrances to the city.
Pomainca, *cacique* of Quiquijana and *Justicia Mayor* of the same by order of
    the rebel. He was shot in the back for lack of an executioner.

In Tinta, sixty accomplices were hanged on April 8, not of as serious crimes
    as the others. [*CDIP,* 195. 1781-V-15, 18]

60. Sentence Pronounced in Cuzco by the *Visitador* D. José Antonio de Areche against José Gabriel Tupac Amaru, His Wife, Children, and Other Principal Prisoners (Defendants)

Spanish reprisals against rebels were usually harsh and swift, with special tortures and gruesome mutilations added to the sentences of many of the leading rebels—especially Tupac Amaru, his wife, and other family members or notables. José Antonio de Areche ordered and supervised the torture and execution of nine leaders on May 18, 1781. Areche was not unaware of the importance of the image of the Inca and Inca rule in the rebellion, thus he also sought to do away with Inca symbols and to undermine people who held authority based on their birth as nobles dating back to the period of Inca rule. Making the victims witness the deaths of their compatriots, and having the youngest child of Tupac Amaru and Micaela Bastidas—Fernando—witness his parents' execution and that of other family members and associates, shows the Spanish determination to teach a very powerful lesson to those who might rise up against their authority, especially with body parts of the rebels being displayed at key places in the insurgent territory such as the pueblo of Tinta in Canas y Canchis. The Spanish, however, were not able to completely erase the memory of the Inca from people's minds. The following are excerpts from Areche's execution order of Tupac Amaru and other rebels along with the provisions taken to secure the region. This document is written in the run-on style that is characteristic of many colonial documents. We have altered some of the punctuation, but much of the original style has been maintained due to the difficulty of altering this document and keeping it readable.

In the criminal case that is before me, and that has been officially brought by Royal Justice against José Gabriel Tupac Amaru, *cacique* of the pueblo of Tungasuca, in the province of Tinta, for the horrific crime of rebellion or general uprising of Indians, *mestizos,* and other castes, planned for more than five years, and executed in almost all territories of this Viceroyalty [Peru] and that of Buenos Aires, with the idea (of which he is convinced) of desiring to have himself crowned as their Lord and of liberating them from what he terms the "miseries" of these classes of inhabitants, whom he has managed to seduce; and he began this [rebellion] by hanging his *corregidor* D. Antonio de Arriaga. . . . [T]he defendant has twice tried to flee from jail . . . [and] in order to bring the most rapid tranquility to the provinces aroused by him, the news of the carrying out of his death sentence will prevent the spread of various ideas that have been extended throughout the nation of Indians, who are filled with superstitions, inclined to believe the impossibility of his execution due to his elevated character and who believe him to be from the principal line of the Incas, as he said himself, and therefore absolute and natural ruler of these dominions and their vassals. I have also kept in view the nature, condition, low customs and education of these same Indians, and those of the other castes of commoners, contributed a great deal to the ease with which the depraved intentions of said defendant—José Gabriel Tupac Amaru— were carried out. Having been deluded [by him], they were submissive, and quick . . . to obey any of his orders and they were among the first to resist the vigorous fire of our arms, even against their natural horror. And he has succeeded in making them express an implacable hatred against everything European or any white face, or *pucacuncas* [rednecks], as they call them, committing himself and them to innumerable ravages, insults, horrors, robberies, deaths, rapes, unimaginable violence, church desecration, vilification of his [Spanish] ministers, and making a mockery of [our] most important weapon, which is excommunication, considering themselves immune or outside its reach. And to assure them of this, with other cursed inspirations, he, whom they call Inca, at the same time he was publishing in numerous convocations, proclamations, and orders (of which there are numerous of originals among these documents) that they were not going against the Church, he deprived it [the Church], as has been stated, of its greatest force and authority, making himself legislator of its most sacred mysteries and ministries, and pursuing this system in his own fashion against his legitimate sovereign, against the most magnificent, benign . . . and most venerable and kind of all the monarchs who have filled the throne up to this time in Spain and the Americas; depriving one and the other high authority of their most particular prerogatives and power: he placed priests in the parishes . . . he named justices in the provinces, stopped the *repartimientos* or tariffs . . . collected the ecclesiastical perquisites, extinguished the royal customs and other levies that he called unfair. He opened and burned the *obrajes,* [also] abolishing the benefits of the *mita.* . . . He ordered the embargo of particular properties . . . and not content with this, he wanted to do the same with the riches of the royal treasury. He imposed the death penalty on those who did not obey him. He built . . . gallows for this end in all the pueblos, executing many. He made everybody pay tribute to him. He managed to mobilize peoples and provinces through fear and his devilish offers, removing those dwellers from their just obedience towards their legitimate and truthful Lord—he who has been installed by God Himself as the sovereign who rules them: to the point that he tried to convince his followers to believe the . . . illusions that all those who would die in battle would arise from death after he would be crowned; making them believe that the cause he defended was just, as much because he was their liberator as because he was the only descendent of the principal blood line of the Incas. . . . He wanted to make patent his oath to all the nation, attributing to himself royal dictates. He had a portrait of himself painted as proof of these clumsy designs, with the royal insignias of *unco, mascapaicha* and others, placing as trophies the triumph attributed to him at Sangarará, representing the dead and wounded with the fire that ravaged the church . . . and lastly he ruled as a king from the beginning of his uprising under the false and frivolous pretext of being the only legitimate descendant . . . of the royal blood of the . . . emperors, especially from the Inca Felipe Tupac Amaru, whose dynasty he usurped . . . without right; as the tribunal of the Royal *Audiencia* of Lima, where this case was pending, had not granted him any right to that ascendancy. . . . [B]ut his pretensions of descendancy, despite their dubious state, have made such an impression on the Indians that they believe him, and they would talk and write to him with the utmost submission and respect, treating him as their Lord, Excellency, Royal Highness or Majesty, coming from various provinces to render him the proper obedience and submission, failing to honor the strict obligations of fidelity and religion that he, as well as all subjects, should have towards their natural king. . . . [H]e pretended that he had orders to execute what he so barbarously executed, something that even the most stupid should not have believed to be legal. . . .

Considering, then, all of this, and due to the liberties that this vile insurgent invited Indians and other castes to enjoy so that they might follow him, even going so far as to offer slaves their freedom, and reflection additionally on the unhappy and miserable state in which these provinces find themselves, altered [by the rebel], and which they will only overcome with great difficulty, or it will take many years to recover from the grievances caused by the aforementioned José Gabriel Tupac Amaro [*sic*]; and, finally, seeing the remedies required to appease these territories through the punishment of the guilty, the just subordination to God, the King and his Ministers, I must condemn, and I do condemn José G. Tupac Amaru to be taken out to the principal public plaza of this city, dragged to the place of execution, where he shall witness the carrying out of the sentences imposed on his wife, Micaela Bastidas; his two sons, Hipólito and Fernando Tupac Amaru; his uncle, Francisco Tupac Amaru; and his brother-in-law, Antonio Bastidas, as well as some of the leading captains and aids of his iniquitous and perverse project or intent, all of whom have to die on the same day. And these sentences having been carried out, the executioner will cut out his [Tupac Amaru's] tongue, and then tie or bind strong ropes [*cuerdas*] to each of his arms and feet in such a way that each of these [ropes] can readily be tied or fastened to others hanging from the cinches of four horses so that, placed in this way, each one of these [horses] pulls in his direction, facing opposite corners or points of the plaza, and the horses, all at the same time, will be ordered to pull so that his body will be divided into as many [four] parts and then, once dead, the parts should be taken to the hill or summit known as "Picchu," where he dared to come to intimidate, lay siege to, and demand the surrender of this city. . . . [His body] shall be burned in a bonfire, which shall be prepared in advance, and then his ashes shall be tossed into the air and a stone tablet will be placed there listing his principal crimes and his death as the only memory and warning against his accursed action.

His head will be sent to the town of Tinta where, after having been on the gallows for three days, it shall be placed on a pike at the most public entrance to the town; one of his arms will go to the town of Tungasuca, where he was *cacique,* for the same [treatment], and the other likewise in the capital of the province of Carabaya; similarly one of the legs shall be sent to Livitaca in the province of Chumbivilcas for the same type of observance, while the remaining [leg] shall go to Santa Rosa in the province of Lampa along with an . . . order to the respective *corregidores* . . . so that this sentence be publicly proclaimed with the greatest solemnity . . . as soon as it arrives in their hands, and on the same day every year hence. . . . Let his houses be torn down or destroyed and [the ground] salted in full view of all the residents of the pueblo or pueblos where he had them or they existed. Let all his goods be confiscated . . . the commission for this being given to the corresponding provincial judges. I command that all the individuals from his family, who until now have not come and may never come under the power of our arms be brought to justice (which sighs for them in order to punish them with equally rigorous and ignominious punishments), will remain infamous and unable to acquire, possess, or obtain, in any manner whatsoever, some inheritance or any succession they may sometime desire or to which they may in the future claim some right. Let the legal proceeding developed to claim his [Tupac Amaru's] descent [from the Inca] be gathered in the Royal *Audiencia,* having the executioner burn them publicly in the public plaza of Lima so that no memory remains of such documents. . . .

[B]ecause of the views of the deluded Indian nation, I advise Your Majesty . . . [that this is an] opportune [moment to make clear] . . . if now, or at some point, someone wants to claim nobility and equal or similar descent, from the ancient kings . . . [this be] absolutely prohibited under the gravest and most severe penalties. . . . This traitor succeeded in arming himself and forming an army and forces against the royal arms by making use of, or seducing and gaining the support of, the *caciques* and their aids [*segundas personas*] who commanded in the villages with his lies. . . . They should not be governed by such *caciques,* but rather by *alcaldes* [mayors] who are elected annually by the vote or nomination of the [leading community members] . . . and the *corregidores* should give preference to those who know Spanish and who are of the best behavior, reputation, and customs in order that they treat their subjects well and with love toward those whom they govern. . . . [Choosing those who have] justly demonstrated their tendency and loyalty, desire, respect and obedience, submission, and gratitude to the greater glory of our great Monarch through their willingness to sacrifice their lives, properties, or haciendas in defense of their country or religion, hearing with valiant scorn the threats and offers of the said principal rebel and his military commanders, yet taking care that these elected leaders are the only ones with the right to be called *caciques* or governors of their *ayllus* or pueblos, without passing on [the position] to their children or others of their generation (family members).

To this same end, you should prohibit that the Indians wear pagan clothes, especially those who belong to the nobility, since it only serves to represent those worn by their Inca ancestors, reminding them of memories which serve no other end than to reconcile them more and more in their hatred toward the dominant nation [i.e., Spaniards]; outside of their looking ridiculous and not in keeping with the purity of our religion, since they wear images of the sun . . . which was their most important [*primera*] deity; and this prohibition be extended to all the provinces of South America [*América meridional*] in order to completely eliminate such clothing, especially those that directly represent the clothing of their pagan kings through insignias such as the *unto*, which is a kind of vest; *yacollas*, which are very fine blankets or shawls of black velvet or taffeta; the *mascapaycha*, which is a circle like a crown from which they hang a certain emblem of ancient nobility signified by a tuft or tassel of red alpaca wool, and whatever other things of this type or symbolism. This shall be published in bans in each province, so that they dispose of, or surrender to, the *corregidor* whatever clothing they may find of this kind, as well as all the paintings or portraits of their Incas which are very prevalent in the houses of the Indians who consider themselves to be nobles and who use them to prove their claim to, or boast of, their heritage. These latter shall be done away with without fail as they do not merit the dignity of being painted in such places, and toward that same end any paintings of them shall also be removed from walls . . . churches, monasteries, hospitals, holy places or personal houses. The duty [to do this] first part rests with the reverend archbishops and bishops of both viceroyalties; and if it is necessary it would be best to replace such adornments with images of the king and our other Catholic sovereigns.

Also, the . . . *corregidores* should make sure that no plays (*comedias*) or other public functions be performed in any pueblo of their respective provinces as the Indians are accustomed to use them to commemorate their said Inca ancestors; and having carried out the order, these officials shall provide a certified account to the secretaries of the respective governments. In like manner, [the *corregidores*] are to prohibit the use of trumpets or bugles that the Indians use for their ceremonies and which they call *pututos,* being the shells of sea snails which make a strange and mournful sound that announces their mourning and the pitiful memorial that they make for their ancestors. And they shall also bring the black clothing [the Indians] are accustomed to wear as a sign of mourning, a custom that is still carried on in some provinces, in memory of their deceased monarchs and also of the period of the conquest which they consider ill fated and we consider fortunate since it brought them into the pale of the Catholic Church and the very loving and gentle domination of our Kings.

Toward the same end, it is absolutely forbidden that the Indians give their signature as "Incas," since it is a title that anyone can take, but which makes a great impression on those of their class; ordering. It is ordered and required that all of those who have genealogical trees or documents that prove in some way their descent from them [the Incas], that they produce them or send them certified and gratis to the respective secretaries. . . . And the *corregidores* are in charge of carefully seeing that such requirements are complied with, verifying and finding out who does not observe them, with the end of having them comply or collecting them with the purpose of sending them [to the proper officials], giving the owners a [legal] quittance.

In order that these Indians free themselves from the hatred that they have conceived against the Spaniards, and that they follow the legal dress [codes], adopting Spanish dress customs and speaking Castilian, schools will be introduced in a more vigorous manner than has been done up to the present, imposing the most rigorous and just penalties on those who do not use them once enough time has passed for them to have learned. . . . They shall be given a period of four years for the people to speak fluently or at least being able to make themselves understood and to explain themselves in Castilian. . . .

Finally, the manufacture of cannons of all kinds shall be prohibited. . . . Any noble found manufacturing such items shall be sentenced to ten years of prison in one of the *presidios* in Africa and any commoner will receive 200 lashes as well as the same penalty for the same time period; reserving for now a similar resolution regarding the manufacture of powder, which will follow [at a] later [date]. And since there are a variety of cannons of almost every caliber in many haciendas, grinding mills, and textile mills, the *corregidores* will gather them once the pacification of this uprising has been completely finished. . . . Thus I have decreed, ordered, and signed. . . .

José Antonio de Areche. [*CDIP,* 195. 1781-V-15, 18]

61. List of the Individuals of the Family of Tupac Amaru Arrested by Me, Colonel D. Francisco Salcedo, *Corregidor* and Commander of Arms of Canas y Canchis (Tinta)

The Spanish went to considerable lengths to bring the family of Tupac Amaru under their control so that they would no longer be a source of problems for the colonial regime. This meant not only executing many of them but also exiling some to Spain and detaining others. The following documents list people who were linked to the family and had been detained but were not major activists in the rebellion. Furthermore, it mentions others who were yet to be apprehended. The very length of the document reveals the extent of Spanish concern regarding the potential for the extended family of Tupac Amaru to be a source of further problems for royal authority.

Cecelia [*sic*] Tupac Amaro [*sic*]

Mariano Mendiguri, son of said Cecelia

Felipa Mendiguri, daughter of the said

Juan Barrientos, grandson of Bartolomé Tupac Amaro, [*sic*] first cousins of the vile José Gabriel and Diego Tupac Amaro [*sic*]

Margarita Castro, sister of Marcela and aunt of the same Diego

Antonia Castro, same same

Paula Castro, same same

Martina Castro, same same

José Sánchez, *cacique* of the pueblo of Surimana, married to the aforementioned Margarita Castro

Francisca Castro, wife of Francisco Noguera, first cousin of José Gabriel and Diego Tupac Amaro [*sic*]

Lorenzo Noguera, son of Francisco Noguera and of Asencia Castro

Paula Noguera, daughter of said Francisco Castro

Antonio Castro, uncle of said Diego

José Castro, uncle of the announced Diego

Cayetano Castro, same

Bernardo Castro, same

Francisco Castro, son of aforementioned Antonio Castro, second cousin of Diego

Patricia Castro, first cousin of Diego

Manuel Castro, son of said Patricia

Asencia Castro, cousin of Diego Tupac Amaro [*sic*]

Maria Luque, daughter of said Asencia Castro
Silvestre Luque, same
Miguel Tito-Condori, father of Manuela Tito-Condori, wife of Diego
Gregorio Tito-Condori, same
Marcelo Tito-Condori, same
Feliciana Tito-Condori, sister of the same
Antonia Tito-Condori, same
Manuel Tito-Condori, brother of the same
Luis Tito-Condori, same
Mariano Tito-Condori, same
Isidora Escobedo, first cousin of the vile José Gabriel and Diego Tupac
    Amaro [*sic*]
Bartola Escobedo, same
Catalina Guancachoque, mother of the referred Isidora and Bartola
Pedro Venero, husband of the aforementioned Bartola
Ventura Aguirre, father-in-law of Juan Tupac Amaro [*sic*]
Nicolasa Aguirre, daughter-in-law of said Juan
Antolin Ortiz, husband of Nicolasa Aguirre
Marcelo Puyucagua, uncle of the wife of the vile insurgent, José Gabriel
    Tupac Amaro [*sic*]
Simon Capatinta, a blood relative of the wife of said José Gabriel
Martin Capatinta, the same in everything
Pascual Cusiguaman, of the same ties
Andrea Uscamanco, wife of the aforementioned Cayetano Castro
Juan Belestrán servant of the said Cecilia
Santusa Castro, sister of Marcela, wife of Diego
Maria Cruz Guamani, *ponga* [servant] of the said Cecilia.
Francisco Diaz, her husband
Pablo Quispe, brother of Manuela Tito-Condori, wife of Diego
Ignacio Quispe, first cousin of the said wife of Diego Tupac Amaro [*sic*]
Gregoria Malque, wife of Manuel Tito-Condori, uncle of the wife of Diego
Juliana Tito-Condori, daughter of said Manuel, and first cousin of the said
    woman
Antonia Cayacombina, wife of José Castro, uncle of said Diego
Paulino Castro, son of José, first cousin of Diego
Antonia Castro, daughter of said José Castro, first cousin of Diego
Santusa Canque, wife of Antonio Castro, uncle of Diego
Margarita Condori, aunt of the wife of Diego
Dionisia Caguaitapa, wife of Marcelo
Puyucagua, uncle of José Gabriel and the rest
Diego Ortigosa, secretary-advisor of José Gabriel and Diego Tupac Amaro [*sic*]
Tomas Araus, confidant and overseer of the farms of Diego

Margarita Cusi, wife of the aforementioned Tomas Araus

Crispin Guamani, one of the most inhumane colonels of José Gabriel and
     Diego Tupac Amaro [*sic*]: he who destroyed Cailloma and attacked the
     column from Arequipa under the command of D. Pedro Vicente Nieto
     on the 27 of May of the past year of 1782

Tomas Jacinto, famous colonel of the Punas of San Pedro and San Pablo de
     Cacha, and the most obedient of the orders of Diego

Eight Indians who were remitted to me from the Punas of Checacupe and
     Pitumarca for the crimes attributed to them

Maria Ramos, born in the pueblo and province of Soroata, concubine of
     Diego Tupac Amaro [*sic*], who, when arrested and pressured confessed
     to where the hole was where the document [*esquela*] was hidden

Those of the Descendants That Remain to Be Apprehended
Juan Tupac Amaro [*sic*]
Susana Aguirre, wife of said Juan
Francisco Noguera
Antonio Capatinta
Juana Coriyuto (alias Bastidas), aunt of Mariano Tupac Amaro [*sic*]
Diego Anco, confidant of Diego, in whose house he maintained his
     concubine

. . . Later [in addition] to the detention of the above mentioned, they
     succeeded in capturing Melchor Ramos, famous partisan of the rebels,
     in the Altos de Checacupe. [*CDIP,* 284. 1783-III-25]

62. Punishments Carried Out in the City of Cuzco with Tupac Amaru, His Wife, Children, and Confidants

*As the following document attests, the day of the executions was met with extra
security and a strange turn in the weather: to some Indians, and perhaps others,
it was an omen intended to alert the Spanish and the crowd to the cruelty of
the situation. The brutality of the executions was almost without comprehen-
sion. The rebels were not simply put to death—their bodies were dismembered
and sent to various locations. Horses were tied to Tupac Amaru's limbs as the
Spanish tried to literally pull the rebel leader apart while he was still alive.*

On Friday, May 18th, 1781, after having surrounded the plaza with the militias from this city of Cuzco, who had their pikes and firearms, and surrounded the four sides of the gallows with the corps of mulattoes and *Huamanguinos,* all arranged with their muskets and bayonets fixed, nine individuals came out of the [church of the] Compañía who were the following: José Verdejo, Andrés Castelo, a *zambo,* Antonio Oblitas (who was the executioner who hanged . . . Arriaga), Antonio Bastidas, Francisco Tupac Amaru, Tomasa Condemayta, *cacica* of Acos, Hipólito Tupac Amaru, son of the traitor, Micaela Bastidas, his wife, and the insurgent José Gabriel. All came out at the same time, and one after the other they walked with their shackles and handcuffs, [and then they were put] inside some bags like those used to carry *yerba* from Paraguay and were dragged behind a pair of harnessed horses. Accompanied by the priests who were assisting them, and guarded by the aforementioned guards, they all arrived at the gallows, and were put to death by two executioners in the following manner:

Verdejo, Castelo, the *zambo* and Bastidas were hanged as usual: the tongues of Francisco Tupac Amaru, uncle of the insurgent, and his son Hipólito, were cut out before the bodies were thrown down the stairs of the gallows; the Indian Condemayta was strangled through *garrote* on a scaffold that was fitted with a metal spindle that was built for this purpose and that we had never seen before around here: all of which the Indian (Tupac Amaru) and his wife witnessed with their own eyes, including the torture of their son Hipólito who was the last to go up the gallows. Then, the Indian Micaela was brought up on the scaffold where they cut out her tongue in front of her husband and then she was put to death through *garrote* from which she suffered immensely as her neck was long and thin and the spindle could not strangle her, forcing the hangmen to tie ropes around her neck and pull them every which way while kicking her in the stomach and breast to finish [killing] her. The last to be executed was the rebel José Gabriel, who was brought to the middle of the plaza, his tongue cut out by the executioner, and after taking the shackles and handcuffs off him, they forced him to lie down on the ground: they tied ropes to his feet and hands, and then cinched these to four horses, and then four *mestizos* had the horses pull in different directions—a spectacle that had never been seen in that city. I do not know whether it was due to the horses not being strong enough, or because the Indian really was made out of iron, [but] they absolutely could not tear him apart, even though after pulling hard for quite some time in such a way that he was suspended in the air, in a fashion that looked like a spider. . . . [T]he *Visitador,* moved with compassion so that the miserable [Tupac Amaru] would not suffer any longer, sent an order from the *Compañía,* to cut off his head, an order which the executioner obeyed. Immediately afterwards, the body was taken back under the gallows where they cut off his arms and legs. The same was done to the women and the rest had their heads cut off so they could be sent to different villages. The bodies of the Indian and his wife were taken to Picchu [a mountain above Cuzco], where a fire had been started so that their bodies would be reduced to ashes that would then be thrown in the air and in the creek that flowed nearby. This was the end of José Gabriel Tupac Amaru and Micaela Bastidas, whose loftiness and arrogance led them to declare themselves kings of Peru, Chile, Quito, Tucuman, and other places including the Gran Paitití, with other insanities of this same tone.

Very many people were present that day, but nobody screamed, nobody raised their voice: many noticed, I among them, that amidst the many people, very few Indians were seen, at least dressed in their customary attire, and if there were some, they might have been disguised wearing capes and ponchos. Some [strange] things seemed to occur as if the devil had planned them, in order to confirm those Indians in their abuses, omens, and superstitions. I say this because, after having enjoyed dry weather and calm days, that day dawned so overcast that the sun did not show its face, [and those clouds] threatened to rain everywhere; and around noon, just when the horses were [trying to] pull the Indian [apart], a strong wind sprang up, followed by a heavy downpour that forced everybody, including the guards, to seek refuge in a hurry. This is the reason why Indians have started saying that the heavens and nature felt the death of the Inca, who was being put to death by inhuman and impious Spaniards who were very cruelly killing him. [*CDIP,* 195. 1781-V-15, 18]

63. Distribution of the Bodies, or Parts, of the Nine Principal Prisoners of the Rebellion, Executed in the Plaza of Cuzco, May 18, 1781

In an effort to put fear into people and quell the rebellion, the colonial state not only sentenced the main rebels to death, it also had their bodies dismembered. The body parts were then distributed to various communities that had been involved in the rebellion, such as those the rebels were from or places that battles had been fought. This was meant to send a clear and powerful message to indigenous peoples who might think of rebelling about what their future would be, while at the same time sending these bloody "assurances" to the loyalists that those who threatened their very being would be dealt with severely. Thus, the severed heads and limbs were used as both a punishment and a deterrent. The following is a list of people who were executed, their body parts, and the provinces and communities to which they were sent following the executions in Cuzco.

José Gabriel Tupac Amaro [*sic*]
Micaela Bastidas, his wife
Hipólito Tupac Amaro [*sic*], his son
Francisco Tupac Amaro [*sic*], [his] uncle
Antonio Bastidas, his brother-in-law
La *cacica* de Acos [Tomasa Titu Condemayta]
Diego Verdejo, commander [Lt. colonel]
Andrés Castelo, colonel
Antonhio [*sic*] Oblitas, executioner

Tinta
The head of José Gabriel Tupac Amaro [*sic*] (pueblo of Tinta)
An arm to Tungasuca
Another of Micaela Bastidas, the same
Another of Antonio Bastidas, to Pampamarca
The head of Hipólito to Tungasuca
An arm of Castelo, to Surimana
Another to Pampamarca
Another of Verdejo, to Coporaque
Another to Yauri
The remainder of his body, to Tinta
An arm to Tungasuca
The head of Francisco Tupac Amaro [*sic*], to Pilpinto

Quispicanchi
An arm of Antonio Bastidas, to Urcos
A leg of Hipólito Tupac Amaro [*sic*], to Quiquijana
Another of Antonio Bastidas, to Sangarara [*sic*]
The head of the *cacica* of Acos, the same
That of [the head] of Castelo, to Acamayo

Cuzco
The body of José Gabriel Tupac Amaro [*sic*], to Picchu
The same with the body of his wife with the head
An arm of Antonio Oblitas, en route to San Sebastian

Carabaya
An arm of José Gabriel Tupac Amaro [*sic*]
A leg of his wife
An arm of Francisco Tupac Amaro [*sic*]

Azangaro
A leg of Hipólito Tupac Amaro [*sic*]

Lampa
A leg of José Gabriel Tupac Amaro [*sic*], to Santa Rosa
An arm of his son to Ayabirí

Arequipa
An arm of Micaela Bastidas

Chumbivilcas
A leg of José Gabriel Tupac Amaro [*sic*], in Livitaca
An arm of his son, to Santo Tomas

Paucartambo
The body of Castelo, in its capital
The head of Antonio Bastidas

Chilques y Masques
An arm of Francisco Tupac Amaro [*sic*], to Paruro

Condesuyos of Arequipa
The head of Antonio Verdejo, to Chumbivilcas

Puno
A leg of Francisco Tupac Amaro [*sic*], in its capital

[*CDIP,* 195. 1781-V-15, 18]

VII. The End of the Struggle: Diego and Andrés Tupac Amaru, Lessons to the Spanish, and Indigenous Afterthoughts

64. Cuzco Lampoon Written after the Death of Tupac Amaru

Creole dissent and problems in the empire did not come to an immediate end with the death of the Inca. Indigenous forces continued to fight for some time, but creoles also let it be known by various means that they too had concerns and grievances. The following lampoon was found in Cuzco and warns against abusive officials and, especially, the visitador *Areche.*

Oh, King Don Carlos III, by the grace of God, if you knew the great danger your kingdom of Peru is in, because of the tyranny of the *corregidores,* the *visitador,* and other tyrants, you would come from Spain and take measures against the persons who are the cause of this hell that we suffer. Know especially that your most distinguished Creole people are not very contented because the [tyrants] wish to monopolize salt, and discontent fills the chests of these your vassals. Although Tupac Amaru is dead, others are not lacking to get rid of tyranny by killing the cruel *visitador.* [*LIR,* 238–39. Translated by L. E. Fisher]

65. Spanish Discuss Exploiting Tensions between Blacks and Indians

In the Andes, peoples of African descent—even slaves—were often placed in positions of authority over indigenous peoples. Serving as agents of those who hired or owned them, the Afro-Andeans were frequently perceived by indigenous peoples as abusing or tricking them. As early as the writings of Guamán Poma, one gets a hint of these racial tensions. During the Tupac Amaru rebellion, peoples of African descent fought effectively against the indigenous rebels, leading authorities to discuss the important role that blacks could play in maintaining the security of the region as they sought to exploit the racial tensions between Afro-Peruvians and castas *against the Indians.*

The Ministry should also foment and expand the introduction of *Negroes* because they, and their descendants, as people of mixed blood (*Castas*) opposed to the Indians, will serve to counteract their [Indians'] forces and they will be beneficial to the support of agriculture and the other professions (*Artes*). No measure has been more effective in the present revolutions than that of opposing some provinces against others, and being natural the antipathy of the *Negro* and his predominance over the *Indio,* we will succeed by this method to present to them [the Indians], in times of necessity, an irreconcilable and powerful enemy. [*RTA,* 727]

66. Letter That a Subject and Resident of Cuzco, Who Respects the *Visitador* (A. Areche), Wrote to a Confidant

Although the Spanish suffered many defeats and thousands killed, they slowly but surely began to turn the tide of battle against the rebels, eventually capturing and executing Tupac Amaru and many others. However, this document, written after the defeat and execution of the Inca, attests to the fact that some loyalists were not happy with the commander of the military forces in Cuzco, Inspector José del Valle. This negative opinion, which was shared by the Visitador *Antonio de Areche as well, refers to del Valle's lack of aptitude for the job and his cowardice. This was especially pronounced following his lack of support for the* corregidor *in Puno and his withdrawal, or retreat, back to Cuzco. The writer, though mentioning the capture and execution of Tupac Amaru, is very much aware that the rebellion has not ended and that Diego Tupac Amaru still represents a real threat. The writer also refers to the important roles played by several "indianos," which in this case refers either to* criollos *or Spaniards who had been longtime residents of the Americas. This is not a common term, and it seems to separate more recently arrived Spaniards from others of Iberian heritage. One can only speculate whether "indiano" was a less politically loaded term in the middle of the rebellion than "criollo," due to the effort of the rebels to recruit* criollos *and the Inca's somewhat more lenient treatment of them on occasion—an attitude not always shared by the rebel army. Unlike the author of document 65, this writer held the Afro-Peruvian forces from Lima in contempt.*

Dear Sir: in January of the current year of 1781 I was writing to you about all that had happened until Tupac Amaru appeared [near Cuzco] so that he might be apprehended on the hills of Picchu, something that was not accomplished due to the lack of aptitude or cowardice of Don Gabriel Avilez, and having lost this opportunity, many thousands [of pesos] would have to be spent trying to get another one that would end the rebellion. Indeed more has occurred than just what was lost, for Tupac Amaru left for the Province of Tinta, and he was ultimately able to get all of the Collao provinces and those of the episcopate of La Paz, Santa Cruz and parts of that of Chuquisaca to rebel. Irreparable damages have been perpetrated against settlements, haciendas, farms, and on the wealth and lives of untold numbers of Spaniards, and on the most sacred lives of many priests in those regions. He was able to reinforce his arms among which are many artillery pieces of a larger caliber than those few of ours, and he was able to fortify himself by constructing walls around Tinta itself.

By the month of March our army left, divided into five columns: the first and biggest with all the colored and other peoples amounting to 10,000 going to a place called Yanacocha and led by the Inspector himself. The second, around the ravines of Quiquijana, was led by Don Juan Manuel Campero; the third, on the outskirts of Paucartambo, was led by Don Joaquin Valcárcel; the fourth, through the ravines of Paruro, led by its *Corregidor* Don Manuel Castilla; the fifth, around Cotabambas and led by Don Francisco Laysequilla; so that the Inspector's column was situated in the middle.

Laysequilla won his battles in Chumbivilcas and killed two courageous enemy generals, Parvina and Bermudez. . . . [He] joined the *Corregidor* of Paruro in order to finish the conquest of that province and then come to Tinta, but they received an order from the Inspector . . . [saying] they should come from where they were. His column was stopped in a place called Pucacasa by the army of the enemy, and also due to his cowardice or lack of aptitude, because he had not taken an advantageous site that the enemy occupied. He was at the point of having the same thing happen to him as happened to those miserable [soldiers] in Sangarará, if a soldier of Tupac Amaru had not come and warned them that at four in the morning there was to be a surprise attack. With this warning, he put our army at ready with their weapons and prepared to open fire. And, thus, when the army came at the aforetold time it was received with bullets and frustrated his [Tupac Amaru's] plans. When day broke the Inspector gave the order to break camp as if we had been defeated, and even in this movement we would have been defeated if the column commanded by Juan Manuel Camparo had not appeared on one side [of the battlefield], the view of which stopped the rebels in their advance.

Our army, going down into the ravine of Quiquijana, took the town by this name and went on to Checacupi where the Indian [Tupac Amaru] had not finished his reinforcement. God disposed that he prepared his army into diverse columns and came to take the city while our forces, with all their weapons, were in that ravine. And from here, when he was giving orders to his troops in Checacupi, our army arrived and he had no choice but to flee by horse for the highlands of the sierra with his wife and children. And going through the pueblo of Langui, in which there were no Indians, two *mestizos* and an old woman captured him, and with the news of this event, aid was sent and brought him back as a prisoner to this city where Tupac Amaru, his wife, his son and other principal accomplices were judged; leaving another son of some nine or ten years free due to this reason [his age].

Diego Tupac Amaru, brother of Joseph, and another of his sons were able to escape. They rallied people and went on to wage two battles near Langui against the columns of Laysequilla and the *Corregidor* of Paruro; but they [the loyalist forces] were able to defeat him. . . . Those two continue their escape and nobody knows for sure where they are, even though it is vaguely rumored that they went deep into the mountains of the Province of Larecaxa.

Once all the [loyalist] columns were gathered together, the Inspector continued to comply with his orders to pacify the region. He reached Puno, where the road was being fought for at the very moment [he arrived]. He did not want to aid [his fellow loyalists] and the next day he decided to return [to Cuzco] without leaving arms, people, or money for the *Corregidor* of the city [Puno]. In view of this the *Corregidor* of this city, who from the beginning had courageously served as an impenetrable wall against the hordes of highland Indians, fled with all the inhabitants. . . . The same was done by all those who survived in the provinces of Lampa, Azangaro, Carabaya, Tinta and all those near Chucuito and the Inspector is entering the city [Cuzco] with his army today.

Everybody in Chucuito was put to the knife, no living soul being spared. From La Paz and all the highlands regions nothing is known for sure, only unsubstantiated rumors. Since the *Corregidor* of Puno fled, it is probable that once this obstacle has been removed, the Indians from the highlands will move in and flood through all the areas that have been left at their disposition. And we do not know what is going to happen to us, for we are in a far worse situation now than we were before.

A thousand armed men in addition to those already under his command would have been sufficient for the *Corregidor* of Puno (who is an *indiano* and who never has been a soldier) to fight and pacify the entire kingdom: but as nobody wanted to give him [this support] and he did not have any more powder or bullets nor anything with which to sustain his people, he has come [to Cuzco]. But it is known he left with two prisoners: a certain Catari, who was acting as [the rebel] Viceroy for the provinces of La Paz and a general, whose name is not known, even though they had carried out the destruction of the city of Chucuito.

The Inspector was not born to hold the job he has as he does not possess the courage that is needed, even though he has a rough character, and is violent and tyrannical in his treatment of his soldiers.

The mulattoes from Lima have shown their unthinkable cowardice, uselessness, vices, and knavery and have caused infinite unfruitful expenses to His Majesty.

It is said that the *Visitador,* who is truly a great man, has shared with Your Excellency the mistake of the Inspector's return and the possibility of his taking command away from him and personally leading the conquests. He [the Inspector] who leads the [loyal] Indians is not brave; rather he is barbarous and stubborn. The Indians themselves do not fear death and fight blindly.

If it were not for the ravines of the Calca and Paruro rivers that serve us as walls, we in this city would already have perished, because we are not more than four leagues from the advancing army of 20,000 Indians who are near Lares, invading all the towns of Calca that are located on the other side of the river. . . . Miraculously, we were able to live and witness the battle of Picchu with some degree of happiness as it was waged by the masses and the Company of Comercio commanded by the *indiano* Don Francisco Laysequilla. The battles of Chumbivilcas and Langui were also won by him and only two others from the provinces, as well as other battles of minor importance such as those in the Pampa of Chita. The *Corregidor* Orellana is also *indiano,* and it is they who have taken the principal roles. Alas! It seemed that all the Spaniards left their courage in Spain, bringing only their jackets with them.

Don Manuel Villalta, who also is *indiano,* sustained the city until the Inspector arrived; and even though he went out with the army he retired from the battlefield to avoid the bad temper of the Inspector, and to avoid dying of rage at witnessing a blunder. May our Lord keep You many years. Cuzco, July 3rd, 1781. [*CDIP,* 207. 1781-VII-3]

67. Prohibition of the *Royal Commentaries*

In the wake of the rebellion, the Spanish were adamant in taking the actions necessary to prevent further revolts and to eradicate the Incas from the memory of the native peoples of the Andes. The immediate family and supporters of Tupac Amaru were executed or arrested, with some even sent to Spain to remove them from their ancestral home. Pictures of the Inca were also removed or destroyed.

In the following document, the king orders that Garcilaso de la Vega's work on the Incas (Royal Commentaries, or History of the Incas) *be removed from circulation, even if this meant having to buy up all of the copies. The book had been an important source of pride for many of the indigenous elite, although most of them remained loyal to the crown. However, Garcilaso's book had been an influence on Tupac Amaru and seemingly on other rebel leaders as well. At the same time, the following order seeks to greatly restrict and control any attempt by indigenous peoples to make claims of, or attain, titles of nobility that usually involved being descended from the Incas. The Spanish wanted nothing more to do with the Incas, their memory, and the continuing allegiance of the* naturales *to their Inca rulers.*

Reserved

There are many sinful ideas shared by the Indian masses of this Kingdom of Peru and other provinces. From them stem their abominable customs regarding many things, such as trying to preserve the memory of their pagan ancestors. Amid that chaos and misplaced enthusiasm one can mainly observe the lack of solemnity and truth, while they are convinced that their ancestral lines or descent from primitive Pagan Kings gives them the right to nobility and to call themselves Ynga [*sic*]. It has been painfully observed how many of those claims have been authorized implicitly and explicitly by the Royal *Audiencia*. This practice is abominable and the authority for it should be abolished.

In view of this habitual disorder, which was not corrected by the magistrates the way it should have been, so that it would have become extinct, the King has resolved for now that Your Excellency should take great care to make the Royal *Audiencia* of Lima understand that they should not accept any such information as valid or supportive of such ancestry, nor any proof or declaration of nobility by any Yndian [*sic*], regardless of which class they belong to. This prerogative, . . . should rest with the Royal Chamber of the Supreme Council of the Yndies [*sic*] to which any petition and related documentation should be submitted. . . .

Equally, the King desires Your Excellency to sagaciously retrieve, with the same care, the History of the Ynga [*sic*] Garcilaso through which those *Naturales* [Indians] have learned many pernicious things, as well as those other slanderous papers from the Tribunals and Magistrates of the Kingdom that were printed when it was believed that they were innocent, even though the supposed prophesy of this History's preface should have never been allowed to be published. To this end I advise Your Excellency, by order of His Majesty, to use all normal means possible, even if it means secretly buying all copies available through trusted third parties who will be paid by the Royal Treasury. It is important to make sure that all [copies] have been retrieved so that these *naturales* will not have any way to verify their bad customs through such documents. Your Excellency will need to coordinate this very serious matter with Don Jorge Escovedo whom will be properly advised so that he can fulfill what was ordered.

God and Aranjuez, April 21st, 1782.
Viceroy of Peru. [*CDIP,* 259. 1782-IV-21]

68. Charges against the Priest Gregorio de Yépez

During the rebellion, the Inca received the support of several priests. One of the most infamous was Gregorio de Yépez, who likened Tupac Amaru to the avenging hand of God for the punishment of European excesses. The priest also made comparisons between several revered personages from the Bible and the rebel leader. Once the rebellion was over, the state began to make people like Yépez account for their actions. As a priest, however, Yépez fell under the jurisdiction of the bishop, who was not likely to be harsh in his punishment because it would draw further attention to the errant ways of some priests, not to mention his own earlier relationship with Tupac Amaru. In this document, the prosecutor makes his case for punishment, in a very respectful manner, to the bishop.

Cuzco, September 12th, 1781.—In the presence of the District Attorney. Provided, ordered, and signed by His Very Illustrious Lord the Bishop; my Lord whom I certified.—The Bishop.—Dr. Bustamante.—Secretary.

Very Illustrious Lord.—The Prosecutor in view of these proceedings, expresses: that the letter on page 1, and the declaration on page 3, constitute the accusation against, and the guilt of, Don Gregorio de Yépez, priest of the Doctrine of Pomacanche. As a consequence of which, he finds himself arrested by verbal order of your Very Illustrious Lordship and the announced declaration [word missing from document] that should be considered as his formal confession; thus this should be considered the formal accusation, so that our Very Illustrious Lordship can impose the penalty that he deserves; and . . . at the very least, he be seriously reprimanded for the excess of writing such a letter, warning him that if he does this again, the law will proceed against him and punish him with all its rigor.

In truth, the letter includes, besides affectionate expressions towards the rebel José Gabriel Tupac Amaru and his wife Micaela Bastidas, expressions that raise suspicion if not of his complicity, at least of his approval, of the iniquitous enterprise of the Rebellion. [Yépez stated] . . . without there being any distortion, the following: . . . "Neither I nor my brother have observed anything relative to the doings of the Governor [José Gabriel Tupac Amaru], for that would be like gossiping about the license granted by the will of God, without whose will not even a tree leaf can move. And so, just like the poor shepherd David was chosen to vindicate the army of Saul, allowing him to defeat a giant such as Goliath; in the same way that he elected Moses to save the people of Israel from the Pharaoh's oppression by raising him in [the Pharaoh's] . . . home; and in the same way as he elected the Prophet Jonah for the conversion of the Ninevites, I have to assume that in the same way he is using Don José Gabriel [Tupac Amaru] as his instrument to correct the many faults and abuses [that exist]. There is much I could say in regards to this, but I will spare you . . . and I only beg you to consider me very much in agreement with God's will."

Even though the phrase, "the license granted by God's will," is used in this letter, and the meaning of the proposition is that the Uprising is in fact and undeniably a result of God's will, to impose the Rebel into this same truth, authorizing him with the examples from Scripture is, in one sense, to promote and confirm his iniquitous intent, especially when it deals with an idiot [Micaela Bastidas] who does not understand the difference between the positive and permissive will of God, and who boasts hypocritically that [the rebellion] was "the heaven's whipping [punishment] of the Europeans," as in other times the tyrant Attila's against all the East.

The excuse of the great fear that the Priest felt because of the Rebel's threats, causing this brother [Yépez] to flee, does not excuse his excesses. He had already written more than one page to satisfy this [argument] and it was not necessary for him to bring into the writing the facts about David, Moses, and Jonah, nor authorize with them the assumption that God had taken the Rebel as his instrument *to correct many faults and excesses.*

Similarly, the letter condemns the Priest for communicating with the Rebel in a familiar style in a period in which he [Tupac Amaru] was excommunicated, and when he [Yépez] could not be unaware of his censure, as it is indicated by its date of March 4th of the current year, where the Priest thanks the Rebel for having sent him a loaf of sugar that he had asked for. And on another issue he ends by saying that he is not of two faces, but that *he is very passionate,* as time has proven. This is another excess deserving the punishment included in the sacred canon against those who deal with the excommunicated, as it is forbidden to deal with them even in the face of great fear, *candante invirum constantem* . . . as it is taught by theologians and canonists.

It is in this framework that the Priest's demerits have been demonstrated and that he deserves the punishment established by law. . . . [I]t will suffice (as Your Illustrious Lordship justly and prudently judges) to decide and order as the prosecutor has expressed, or whatever your superior judgment would consider. Estudio, October 3rd, 1781.

—Dr. Iturrizarra. [*CDIP,* 222. 1781-IX-12, 1782-V-13]

69. Letter Written in the Pueblo of Mojo by Sergeant Major Don Pablo Angel of Spain to His Wife, Resident of the City of Arequipa

Deception is almost always a part of warfare. The following document, written by a Spaniard near the end of hostilities, makes apparent the deceitful strategies of indigenous rebels in the northeastern region of Lake Titicaca who took advantage of the situation in which the nearly victorious Spanish were trying to put an end to fighting by pardoning rebels. These rebels pretended to accept the pardon only to use the time gained to gather forces and attack once again. However, because some rebels did accept the pardons, the Spanish were not sure who would stay pardoned and who would deceive them. The author of the following document experienced the dangers of this complex time and came through the battles unscathed, for which he gives thanks to God. This letter was addressed to the author's wife and was meant to be shared with their friends.

After having been in this pueblo of Mojo for eight days, where the Indians received us with great submission, obedience and contrition upon being pardoned, we left for the pueblo of Huaqui and stopped two leagues from it on the 28th, which was Thursday of Easter Week. We spent that night without novelty, and Friday at eight A.M. we began our march toward that Pueblo, two leagues distant through the ravines. Before we entered them, God allowed us to spot Indians on the surrounding hills. We became more careful and decided to unload the cargos we were carrying when a great number of Indians started attacking us from all sides of the camp. We immediately raised the Flag of Peace, while they raised that of War telling us that they wanted to fight and they began to furiously throw rocks at us. I was with eighty men, under the command of Captain don Josef Luis Espejo, his Company composed of fifty musketeers and the rest Cavalry. The fighting lasted for two hours with the enemy being . . . defeated, even though the terrain was advantageous to them. Several of them were killed and many wounded. The greatest number of Indians, some 200, appeared on the other side of the ravine . . . and they were so enraged by the killing of the other Indians that they threw themselves . . . [at us] . . . and five of our [men] died. At eleven A.M. we loaded up and left for . . . a better location. They chased after us all the way through the hills, and through the narrow passes where they wore us out completely. Close to the time of prayer we descended to some fields to make camp in a place where there were some corrals and a spring. In this particular place the Indians, who had already been pardoned twice, ambushed us. These rascals attacked us with rocks and the muleteers were forced to abandon their cargos even though they tried very hard to defend them. Seven of ours died in this confusion and eleven were wounded. The traitors took everything from us and our soldiers. I was the one who was best off as I was able to salvage a bed, even though they took chests, trunks, tarps, etc.

Saturday the 30th, the day before Easter, dawned with the hills appearing to be covered with Indians who were crying out at the top of their lungs and at three P.M. they encircled us. We took up our arms to defend our lives against the attack of an . . . army of ten to eleven thousand, according to the testimony of an Indian we captured. . . . [We] were attacked from all four sides and we fought, in close combat, for three hours with these very undisciplined people. We were able to kill 400 and wound many more, one of our stone firing cannons ripping them apart. On Easter Sunday they received reinforcements from Larecaxa and Carabaya and at two in the afternoon the yelling started again. They were insulting us badly and attacking us with incredible fury, but we were able to defeat their knavery with a great loss of life on their part so that, seeing our perseverance and the serious carnage that we were inflicting on them, they presented their white flag begging for forgiveness. Peace was brokered in this situation, although perhaps it would have been better not to do it as we would have liked to have finished with all of them right there. Our Chaplain went to negotiate with their Colonel who located himself about a block's distance away from us. They were told that they would be forgiven if they would surrender their arms, without bringing up [the matter of] all that they had stolen from us as we thought there would be a better time for that. The rebel indicated that he was going to talk to his comrades, Pedro Vilca Apaza and Carlos Tupac Catari—the main leaders, and that the next day the peace treaties would be confirmed. That night they retreated taking with them all the herds and what they had robbed from us. The Indians . . . ambushed us in the narrow passes along the road, so that we were in the middle of a jail made out of hills and ravines. Having witnessed the events of Friday—the riot and confusion—the surgeon Villanueva took a horse on his own authority and left for Azangaro that same night to request the Inspector to come and help us, but he [the Inspector] was not there as he was in Santa Rosa. But Fernando Guamanvilca immediately rallied some 300 men, and came to help us even though by then we were already free. Said Villanueva, along with a soldier who went with him, was almost killed by some Indians in Azangaro. Guamanvilca caught [these Indians] . . . and wanted to hang them, but Villanueva interceded on their behalf and pardoned them. We will be leaving shortly for Azangaro and Vilques so that we can recover, for neither the soldiers nor the officers have anything on which to subsist. Even though the Indians took all our animals, we have not been lacking food, because we have been subsisting on some chickens and pigs we have found on the ranches of the fugitive Indians.

Our Lady of the Rosary has favored us infinitely but especially me, as I have not received any blows and strangely enough I have not been wounded by a rock, stick, spear, or bullet. The black [man] lost his mule and he escaped on foot with only his spear. It has been a full month since we have even been able to remove our clothes. I barely have been able to find this piece of paper to write on and I do so sitting on the ground and [writing] on a drum. Please inform my friends of all I have shared with you so that they can help us thank God for such a well deserved victory. Mojo, April 4th, 1782. [*CDIP,* 255. 1782-IV-4]

70. Letter from Arequipa Dated May 2, 1781, That Recounts the Ravages Done by the Indians Who Rebel

With the distance of time, we tend to think more of the causes and consequences of the rebellion and the Spanish reprisals, but the Tupac Amaru rebellion was a very bloody and vicious struggle. Although it was written in Arequipa, the following account deals more with battles and massacres in other locations, especially in what is now Bolivia. The graphic descriptions of the killings, the willingness to kill priests and insult the Catholic religion, and the killings by people who knew one another and even were on friendly terms when they killed their old acquaintances were not unusual as race became, for many, the most important divide in the rebellion. This account, mainly of indigenous killings of people of European descent (although the rebels also killed other Indians who did not join the rebellion) was meant to instill fear and a sense of urgency into those loyalists who seemed to ignore what was happening in the provinces.

I cannot, without tears, fully relate the recent happenings in Chuquisaca, Sicasica, Caracoto, Chucuito, Juli, Carangas, Chayanta and other provinces. There is no Tupac Amaru there: even worse, there is no true Catari; for he has died, and it was he who was the most offensive. But what does it matter when each Indian names himself "Catari" and under this name keeps his head held high and tries to distinguish himself by his insolence. I do not want to offend the sane judgment of those individuals who do not reside in those places; but I can truthfully say that they are . . . being duped. They perceive danger as being far away. They see themselves as well protected (and this includes those in populous cities like Lima and Buenos Aires) and do not receive news that has not been disguised by the coarse pens of men of little substance who disseminate it, or malicious news from those who affect incredulity, perhaps hiding the venom to allow [these events] simply to pass. The pure truth is that this [rebellion] is daily growing larger. Such execrable atrocities and sacrilege are being executed, that it horrifies the tongue to relate it. The latest ones that have been communicated from Chuquisaca in a letter from March 26th written by Dr. Josef Domingo Torres, and another letter of almost the same date by a nephew of Don Luis Barrios are the following.

The City of Chuquisaca is under siege; they intend to take the city by hunger. Even school children of eleven years of age can be found with guns in their hands and in combat. In one of the battles the Indians initiated, many people we knew have died, among them Don Pedro Revilla.

In the province of Lipes, they killed their *corregidor,* Don Francisco Revilla, and his family among many others. And they would have done even more damage if 275 troops that were coming from Buenos Aires did not descend upon them, and 400 more [troops] are expected. These last [troops] accelerated their pace and, during the night, surrounded the town of Tupiza and apprehended twenty-eight of the seditious [rebels] who were unable to flee, and who by this hour will have been hanged.

In Chichas which was considered to be the most quiet and secure, they have killed . . . their *Corregidor,* Don Francisco Prado, in the city of Tupiza, along with two of his dependents, Don Luis Velasco, Don Salvador Pacsi, and somebody by the name of Cerdio. And in the settlement of Chocaya they killed more than five mine owners. . . . For this reason one hundred soldiers were dispatched, along with 1,500 provincials, to contain and punish the Indians who were dedicating themselves to theft.

In the villages of Toracari and San Pedro de Buena Vista not even the priests were spared. The Insurgent who carried out the destruction is an Indian by the name of Simon Castillo, who had the energy to put to the knife over a thousand souls inside the Church along with six priests. The priest who questioned these sacrilegious acts, Dr. Don Ysidoro Herrera, told him: *Is it possible, my son, that you would even do me in, me who raised you, who brought you to God, who fed you?* And the Yndian [*sic*] responded: Don't tire yourself, Grandpa, because you have to die the same [as everybody else]. Then the Yndian [*sic*] killed him, beating him to death while the victim clutched the monstrance; he then did the same to his brother Domingo Herrera. After he [the priest] died, an Yndian [*sic*] woman took the monstrance and filled the sacred vessel with coca [leaves], and spitting at God, she said that it was a lie, that He was not there, that it was just dirty flour that she herself had brought from the Valley. They also took the ciborium [receptacle containing the consecrated bread] of sacred hosts, and after spreading them out and stepping on them, they drank *chicha* from the cup with infamy and opprobrium. Rivers of blood have flowed inside the temples themselves, and sacrilege has been committed that only astounds and horrifies. Dr. Arenas was killed while holding the monstrance and wearing a cape from the chorus. He was the priest of Cochabamba, but of the *Cochabambinos* who left to contain the immediate pueblos in rebellion, 5,000 Indians have died, and many more were taken prisoner. All the miners in Tarata have been killed at the hands of the rebels: as well as many *Corregidores.* La Paz has been surrounded by a considerable number of Yndians [*sic*]. The same has happened to Sorata, without knowing what their end will be.

Three priests were killed in Sicasica, one was hanged right after finishing mass. . . . [The rebels] have executed many without even sparing those of their own nation [Indians] who wore shirts and did not immediately change into their traditional [non-European] clothes.

In Amaya, a town of the province of Chayanta, the Yndians [*sic*] killed all the Spaniards; and entering the church they grabbed a miraculous image of Our Lady. The women ripped Her clothing and left their pins [*topos*] sticking into Her body.

In Tupacari and Arque, which are two ravines in the Province of Cochabamba, the Yndians [*sic*] killed more than 300 Spaniards and while they were getting ready to bury the Spanish women alive, the *Cochabambinos* arrived, killing over 1,500 rebels.

On April 18th the rebels of Tupac Amaru entered Caylloma once again, led by his brother Diego, and Mariano, the nephew of José Gabriel, along with 6,000 Yndians [*sic*]. They killed 111 Spanish, *mestizo* and Yndian [*sic*] men and ten women even though the . . . [Spanish forces] were only two leagues away from the city. While destroying the church, a priest from San Francisco, with the monstrance in his hands, tried to appease them. But they did not obey him, saying: *there is no more mercy, there is no sacred host, nor God that exists,* and they beheaded everybody who tried to protect themselves under it [the monstrance]. And having heard that the Expedition was approaching, they fled with the depraved intention of exterminating all Yndians [*sic*] who had not obeyed the orders of the imprisoned Tupac Amaru. . . . The Yndians [*sic*] of Paria went to Colcha and broke the priest's head. He fled, but was killed by two assistants. They did the same in Llany and Orizquiavi, whose priests were killed. Then they went to Colquimarca where they killed the priest and eight landowners who were surprised in their homes, and they destroyed their haciendas.

In Tarata all the Spaniards and *mestizos* were killed. Dr. Urbina, Frey Vicente (a Dominican), and another Franciscan have been imprisoned. Not many days ago in Copta (Altos of Arica) many Yndians [*sic*] from Carangas came, and in concert with the locals, they attempted to finish off the Spaniards. The priest thought he could contain them with his admonitions, but the result was that he was beaten with sticks to the point of his head splitting open.

Seeing himself bathed in blood, and that there was no respect for anything sacred, he attempted to consume the Holy Host. To put it in a more reverent manner, he began to celebrate Mass, and while preaching the gospel, he was dragged from the altar to the cemetery, where he was stripped of his adornments, tied, and burned alive. They captured his assistant and did the same to him.

All this is very true; nothing is left for doubt nor interpretation, not even other innumerable similar or more serious accounts which I know from very good sources such like from the mouths of the unworthy traitors themselves who are imprisoned here. They [the loyalists] think that with the imprisonment of José Gabriel Tupac Amaru all this will be swept away, but they are experiencing just the contrary. His son Mariano, and his uncle Diego, each on his own, are recruiting people to finish off all pueblos and provinces that will not submit to their authority. *They know they will not be acquitted nor given pardon and it is because of this that they influence their leaders to die killing.* This has been observed in the Province of Chumbivilcas with the famous Captains of the Rebel José Gabriel, named Parbina and Bermudes, who were killed next to an artillery cannon that they used to battle our troops. Indeed, let us hope that God wants our Catholic Monarch to triumph on the ocean and on land over such an iniquitous Swine. Arequipa, May 7th, 1781. [*CDIP,* 189. 1781-V-7]

71. Diego Tupac Amaru Offers to Surrender

After the capture and execution of the rebel Inca, his brother Diego took command of the insurgent forces and continued the fight with great vigor, especially in the regions around Lake Titicaca. However, by late 1781, the situation was such that Diego was willing to surrender if he and his forces were given certain terms and protections. The following is the letter of Diego Tupac Amaru in which he offers to surrender.

I, the said Tupac Amaru, offer to surrender, and I command and will not permit any native to offend the Spaniards. At the same time they shall be assembled in their towns and live with the Spaniards in peace and union, as God commands and our Catholic monarch wishes. After hostilities have ceased and precautions are taken to prevent future injuries, everything will be peaceful and there will be harmony between the Spaniards and the Indians, so that commerce may be carried on, the farms repopulated, the mines worked, the Indians instructed by their respective priests, and finally we shall live as true vassals of the Catholic king of Spain. [*LIR,* 361–62. Translated by L. E. Fisher]

72. Diego Tupac Amaru Surrenders, January 1782

Early in 1782, Diego Tupac Amaru surrendered to Spanish forces. He asked that his freedom be respected, and he told his captors where cannons had been left so they could be destroyed. He claimed ignorance of the Inca's real designs and said he followed him because of family loyalty, but he did not denounce José Gabriel. Thus, facing dire circumstances, he still tried to walk a tightrope between family loyalty and his commitment to some of the goals of the rebellion on one hand, and the implications of his surrender on the other. It was a tightrope on which it proved difficult to stay balanced.

In this illustrious council . . . I, my family, and all other erring vassals are now going to receive that most generous pardon, which in future ages will be regarded with astonishment. Behold, Sir, prostrate at your feet, that scandal of Peru, he whose conduct and excesses have proved him a conspicuous leader in the innumerable calamities which have befallen this kingdom. It is I, Diego Cristóbal Tupac Amaru, brother of that unfortunate José Gabriel, the principal promoter of the rebellion, whose steps I followed and whose commissions I executed, not from ambition or selfish motives, much less with disposition to rebel against my king and Lord, however much appearances may seem the contrary. I was, in fact, totally ignorant of my brother's intentions; he never communicated to me his plans or projects, although he called me his son, and as such he always treated me. When he committed his first crime in Tungasuca by putting the *corregidor* to death, he enjoined me, at the peril of my life, to pursue the line of conduct which he was to point out. I punctually executed his commands, mastered and excited the Indians. . . .

These are the arms with which I have offended my sovereign. I now surrender them with the serious intention to use them never again, not even in defense of my own life. At Azangaro I left several pieces of cannon, which I did not bring with me lest the Indians should think I was preparing a new revolt. You may dispose of them for the best service of my king and Lord. Do also the same with me and my family. I only pray you not to reduce me to so hard a fate as to deprive me of my liberty and honor; rather than that, I am ready to sacrifice a thousand lives, if it is possible, to appease my offended sovereign. If I am allowed, I will endeavor to restore my name and reputation and blot out the stain which my conduct has cast upon my family. [*LIR*, 366–67. Translated by L. E. Fisher]

73. Proclamation Published in Lima on February 20, 1782, for the General Tolling of the Bells and the Lighting of the Streets to Celebrate the Pacification of All Provinces

The surrender of Diego Tupac Amaru and his forces represented the defeat of the rebellion and the return of control to the royalists. It also meant peace on Spanish terms. Upon receiving the news of the surrender, the viceroy ordered that lights be lit for three nights throughout the kingdom. In the following document, the viceroy gives special thanks for the blessings God bestowed on the Spanish, as the Spanish viewed it, in their triumph and in getting people who participated in or supported the rebellion to surrender and to abandon the thoughts and ways that guided them during the uprising.

Sr. Agustín de Jáuregui, Knight of the Order of Santiago, member of His Majesty's Council, Lieutenant General of His Royal Armies, Viceroy, Governor and General Captain of the Kingdoms of Peru and Chile and President of the Royal Audience of this City.

Through letters written on the 27th and 31st of January, documents written in the town of Sicuani, one by the General Inspector Don José del Valle and the other by the Very Illustrious Bishop of Cuzco, I was informed of the pleasant news of the . . . surrender of Diego Christoval [*sic*] Tupac Amaru having been solemnly announced in the Church of the pueblo on said 27th with the promise of perpetual loyalty and obedience to the King, subordination to his laws and orders and those of his Magistrates and Judges, with serious promises that from now on he will be one of the most loyal subjects of his Majesty, and that he will work toward the total pacification of the pueblos in rebellion. By his example, and by the presence of humanity and the good treatment he has received since entering that pueblo, thousands of Indians have been arriving; they crown the hills, not only in the immediate Province, but also in Larecaxa, La Paz, Pacages, and even into the Andes, to ask for absolution from the excommunication that was imposed on them at the beginning of the rebellion by the Diocesan Bishop and to pledge obedience to His Majesty, all of which they were hoping to be granted during the successive days, along with other particularities worthy of the greatest estimation. . . . [T]hese happy events were most interesting to the Church and the State for some of the unequivocal testimonies denouncing the errors through which fanaticism had been propagated in the heart of this Christian Nation, fostering a spirit of irreligiousness and indolence clearly demonstrated by the horrible and ruinous consequences of the chain of errors unleashed by the miserable and naive dreamers. And once they are disabused of their fanatic sentiments, they have been brought by the immense pity of God to the knowledge of what matters and is vital to them in order to follow an ordered life adjusted to both Divine and human laws and to the salvation of their souls, wandering until now from the path of truth and on the verge of eternal perdition. We must recognize the All-Powerful as Author and origin of these happy events; not only does Christian Charity inspire the just satisfaction of the well-being of these unfortunates, so it inspires the most humble prayers to the All-High, asking His continued pity to soften their hearts a bit more every day with the abundant light of His grace. I order and direct to proclaim in the proper manner a solemn Public Mass of thanksgiving, in accordance with his Very Illustrious Archbishop of this Holy Metropolitan Church as a token of our reverent thanks and recognition of the Divine Majesty for the great benefit of peace that He so generously has given us. For this the streets of this city should be lighted for three consecutive nights starting today, and that the same is to be done in the other cities and towns of this Kingdom, with the corresponding provisions that His Most Illustrious will send to the respective Vicars along with the letters that have been written from my Secretariat to those Reverends and Colleagues so that this news will get to everybody. It should be published as edicts and put in the usual places in this Capital and in other cities and heads of Dioceses and Provinces, printing enough copies so that they accompany the mentioned letters that should also be sent to the Governors and *Corregidores* of Districts in this Viceroyalty. Lima, February 20th, 1782. Don Agustín de Jáuregui.

—Juan Maria de Gálvez. [*CDIP*, 250. 1782-II-20]

74. The Viceroy Expresses Doubts and Suspicions about the Loyalty of the Former Rebels

In the wake of the rebellion, Spanish officials expressed doubts about the sincerity of rebel leaders who had been pardoned. The viceroy, in the following letter to Minister of the Indies José de Gálvez, expresses the opinion that it would be best to remove the former leaders of the insurgency from their Andean homeland and either bring them to Lima or send them into exile. This opinion would become a reality as the Spanish exiled, and found reasons to execute, the main leaders who had been pardoned or the family members of important rebels.

Dear Sir.—Based on the experience of many years, I have come to know the inconsistency and fickleness of all indigenous operations and of the little faith that one should place in their words. I have always been suspicious of, and very unsatisfied by the offers that the rebels made when they learned of the general amnesty that I granted them. I have always been convinced that it is indispensable in securing the public tranquility to remove and extradite all Indian leaders and principal caudillos from the Kingdom. In order to achieve this goal with greater security and only minor risk of disturbing or altering their spirit but also in an effort to observe them closer, I chose the alternative that I thought conformed the most with the wise intentions of His Majesty and the just wishes of Your Excellency. [*RTA,* 737]

75. Andrés Mendigure Becomes Andrés Tupac Amaru

Family members such as Diego, the Inca's half-brother, took over the leadership of the movement after the capture and execution of José Gabriel. Another such person was the rebel leader's nephew, Andrés Mendigure. He changed his last name to Tupac Amaru, the name associated with leadership of the rebellion. He also claimed that he was the son of the Inca. In the following selection, Andrés makes clear his opposition to Spanish policies, yet he still maintains verbal loyalty to the Spanish monarch.

In the name of King Charles III, Andrés Tupac Amaru, Marquis of Alcalises, Inca descendant of the royal blood and principal throne of the monarchs, who governed these kingdoms of Peru, makes known to all natives of the province of Pacajes, Sicasica, and other places . . . that the King, our Lord, being informed of the great excesses, disorders, and abuses which were caused by the *corregidores,* customs collectors, and usurper *chapetones,* sent his commission from Spain, directed to my father, José Gabriel Tupac Amaru, Marquis of Alcalises, Inca descendant of the royal blood and principal throne of monarchs, who governed these kingdoms of Peru, and told him that the *corregidores,* customs officials, and *chapetones* should be removed and punished; and that at the same time the *mita* of Potosí should be abolished. The *corregidores* pretended that a just opposition should be made, as they did it, bringing together many inhabitants, soldiers, and creoles; on account of this many of them were punished and the same *corregidores,* who fled, were overthrown; and by virtue of the royal order these were acts of justice. [*LIR,* 243. Translated by L. E. Fisher]

76. Sentence against the Prisoner Diego Cristóbal Tupac Amaru and His Accomplices

Spanish officials were leery of the former rebel leaders. When a plot against the Spanish was discovered in the province of Quispicanchis near Marcapata, the troops were sent and the head of this plot, Santos Huayhua, was torn apart by horses as they had tried to do to Tupac Amaru. A cousin of José Gabriel, Juan Velasco, rose in revolt in the region near Huarochirí, taking the name of Tupac Inca Yupanqui. He and his followers were defeated, and he too was executed. These incidents, along with other rumors, were enough of an excuse for the Spanish to maintain that Diego Tupac Amaru had violated the terms of his pardon. The colonial rulers were not going to take any chances. Diego, his family, and some associates were arrested. Diego was not only to be killed, flesh was to be ripped off his body with tongs that had been heated in a fire. His mother was to be executed, her body quartered and then burned before Diego's eyes. Thus ended the life of the Inca's brother who had carried on the struggle to free their people from the colonial yoke following his brother's execution.

I, Don Francisco Calonje, scribe who has been given the task of compiling the [criminal] case against Diego Tupac Amaru and his accomplices, presented by Don Benito de la Mata Linares, member of His Majesty's Council, *Oidor* of the Royal Audience of Lima and Judge commissioned by His Excellency the Viceroy of these kingdoms, to proceed in accordance with Don

Gabriel de Aviles, colonel of the royal armies of His majesty, Commander in Chief of the arms of this city and its provinces, I certify that in the case formed against the previously cited Diego [Cristóbal] Tupac Amaru and his accomplices, the sentence pronounced by said gentlemen is included in the trial record, from which I excerpted the testimony that follows which has been copied verbatim and which is as follows:

In the case pending before us, ordered by His Excellency the Viceroy of these kingdoms and which has been followed against Diego Cristóbal Tupac Amaru, Marcela Castro, Manuela Tito-Condori, Simon Condori, and Lorenzo Condori, in which Don José de Saldívar, lawyer of the Royal *Audiencia* of Lima, Protector of the Natives, acted as lawyer for the prisoners . . . we gave sentence, mindful of the proceedings and as a result of the serious crimes committed by the prisoner Diego Cristóbal Tupac Amaru whose behavior was based on the falsities and lies with which he accepted the pardon that was given him in the name of our most benign Sovereign who, thank God, may continue to reign for many years. Without respecting his pardon, he [Diego Tupac Amaru] maintained correspondence with the *naturales* of these lands, caressing them [with words], regaling them with offerings of his patrimony and defense without any respect [to the Sovereign]. He even usurped, in the letters he wrote to them, the dictates of Padre, Governor and Inca. He brought them to his side with the sweet and soft name of sons, which added to his deceitful promises, so that those from the province of Tinta, and from others as well, would contribute provisions [to support the rebellion]. They would show him not only their respect and submission but their most pernicious love that they maintain for him. He would give them the title of Governor, *Justicia Mayor* and others, so that they would administer justice among themselves, requiring them to come to him with their fights and written requests. He hid the fact that he had taken riches and arms from them without any retribution whatsoever. [These accusations violated] the precise conditions under which his pardon was conceded and accepted. His ultimate goal was to take these dominions away from His Majesty, giving Indians orders to keep their arms so that they could be ready to use them when he would order them to do so. He also warned the Indians to mistrust the Spaniards and to not give them any taxes, as these should be distributed among the *ayllus*. He told them they would have no *corregidores*, only *Justicias Mayores* and inspired them to help him wherever he was working or in prison, or to rebel while at the same time allowing them to praise him and call him *father*. He reminded them of all the benefits they owed to him from his placing his life in danger to free them from such great oppression, plucking out the thorn with which [the Spanish authorities] had pricked them and in this way permitting them to acclaim him. Marcela Castro was also convicted for having been present in the conversations pertaining to the rebellion in Marcapata without having opposed or denounced them and for keeping the Indians ignorant and disaffected, addressing them as her *sons*. Equally convicted were Simon Condori and Lorenzo Condori who headed the rebellion in Marcapata, mobilizing the Indians by wearing a sash sent by Mariano Tupac Amaru so that they would be thought to be his messengers and they [the Indians] would obey him so that they could put their iniquitous ideas into practice as they have confessed. Taking into consideration that they have renewed the crimes they committed prior to the pardon, we ought to condemn and we condemn the said prisoner, Diego Cristóbal Tupac Amaru to be put to death. . . . And justice mandates that he be taken out of the jail where he is a prisoner and be dragged from the tail of a pack animal with an *esparto* [grass]-rope around his neck and with his feet and hands tied, with a town crier calling out his crimes. He should be taken like this through the usual streets to the execution place where a fire shall be built next to the gallows [to heat] large tongs so that in sight of everyone he should have [his flesh ripped off] with the tongs and then hanged by his neck until he dies naturally without anybody coming to take him down without our permission under the same penalty. After this, his body will be quartered and his head taken to the town of Tungasuca, one arm to Lauramarca, the other to the town of Carabaya, one leg to Paucartambo, the other to Calca and the rest of the body shall be put on a pillory on the road to this city's water tank. All his estate shall be confiscated and given to His Majesty's exchequer and his houses destroyed and salted, all of which should be done by the *corregidor* of the province of Tinta.

Marcela Castro should also be condemned to be taken out of her prison cell to be dragged by the tail of a pack animal with an *esparto*-rope around her neck, with her feet and hands tied and a town crier proclaiming her crimes. She will be taken like this, through the usual streets to the place of her punishment where, next to the gallows, her tongue will be cut out and she will be hanged by her neck and let die of natural death without anybody taking her body down without our permission. She will then be quartered: with her head put on a pillory on the road to San Sebastian, an arm be sent to the town of Sicuani, while the other should be sent to the bridge in Urcos, one leg to Pampamarca and the other to Ocongate. The rest of her body should be burned in a fire in the main square of this town and her ashes thrown to the air.

Simon Condori should be condemned, and is condemned, to the death penalty and for justice to be served we order that he be taken out of jail, dragged by the tail of a pack animal with an *esparto*-rope around his neck, and his feet and hands tied and a town crier proclaiming his crime. He should be taken in this manner through the usual public streets to the execution place, where a gallows will be installed where he will be hanged by the neck and hanged until he dies naturally, without anybody taking him down without our permission. It is ordered that he should be quartered, his head taken to Marcapata, one arm to the capital of the province of Azangaro and the other to the *ayllu* of Puica, one leg to Apo, next to the mountain of Quico and the other to the glaciated mountain of Ansongate, and all his property confiscated for the exchequer of His Majesty.

Lorenzo Condori should also be condemned and we condemn him to die. He will be taken out of the jail where he is now imprisoned and dragged by the tail of a pack animal, with an *esparto*-rope around his neck, with his feet and hands tied and a town crier proclaiming his crime. He should be taken in this manner through the usual streets to the execution place where the gallows should be ready. He should be hanged until he dies a natural death without anybody taking him down without our license. He will then be quartered, his head taken to the site of Acobamba, one leg to Lampa, the other to the farm of Chilca in the parish of Pitumarca, one arm to the bridge in Quiquijana and the other to the town of Tinta. All his property should be confiscated. All this should be executed without any appeals, petitions, or any other recourse. . . . A copy of this sentence is being sent to the provincial *corregidores* so that they will publish it through edicts, so that everybody complies with the actions that pertain them and sends confirmation that they had done so. . . . In regards to Manuela Tito-Condori, we condemn her to perpetual exile from these provinces, reserving her final destination to the decision of His Excellency the Viceroy of these kingdoms who has been informed of everything.

Gabriel de Aviles, Benito de la Mata Linares [*RTA,* 743–44]

77. Andrés Tupac Amaru Tries to Get Creole Support in La Paz

During the siege of La Paz, the rebel forces used not only force but also psychological warfare to try to gain support. In the brief selection that follows, Andrés (Mendigure) Tupac Amaru tries to convince the creoles of La Paz to join him by sending a message to them in the name of the creoles he supposedly has on his side and promising them mercy.

With the coming of the Marquis we have obtained and enjoy all his protection and clemency, since we have surrendered to him. He has pardoned us and received us into his . . . true love, as the best father or dearest mother.

The Marquis takes care of our needs, quenches our hunger . . . and has clothed us with the best clothes, without permitting us to suffer need. With this intelligence, you who see or know the contents of this letter can decide to ask for the same mercy that we enjoy, for at the hour you wish it, you shall receive it as soon as possible, or when you reply to this letter and show submission. [*LIR,* 306–7. Translated by L. E. Fisher]

78. Notice of the Indians Being Taken to Spain as Prisoners of the State Who Have Died on the Ship *El Peruano* en Route from Lima to Rio de Janeiro

Travel on the high seas was always dangerous, especially because of the diseases that broke out onboard ships. Many of the relatives of the rebels were sentenced to exile in Spain, but some of them never arrived. The following is a list of the exiles who died in the portion of the trip from Lima to Rio de Janeiro. It also mentions other important prisoners, such as the young son of the Inca and Micaela Bastidas, Fernando. In the second leg of the journey from Brazil to Spain, the ship he was on went aground and broke up, but Fernando survived. He died in Spain without ever being allowed to return to the Andes.

Mariano Cóndorcanqui [*sic*], died June 27.
Miguel Gutierres, died July 21.
Isidro Pérez, died June 26.
Josep Mamani, died July 30.
Pascual Huamán, died June 8.
Mateo Condori, died May 11.
Josef Sánchez, died June 19.
Cayetano Castro, died June 21.

Wives of These:
Antonia de Castro, died May 20.
Andrea Cózcamayta, died August 3.
Nicolasa Torres, died June 1.
Susana Aguirre, died April 20.

Minor Children:
Gregorio Tito, died May 27.
Juliana Tito, died August 5.

Mariano Tito, died July 10.
Feliciana Tito, died June 1.

Aboard . . . [*El Peruano*], anchored in the port of Rio de Janiero, August 10, 1784.

Most Excellent Sir . . . ; With the date of the 5th of the current [month]. . . : "Among the prisoners taken from Lima at the disposition of the ships of war of Your Majesty that wait in this port. . . are Mariano, Fernando and Juan Córdorcanqui [*sic*] (Tupac Amaru) and Andrés Mendiguri [*sic*].". . . [*CDIP*, 300. 1784]

79. Letter from Juan Bautista Tupac Amaru to the Liberator Simón Bolívar

Juan Bautista Condorcanqui Monjarra Tupac Amaru was a half-brother of the Inca. After being taken prisoner, he was sentenced to 200 lashes and ten years of exile in Spain. In 1784, he and several others who had participated in the rebellion or were relatives of the extended Inca family were put onboard the ship El Peruano *and sent to Spain. The trip was arduous, and his wife, Susana Aguirre, died in the passage, as did many others.*

Even though his sentence was for ten years, he was not freed until 1820, when he was some eighty years of age. After the turmoil that followed the French invasion, he was finally allowed to leave Spain. He returned to the New World, landing in Buenos Aires in late 1822. He had not forgotten the Incas, his family, or the injustices that had been perpetrated on himself and his people by the Spanish. He referred to the Spanish king as ferocious and a usurper. He was filled with joy when the wars of independence finally freed his people from the Spanish yoke. In the following letter, he thanks Simón Bolívar, the man he calls "Liberator," for finally finishing the work of his brother, Tupac Amaru, and the thousands of others like himself who had fought for this freedom.

If it has been a duty of the friends of the Homeland of the Incas (memories of which are among my most tender and respectful) to congratulate the Hero of Colombia and the Liberator of the vast countries of South America, I am obliged by a double motive to manifest my heart filled with the highest jubilation. I have survived to the age of eighty-six, despite great hardships and having been in danger of losing my life, to see consummated the great and always just struggle that will place us in the full enjoyment of our rights and liberty. This was the aim of Don José Gabriel Tupac Amaru, my venerated and affectionate brother and martyr of the Peruvian Empire, whose blood was the plow which prepared that soil to bring forth the best fruits; [but it was left to] the Great Bolívar to harvest them with his valiant and very generous hands. I also aimed [to free our people] and although I did not have the glory of spilling the blood of my Inca fathers which runs through my veins, I spent forty years in exile and in prison. [This was] the fruit of the just desires and efforts that I made to take back the liberty and rights that those tyrannical usurpers took with such cruelty. I, in the name of the spirits of my sacred ancestors, congratulate the American Spirit of the Century. . . .

God is very just. God favored all the undertakings of the immortal Don Simón Bolívar and crowned his efforts with laurels of immortal glory. . . .

I, sir, considering the series of hardships that to this day I remember, harbor in my breast the pleasurable hope of breathing the air of my homeland. . . . [T]he incalculable grief and hardships [I have suffered] would seem as nothing if, before my eyes close, I might see my Liberator, and with this comfort I could go to my grave. . . .

Juan Bautista Tupac Amaru [*CDIP,* 327. 1825-V-15]

PART TWO

The Catari Brothers and Rebellion

in Chayanta and La Plata (Bolivia)

VIII. *Kurakas, Corregidores, Repartos,* Protest, and Defiance

80. Description of Chayanta, 1787

A few years after the rebellion, the intendant (governor) of Potosí, Juan del Pino Manrique, gave the following description of the province of Chayanta. It is interesting that he viewed the province as relatively prosperous and containing a number of rather "civilized" people. This description causes one to ponder the political implications of such a description on the heels of an insurrection. Was this wishful thinking, a cover-up, or a reality after the reparto *had been terminated?*

Chayanta or Charcas is the most distant of the provinces of those in this Intendancy. It is bordered on the north by Porco, Cochabamba and Mizque; on the south and east by Yamiparaez; and on the west by Paria. It stretches some 70 leagues from north to south, 60 from east to west, and it is 210 in circumference. It has twenty parishes distributed evenly in the *punas* [highlands] and valleys, with this wonderful advantage: the *naturales* never have to leave the province for their plantings or harvests of grains because they possess lands in various climates and from them they harvest what they need. Because of this the Indians from all districts [of Chayanta] are those who find it easiest to pay their tribute. And among them it is not so rare to find some who are more civilized than others [those of other provinces?]. [*RTA*, 347–48]

81. The *Kuraka* of Pocoata Complains the People He Governs Will Not Do Customary Free Work for Him

In a normal, reciprocal relationship between the people of a community and their kuraka, *or sometimes even their priest, a degree of labor was typically provided by the people without expected payment. Those* kurakas *or priests who were the recipients of this labor were often expected to help the people or to reciprocate in some way—perhaps through festive largess, diligent protection, the provision of "social services" that helped people out of difficult situations in times of need, or some other means or combination of the above. When the relationship soured between a community and the person receiving the free labor, the reciprocity broke down. In the selection that follows, the* kuraka *of Pocoata complains that people will only work for him and his family for pay, and that they do not take good care of his animals. He, in turn, portrays himself as fulfilling his role as* kuraka *in a just manner. One can only wonder what actually transpired in Pocoata.*

[T]o the Indians going to the *Mita,* I have to provide everything, so that they have the necessary support to maintain themselves. I am always subsidizing them and giving them whatever they lack and I go through lots of trouble to ensure that they go to the *Mita,* as if it were not just their obligation. I also marry them at my expense just to make them happy. [However] they do not want to cultivate for us plots in the common lands whether in the valley or the *puna;* only my relatives and compadres help me in cultivating my scarce plots, and the rest, instead, try to take away from me the pieces of land that my ancestors used to sow. If all the Indians were to cultivate my plots, I would have to pay them, and I cannot have any services from them, since they only do it for pay, and if we tell them to take care of some of our mules, they break their feet and ruin them. [*SCA,* 40. Translated by S. Serulnikov]

82. Judge Francisco de Arsiniega Comments on Indigenous Complaints and Behavior Related to the *Mita* and Their *Kuraka*

In August 1750, a colonial judge, Arsiniega, tried to take testimony about problems that stemmed from kuraka *abuse, especially those related to tribute and the Potosí mita. The following documents concern the villagers' discontent with their* kuraka, *whom they saw as profiting from their labor for the Crown in Potosí and cheating on their tribute. The first brief statement, by Arsiniega, notes that the indigenous people carried sticks and clubs, which—along with their drinking—was enough to keep the judge from trying to engage in any work as he sought to take testimony from them. The second statement, made to Arsiniega by the Pucara people, comments on the* kuraka's *misappropriation of tribute monies and charging people for being exempted from the* mita. *The* kuraka *was exploiting the people he governed and deceiving the government. Such a complaint may also have reflected divisions in the community between those who could afford to buy a* mita *exemption and those who could not, or those who were favored by the* kuraka *and those who were not.*

Document 1: Arsiniega
On the sixteenth day of [August] which was when the list [of *mitayos*] was made and the Indians gathered in the town, we did not summon the Indians because they were all drunk since dusk to dawn *making several displays in the plaza and streets of this town* [of Chayanta] *as well as in the pampa and the place where the said list is carried out, many of them carrying sticks and clubs.* [Italics added.]

Document 2: Pucara Testimony
When the governor Don Marcos Tococari goes to hand over the tribute to the *corregidor* of this province, of the money that he takes, he usually has about 500 pesos left over after paying them, which they assume is left over from the tributes that he charges. . . .

When the Indians who go to the Potosí *mita* are appointed, every year the governor Marcos Tococari made up the list with forty-one Indians and some-times thirty-five, of all these only about twenty-one actually go to Potosí, the rest he charged eighty pesos as an exemption fee from the *mita*. [*SCA*, 39. Translated by S. Serulnikov]

83. The Peoples of Chullpas Complain about Exploitation by Their *Kuraka*

As early as 1761, nearly two decades before the Chayanta uprising, the villagers of Chullpas complained about being exploited by their kuraka. *They said he used their communal resources and the fruits of their work, claiming the prod-uct as his own "expenditures." In the following selection, the people of Chullpas complain to a judge about the exploitative behavior of their* kuraka. *Implied in the discussion is the fact that the* kuraka *did not reciprocate with his people as he should; therefore, he was not behaving in accordance with custom. This, in the eyes of those he governed, undermined any authority or legitimacy he may have had. He was only one of many* kurakas *who fell into this category. When the insurrection began years later, these abusive* kurakas *would be one of the primary targets of the rebels.*

[N]othing comes out of [the *cacique's*] pocket [during festivities], because instead of supplying the *mitayos* he tells them to make *chicha*, and he buys *coca* selling the harvest of the plots that, under the name of commons, all the

Indians sow using their own oxen and ploughs. So it comes from the same Indians' pockets because they work on it, but since the harvest is kept by the governor, he claims that it is his expenditure. Even if there were an accurate accounting of such matters, he would have a surplus because the expenses in such celebrations are no more than twenty jugs of *chicha,* and two *coca* baskets are worth four *reales* and maybe one or two *arrobas* [one *arroba* equals approximately 25 pounds] of brandy [*aguardiente*], which is mainly drunk by the governors and their principals. And he does not spend anything in mules because the Indians plant barley and take it to his home, and they do the same with maize, potatoes, and wheat which they grow in the best areas of the communal lands, so that the governor, after living off such harvests, and paying for the said celebrations, still has some leftover to sell, even though it has not cost him a cent, other than rigorously giving orders to do so, and taking care that he keeps seed for the following year. [*SCA,* 32–3. Translated by S. Serulnikov]

84. Abuse of People of Macha by Priest

Tensions among indigenous peoples in Chayanta, colonial authorities, and some priests developed long before open rebellion. In the following document from 1772, the leaders of ayllu *Majapicha, the same Macha ayllu to which Tómas Catari belonged, complain about abuses by the assistant to the priest, Don Lorenzo Morales, with regard to the list of prices* (arancel) *that priests charged for their religious services.*

We were hoping to have some relief from the said publication of the *arancel,* [but] the current assistant, Don Lorenzo Morales, has been even more rigorous with us not only in the abuse of forcing us to pay fees but also in the way that he mistreats us, punishing [us] for the slightest offense through lashes and beatings. . . . In this way, nowadays we are even more grieved by the said assistant than we were before, because he has posted at the doors of the church an *arancel* that is very different from the true one that was recently approved, since no poor person can be buried free, and there is not any feast that costs less than one hundred pesos . . . and even for just tasting the salt of the food that the *alfereces* are required to donate to the priests, we have to pay four pesos to the cook, even though she has no other job than the said one. [*SCA,* 102. Translated by S. Serulnikov]

85. Indians of Aymara Complain of Abuse by Priest and Forcing People to Marry

Priests were often at odds with the ayllus *and communities they served. One of the differences that caused considerable tension was the forcing of indigenous people to marry before they were ready to do so. Married couples were the backbone of the community. Indigenous people took their time solidifying this relationship because of its importance not just to themselves but to the community as well. Before an indigenous couple decided to marry, they typically cohabitated and frequently had children. This caused a problem for some priests, who wanted couples to formally marry; the priests objected to cohabitation and having children before formal marriage on religious grounds. Many priests were understanding of the situation or ignored it. However, sometimes tensions arose between a priest and the community when he forced couples to marry. Marriages were forced usually as a result of disagreements over economic and service issues, and not over religious issues.*

*According to the following 1778 document, Mateo Choque was punished by the priest, Domingo Cortés, for complaining about his daughter being forced to marry. Other indigenous people, such as members of the Bello family, were imprisoned for speaking badly about the priest at approximately the same time. In 1781, when the political situation had changed dramatically, indigenous people attacked the priest and beat him to death, saying "*Cura ladrón, que por tu causa estamos desnudos*" ("Thief priest, we are naked because of you"). Others were reported to have said that "killing priests was not a sin." Part of these tensions stemmed from actions such as those against Mateo Choque a few years earlier. An observer wrote that the priest had forced the daughter to marry "as he is accustomed to do," and that Choque had protested.*

[Choque] was dragged along the streets in the most shameful manner, making him shout at every street corner and square the following words: "I, Matheo [*sic*] Choque, a dumb and litigious Indian who went to complain about the priest, give myself these lashes in order to serve as an example for those who would go against the priest and the *corregidor*. They will suffer the same fate!" [*SCA*, 106. Translated by S. Serulnikov]

86. Petition of Tomás Catari to the Viceroy, on the First Days of January, 1779

Far from avoiding the colonial legal system, leaders such as Tupac Amaru and the Cataris sought to work within the system and use the legal possibilities and remedies available to them within the colonial legal apparatus. In the following document, Tomás Catari addresses the viceroy to complain about their kuraka, *Blas Bernal, and his usurpation of tributes as well as his bad treatment of community members. He also draws attention to the fact that the* corregidores *have not enforced the decrees of the viceroy, which would have put Catari and others in charge of tribute collection. He draws attention to the vulnerable state of the indigenous people and the lengths to which they have gone to try to restore proper order within the system, as well as how much personal sacrifice this has involved. In this way, he makes it clear that they do not see the king as the enemy. The language of the document is very complex, and we have chosen selected excerpts. The run-on sentences have been somewhat shortened and given punctuation that makes the document more intelligible, but the reader can still appreciate the complex writing style of the colonial era.*

Don Thomas [*sic*] Catari, Indio Natural and principal of the Town of Macha. Province and *corregimiento* of Chayanta, having the right and with the most respect, I present myself before your Excellency and state that I have been made to understand that the representation of my first relation of these events made to Your Excellency by brief the *Protector de Naturales* was very incomplete on the events [that had transpired]. . . . This probably was because he did not master my native language, making the explanation confusing and defective in the details. But this was done unintentionally, and based on all the good faith of which he was capable. [Now] I submit to your Excellency this brief (*escrito*) dictated to a person more literate in my language and based on the . . . truth that I and another Indio principal by the name of Isidro Acho, father of my friend who is here with me, present, because of our love of our sovereign and our sadness to witness the serious usurpation of the royal tribute. For many years Don Blas Bernal, one of the four *caciques* of the pueblo of Macha who collects the tribute from the *ayllus* or *parajes* by the name of Collana and Picha, has usurped [tribute monies] . . . from the Royal Treasury of Potosí and we have denounced this usurpation. We have sent an official communication to our *corregidor* Don Nicolas V[U]rsainque so that we be named senior collectors of all the monies collected from the hidden Indians from whom . . . Don Blas Bernal has collected annually. . . . The Royal *Audiencia* of La Plata . . . after confirming the information and approving of the actions taken, gave us the title of collectors and excluded the *cacique* Don Blas Bernal from any collection efforts. But what happened is that when arriving to our town and informing our *corregidor* Don Nicolas V[U]sarinque [of the changes] and after him the new *corregidor* that succeeded him, Don Joachin de Alos [*sic*], of the aforementioned briefs, one from the Royal Cashier and the other from the Royal *Audiencia*. . . . Neither of them complied with what had been ordered, which was to install us in those offices. . . . The new *corregidor* very unpleasantly informed us that we should not have gone a second time to submit our petition to the officials . . . of the Royal *Audiencia* to complain about their delays and refusal to comply with what had been ordered. . . . They refused to accept the monetary guarantees presented [for us to be collectors], claiming that they were insufficient when they were not. In fact they were plenty. [The monies] came from three individuals who were very affluent with some . . . 17,000 pesos respectively that represented the whole year of such tributes that we needed to collect. . . . They [the *corregidores*] have threatened us with prison if we collect such monies and with whips, exile, and other similar penalties if we would submit such briefs another time to other tribunals. We had already been punished for previously having submitted such claims, and . . . so that they could relieve themselves of their hatred they paraded us through the streets and plazas all tied up as if we were common criminals. And they threw us in jail and put us in stocks. . . . [W]e escaped the next day so that we would not die there or suffer through even greater punishments than I had already suffered before . . . when I spent a month in jail being brutally whipped. . . . I had to suffer the *cacique's* [Bernal] cruelty for just having defended my small pieces of land from a woman intruder who is protected and favored by him in a clandestine manner, something that is very common in this pueblo. . . . He even takes land away from deserving Indians and gives it to *mestizos* and other strangers in defiance of the . . . [the law]. . . . [He does this] along with other dubious businesses that are too numerous to mention and which accumulate to the detriment of all of us Indian commoners who find ourselves in this predicament without our land titles, with no recourse to have our rights respected, and with no assurances vis-à-vis the superior authority that this hated *corregidor* [will be dealt with]. He resents us and submits us to twenty abuses and opprobrium. . . . [T]he *cacique,* who has the support of the *corregidor,* is not controlled nor is he afraid of anyone in the pueblo and he is upset with us for having justly submitted our complaints. Thus, it was expected that he would get zealously prepared in spirit and disposition . . . to persecute us and fiercely cover himself in the blood of our defenseless people. Having experienced his cruelty and the aforementioned punishments that were unfairly inflicted on us, and looking for some redress but also observing that the new *corregidor* regards even the superior orders of the Royal *Audiencia* with contempt, we have chosen to come humbly before you seeing this as the best and only means [of getting justice], despite the great hardships and untold miseries that we have suffered throughout our pilgrimage to do this, having left behind our women and children . . . to put ourselves under the Royal and charitable protection that is presented by Your Excellency. You are so well informed, and a pious, zealous . . . soul reverberates in your Highness. We beseech you for a remedy to our sufferings and we hope we will be granted it by your generous hand. . . .

Bernal and the other *caciques* that are presently in office are neither by blood or legitimate succession [true *caciques*]. Nor are they true Indians, as they should be for this service. They are just . . . *mestizos* who have been made *caciques* through appointment by the *corregidor,* whereas we are part of the lineage and blood of the *caciques* as we have so declared. . . . I swear to God and the Holy Cross, in good faith and without malice. . . .

Thomas [sic] Catari [RTA, 801]

87. Tomás Catari Implores New Tribute Collectors to Take Care in Doing Their Work

One of the ways in which kurakas *exploited the villagers over whom they governed was through overcollection of taxes owed such as the personal tax or head tax known as tribute. This was a tax owed to the Spanish crown by male members of a community with access to land and other legal rights. In the following section Tomás Catari warns the new tax collectors not to be abusive like the* mestizo kuraka *Bernal.*

[Catari warned the tax collectors to] take care of the four *comunes* . . . with which the *mita* workers will be maintained, and I bring now new orders from the Sr. viceroy [so that it will] no longer be all robbery as before. . . . That this *mestizo* [Bernal] could no longer do harm [is] because he cannot claim obedience since he was not appointed by the *Audiencia* nor the treasury [of Potosí]. [*SCA,* 130. Translated by S. Serulnikov]

88. A *Cacique* of Macha Denounces Tomás Catari

Tomás Catari sought to undermine the authority of the caciques (governors) in his community that he saw exploiting his people. He eventually went to Buenos Aires and obtained an order from the viceroy that installed himself as head cacique. In the following document, Ignacio Burgoa, a cacique of Macha, complains that Catari has told people not to listen to Burgoa or pay tributes to him. In this way, the future rebel exerted his power and undermined that of the caciques that were abusing people through their demands and treatment.

Señor *corregidor*—
[I,] Don Ignacio Burgoa, Governor of Ayllu Majapicha in the Pueblo of San Pedro de Macha, Province of Chaianta [*sic*], present myself before Your Mercy . . . and state: I am bothered by an Indian named Thomas [*sic*] Catari, who influences the people under my charge, telling them not to pay me the Royal Tributes. He is saying that he is the Governor and he is naming his assistants (*segundas*) and tax collectors and that the Tributes are to be delivered to the Royal treasury. Under his influence none of the Indians hold me in respect. And so that I may take charge of the aforementioned Tributes of the Royal *Mita* as soon as possible, I appeal to Your Mercy to quickly resolve this issue, having already received from me certain Information to which I have referred and which proved to be true. I ask and beg Your Mercy to order him to [desist] and with this lesson I will again have the liberty to collect [Tributes] as well as name *mitayos*. . . .

Ignacio Burgoa. [*RTA*, 809–10]

89. Petition to the President of the *Audiencia* of Charcas by Tomás Catari, 1779

In 1779, Tomás Catari was imprisoned in Potosí on the orders of the corregidor *of his province, Chayanta. Catari tried to get his case heard by higher authorities and to obtain the aid of the Protector of the Naturales, but the* corregidor *apparently was able to block his efforts. Finally, Catari was able to send the following letter to the president of the* Audiencia of Charcas (Sucre), *in which he complains about his situation—the suffering he and his family have endured—and asks for justice from a higher authority.*

Very Honorable Mr. President.—Sir—With all due respect, and with the veneration that I owe you, I will now express my complaint to your blessed ears and expose my long imprisonment in this public jail of the City of Potosí which has lasted over four months, with no more merit than the mere whims, atrocities, and passion with which my *Corregidor,* from the Province of Chaianta [*sic*], executes [his office]. . . . The main reason for my imprisonment has been for having denounced the usurpation of the royal tributes by the *cobradores* [collectors] and having informed the Governor of this town of such through an official letter. . . . [U]p until this date I have not been informed of the reasons for this extended imprisonment of four months. Nor have I been informed of any sentence . . . as is the custom. Nor have I been granted a hearing. Nor [have my] petitions to the Protector [legal officials designed to serve the indigenous population in their legal interactions with the colonial legal system] of this town been attended to. Nor does the Protector have any record of them. Nor have they been acted upon judicially or extra-judicially as far as said Governor is concerned. . . . I have, in vain, submitted my petitions three times to the General Protector, who instructed the Protector of this town to use efficient means to get me out [of jail] with no success. . . . [I]t seemed to me that it was best to inform you of my imprisonment (taking into consideration that your Excellency knows I have been named Governor and *Cacique Principal* by you and because it is my inherited right) so that, because of your position, and as exclusive judge, you issue a Royal provision to the Governor of this Pueblo so that I may be transferred to the royal prison of that city and have the accusations against me cleared, and if I have committed [any crime] to be severely punished. Otherwise, Sir, the situation through which my family and I are suffering is very bad, and having a lot of expenses to be covered [I hope they may be] charged against the royal tributes that I contribute to your Majesty. I hope for mercy from your hands. . . . May God our Lord protect you for many years to come, in prison, December twelfth, seventeen hundred and seventy-nine. At the feet of Your Excellency, your humble subject,

Thomas [*sic*] Catari. [*RTA,* 813–14]

90. Tomás Catari Declares the "Truth and Justice" of His Cause, 1780

Catari and his followers, like many other indigenous peoples, used the colonial legal system to the extent that they could and often claimed to have an abiding faith in the eventual justice of the Spanish Crown. In the following statement,

Tomás Catari, having been warned that the Audiencia *might order his arrest, makes a defiant statement to the effect that truth and justice will win out. He was, however, arrested shortly thereafter.*

[Catari stated that] he was not afraid of being arrested again because he was innocent and wanted to declare his truth and his justice; and for that reason, he was going to place himself at the gates of the *Audiencia* daily, so that all might see him and know of his presence. [*SCA*, 123. Translated by S. Serulnikov]

91. Catari Instills Fear in *Kurakas* and Government Officials

As the situation became tense and more violence erupted, many nonindigenous people began to fear what Catari and his forces would do. Some feared for their very lives. In the first of the following short sections, four kurakas *from Macha resign in fear of their lives. In the second,* Corregidor *Alós tells of the power Catari has over his followers. In the third section, an attorney of the* Audiencia *tries to explain Catari's appeal by noting that Catari claims to have orders from the viceroy, just as Tupac Amaru claimed to have royal orders for his actions.*

Document 1: *Kurakas* of Macha
[In June of 1780, four *caciques* from Macha informed Joaquín Alós that] the powerful arm of royal justice that your majesty administers has not been able to contain the sedition and arrogant uprising of this criminal [Tomás Catari] who believes himself to be beyond the reach of the law because of the support he receives from the Indian communities . . . that zealously protect him from royal justice.

Document 2: Alós
[Alós wrote that] the control that Catari exercises over the Indians leaves them so completely enthralled that they no longer obey the law and submit even less to their *Caciques.*

Document 3: *Audiencia* Attorney
[Attorney Juan de Pino Manrique noted] Catari thought nothing less than to carry out [the viceroy's order]. . . . He reduced everything to seductions, disturbances, and riots, seeking not to employ moderate methods, or at least

methods that would ease the shock of his exorbitant ends, but rather the most irregular extremes. [*SCA,* 132. Translated by S. Serulnikov]

92. Catari and Supporters Seek Justice from the Colonial Legal System

Indigenous representatives and leaders constructed statements that would appeal to Spanish legalism in making their case. The following selection contains two parts: one is by indigenous peoples and describes the good character and rectitude of Tomás Catari, and the other is by Catari himself with regard to his legal situation. They make the point that Catari would be a good leader, and that he cannot obtain justice from the corregidor *Alós. These statements make it clear that indigenous people were open and frank in the presentation of their case to the Spanish legal system, and that they expected justice.*

Document 1: People Support Catari
[After his detention by the *Audiencia,* Indians complained that Tomás Catari] had been treated as a criminal without our knowing why he had not been permitted to take office, as we expected. . . . [For] there is no other person who would be more scrupulous and vigilant in the collection of tributes and would give us the good treatment so recommended in the laws so that we do not experience even the slightest harm or abuse.

Document 2: Catari
[And before the *Audiencia* Catari stated that he knew the court] has ordered Joaquín Alós to conduct my trial and to find evidence of the charges against me. In this particular . . . I must say to your Highness that the said *corregidor* has been and is my mortal enemy, and as such has tyrannically persecuted me throughout that province. . . . As I could not bear his violent methods anymore, I came to this court in order to continue my claims; it is also apparent that if I were the type of criminal [I'm alleged to be], I would have never come to seek the justice that the well-known mercy of your Highness administers. [*SCA,* 146. Translated by S. Serulnikov]

93. Indians Demands *Mitayos* Be Freed from Tribute Payment

The Spanish colonial system often passed laws designed to alleviate some of the suffering and exploitation of the indigenous peoples, but on the ground the practical realities of necessity and greed often trumped more humanitarian laws. Hence, the colonial adage: "I obey, but I do not comply." A hacendado *and former* corregidor *named Juan Antonio de Acuña, acting on behalf of Spanish authority after Alós had been thrown out, was confronted by the people of Micani. They demanded the enforcement of a 1692 order by Viceroy Conde de la Monclova that* mitayos *not pay tribute. Acuña tried to avoid proclaiming the validity of the order; however, the situation quickly grew tense, and he came to see the wisdom of making the order valid. In the following statement, Acuña describes his actions.*

. . . [I]n view of the demeanor of the Indians who were inclined to kill me and my retinue, I decided right away to climb to the top of an oven for baking bread—which was the most elevated spot in this plaza—and tell them from there: "the order of his Excellency [Viceroy Conde de la Monclova] must be obeyed." And I also said, "Long Live the King," which all the people repeated with much rejoicing. The Indians, then, carried me in their arms from the oven to my room, kissing my hands and feet, and hugging me. After that, they left me alone. [*SCA*, 181. Translated by S. Serulnikov]

94. The Priest of Sacaca Expresses Fear of Indians and Sarcasm about Their Rule

Spaniards, including priests, feared for their lives during the rebellion. They continued, however, to express contempt for those who threatened them, and sometimes this contempt was mixed with a fair degree of sarcasm as they awaited what would befall them. The priest of Sacaca, Idelfonso de Mina y Escobar, provides a hint of these raw nerves and contemptuousness in the following letter he wrote to Tomás Catari.

Fall all the plagues upon you, for you are the cause of [all the trouble], as all the Indians are voicing it; the Indians, who are already more than four thousand, invaded this town and inside the church took away from my own hands, in the presence of Our Lord Transubstantiated, [Sacaca] governor Manuel Ayaviri, who was sick and suffering. Look at what they do! Be afraid of God! That you are mortal and when you expect it the less, God will throw you to hell for all the eternity. . . .

Let me know how I must henceforth address you, because I want to exchange letters with you, if as Majesty, as Excellency, as Your Lord, so that I do not err since I ignore everything, and I only suffer in your name, all we suffer in our parish, and the priests of the valleys in theirs. So, I wait for your answer because it would be against reason that a man of such high qualities does not answer. [*SCA*, 171. Translated by S. Serulnikov]

IX. Rebellion, Defeat, and Death

95. The People of Pocoata Complain of Abuse by Their *Kuraka*, Florencio Lupa, 1775

Florencio Lupa's death at the hands of the people he governed was a turning point in the events in Chayanta, as people moved beyond legal protest against their oppressors to executing them. Before his death, Lupa, an appointed kuraka *and a* mestizo, *became a lightning rod for indigenous complaints in the communities he governed. This was due in part to his behavior, which was often exploitative. It was also because of the fact that he lacked legitimacy in the eyes of many of the indigenous people he governed. They felt that he did not represent them well, in addition to being a* mestizo *and appointed. Because he ruled over different ethnic groups, he appeared to have divided, if any, loyalties. He took office in Moscari in 1753, and his power grew significantly over the years. He was installed as* cacique *over the people of Pocoata in the early 1770s. He ruled until he was killed by people he governed in 1780. In the first document that follows, people from* ayllu *Chanca in Pocoata complain of Lupa's exploitation, especially in relationship to the church. The second document, also by people of Pocoata, points to other complaints and dissatisfactions with Lupa. In the third document, Lupa himself fears for his life at the hands of the people of Pocoata and others over whom he rules.*

Document 1: People of Pocoata

. . . [I]t is the truth that the governor compels us to go to mass, to confess, and to attend doctrine. But it is also true that there are other Indians who can be Governors without demanding these new taxes and allowing Indians to keep their old customs to which they are so attached. . . . It is apparent, too, that all the Indians are dissatisfied with this governor's behavior because they no longer have any break during the services to the Church since he charges them the tribute. . . .

Document 2: People of Pocoata

The countless complaints that against [Lupa] have been made . . . must have made [the tribunal] realize the pernicious behavior with which he manages; for it is apparent that since his assumption we do not have peace and quiet anymore, nor do we believe we will until his expulsion be secured.

Document 3: Florencio Lupa

. . . ['I']he insolent spirit of these people grew so big that they seriously arranged to kill me in case I tried to make this collection, and also to kill don Nicolás Ursainqui if he took repressive measures. [*SCA,* 109, 111. Translated by S. Serulnikov]

96. Florencio Lupa's Links to Spanish Authorities

After Lupa was killed, others commented on his relationship to Spanish author-ities. These ties were seen as the reason for his death, because people understood that he had a better relationship with the Spanish than with the people he gov-erned. Dating from 1781, the first of the following documents—which is anonymous—discussed Lupa and his ties to the Corregidor, *and his extraction of money from the peoples he governed. The second very brief quote from Tomás Catari also discusses Lupa's ties to the Spanish.*

Document 1: Anonymous

In this city used to live an Indian governor named Lupa, he was so well known for his actions that he had province-wide influence. In such a way that the *Corregidor* who was in harmony with him, left the province in very good shape, and those who were not, he attacked them until they fell. Since he was so sovereign in his actions, all tributaries used to give him half a *real* per annum, which he saved to defend provincial causes. He used the money to bribe the system of justice for his just or unjust causes.

Document 2: Tomás Catari
. . . [Y]our Majesty ought to know that Lupa was the favorite of your ministers due to the gifts and bribes he used to give them [and] that Lupa had amassed a huge fortune out of the blood he stole from the miserable Indians. [*SCA,* 65, 66. Translated by S. Serulnikov]

97. *Kuraka* Florencio Lupa Is Killed by Indians He Governs

Florencio Lupa was one of the appointed kurakas *who was disliked by many of the people over whom he had authority. He was not considered legitimate by many villagers who lived under his rule, and he did little to make himself popular. Lacking legitimacy and support, he was killed by the people of Moscari, who chafed under his rule. The following reading explains the decision—which was not unanimous—to execute Lupa and take his head to La Plata.*

. . . [M]any were opposed [to murdering Lupa], arguing that it was better to bring him alive to this city [La Plata] to submit him to the *audiencia*. And although many agreed to this at the time, they changed their mind during the night and in the midst of confusion, shouting, and uproar, they cut his head off. In the morning, there was a meeting in which . . . they resolved to bring [Lupa's head] to this city and put it during the night on a cross called Quirpinchaca, as they did between one and two o'clock in the night and then they came back to Moscari without making stops. [*SCA,* 159. Translated by S. Serulnikov]

98. The Head of Florencio Lupa Is Brought to La Plata, 1780

By early September 1780, violence and fear were already gripping the residents of La Plata (Sucre), where fighting had erupted. On September 5, a particularly ominous event occurred when the head of the unpopular kuraka *Florencio Lupa was delivered to the city. The following selection gives a sense of that fear.*

[A resident of La Plata] noticed that the people's sense of alarm and restlessness grew by the second, so that they opened and closed their doors at the same time, closing them to take refuge and opening them to defend themselves, taking sticks, knives, stones, or whatever happened to be at hand as weapons. [Another observer claimed] this city was shaken in such a way that its inhabitants believed that this was going to be the last day of their lives. . . . [It was also noted that] outside the walls of the city, in the area commonly called Quirpinchaca, a considerable number of Indians [are] gathering, raising flags and playing cornets with the obvious purpose of falling into this neighborhood and invading it. People [believe] that these Indians [are] coming from the rebellious province of Chayanta.

[During the night Lupa's head was placed in Quirpinchaca and later it was brought to the *cabildo*. Officials] along with the town clerk went down to the cell of the jail where the head was shown wrapped in a blanket, and we recognized that it was Lupa's head and we ordered that it should be safeguarded in one of the dungeons of the jail until further notice; when we came out from that place we found that the patio was so full of people that we could not leave it . . . various people who had known the *cacique* while he was alive [examined Lupa's head]. [*SCA,* 54–55. Translated by S. Serulnikov]

99. Spaniards Comment on the Killing of *Kurakas* Bernal and Lupa

Spaniards were not unaware of indigenous complaints about their kurakas *with regard to exploitation and abuse. They also knew that many of the* kurakas *who had been appointed were not Indians, and some were not even from the communities they governed. The following selection, which reflects on the causes of the rebellion, shows that the Spaniards understood that the peoples of the communities may have killed the* kurakas *Bernal and Lupa because they were* mestizos *and were closely tied to the* corregidor.

[A Spaniard noted that] seeing that the collection of the Royal tribute was not in the hands of pure Indians as they are, since they are spiritless and fainthearted and do not accept others to command them, and perhaps this is the explanation of the murders that took place in Macha and Moscari of their governors Blas Bernal and Florencio Lupa who were Hispanicized *mestizos* with whom they always were upset. [*SCA,* 61. Translated by S. Serulnikov]

100. The City Council of Chuquisaca (La Plata) Discusses the Role of the *Corregidores* and the *Reparto* in the Rebellion

In Alto Peru, as near Cuzco and throughout the Andes, the reparto *system— with its forced sale of goods at high prices, many of which were of questionable value to the indigenous population—was a source of growing conflict and tension. Those villagers and others who were subject to the* reparto *were often at loggerheads with the* corregidor *and his aids. Sometimes this conflict also included* caciques *and other indigenous officials who aided the* corregidor. *Tomás Catari focused on the* reparto *as the primary abuse of many that his people suffered.*

In the following document, the city council of Chuquisaca (La Plata, Sucre) expressed their belief that the corregidores *and the* reparto *were largely responsible for the rebellion. The city council argued that the avarice of the* corregidores *led them to ignore their duties and abuse the Indians to collect exorbitant charges for the* reparto *items. The document also shows the divisions that existed between various levels of Spanish authority because they perceived their interests and the interests of the Spanish colonial regime in different ways.*

Concerning the origin of the widespread seditious Commotion that exists in all of the Peruvian Kingdom, it is believed that it was the conduct of the *reparto* by the *corregidores,* along with their deputies (*Thenientes*) and the many more domestic servants and dependents, who carried out unspeakable extortions, persecutions, and molestations of the Yndios [*sic*] in their collection [of the *repartos*]. For the sake of collecting [the *reparto*] they studied all means [at their disposal], including imprisonment, and all manner of torments. . . . [What they take] is only the profit from the labor of the Indian (who is left perhaps without sufficient provision for himself), for the convenience of the *corregidor,* and all his men, who proportionally gain from the sweat and fatigues of the oppressed Indian, [who is] always filled with anguish and fatigued, in order to pay for the *reparto* merchandise that is given him at an excessive price. And perhaps the Indians have no need of it [the *reparto* merchandise] because it is worthless or unusable. From the moment he enters his Province, it is the sole purpose of the *Corregidor* (with the occasional exception of those who have a fear of God) to procure with anxiety and greed the *repartimiento* of effects from the people of his province and redistribute them at his pleasure, as if this were the only obligation under his charge. If only he fulfilled the Administration of Justice (the principal object of his office and employment) with similar care. . . . Thus, one has to think that the present commotion has been directed since the beginning against the *Corregidores* and their henchmen, and [this conclusion] has been borne out by experience. Only those [*corregidores*] who fled have managed to escape with their lives. [*RTA,* 721]

101. Lampoon Placed in La Plata in 1780

The following lampoon, like most of those placed in Arequipa and La Paz, had to do primarily with the new customs duties, but it also mentions other exactions by the colonial state and the bad behavior of colonial officials. It calls for "Death to bad government" and to those "who stole insatiably / under the pretext of the Customhouses." It is meant for the literate urban audience and must predate serious concerns about indigenous insurrection.

Already Cuzco and Arequipa
with La Paz and Cochabamba
seeing the systematic robbery
and using the Customs as a pretense
have been forced to resolve
to defend themselves with their arms.
Potosí also intends to defend itself,
but due to its strange loyalty
it has been waiting for Chuquisaca's clamor;
but that noble city in its strange loyalty
has always concealed
the most tyrannical thoughts;
but now that it finds itself
between the Sword and the Cross
(for its continued loyalty),
declares its intentions,
advising that for being so privileged
its defense is warranted,
even in the worst of luck;

and that in this consequence,
upon seeing themselves today distressed,
if the inhabitants persevere with their hearts
they themselves will take vengeance,
for in their [current] consent is the disgrace
of this Kingdom.
While Potosí floods the city
with its waters,
our ready anger will
reach the Pampa.
Cochabamba will take the
slopes of San Sebastian,
while we start with the President
and robed justices,
the Mayors, notaries public,
Officials of the Treasury,
Tobacco monopolies
and many other pirates,
and because those infidels wanted
to leave us without a cloak,
Death to bad government,
and Long Live our King!
Death to the false Ministers,
and Long Live La Plata!
But in order to live we ask
for characters of substance,
and Death (as they deserve)
to those who trampled the law
and those who stole insatiably
under the pretext of the Customhouses.
[*CDIP,* 44. 1780-III]

102. Presentation of Tomás Catari to the Viceroy Vértiz

In November 1780, Tomás Catari once again sent a letter to the viceroy in Buenos Aires asking for his help to obtain freedom for some indigenous people who had been taken prisoner. He also tried to calm the situation by insisting that, when the villagers had risen up in August, it was not against the government but against bad and greedy officials. Of major concern to Catari was the abuse of the reparto, *which he saw as impoverishing the people of his region. He also praised his priest, Gregorio Josef Merlos, for helping his people, and he condemned other priests for doing the work of the* corregidor. *He asked that the bad officials be removed and replaced with those who were more sympathetic to the Indians. In addition, he pointed to the* Audiencia *as a source of further problems rather than solutions. The document is repetitive, but it emphasizes the urgency of the request to end the abuses and exploitation, and it demonstrates Catari's effort to seek understanding and legal help from higher authorities.*

Buenos Aires December 16th, 1780
Let it be registered where it belongs.
Most excellent Sir,
[signatures of Vértiz and Rospigliosi]

Don Tomás Catari, Indio principal of the Pueblo of San Pedro de Macha, Province of Chayanta and present governor named by the Royal *Audiencia* bent at the feet of your Excellency in his name and in the name of all this Kingdom, especially the Province of Chayanta [express with utmost respect]: I find myself accused of several crimes that I have not committed, but which have been easily imputed to me by my enemy *Corregidor* Don Juachin Alos [*sic*]. I have said that it has been easy for him to accuse me, my Lord, because a *Corregidor* in his province does whatever he feels like doing and writes whatever deposition that he wishes. And if up until now no *corregidor* has justified that Luther is more saintly than San Francisco it is only because it does not benefit his interests and because they do not deal with matters of sanctity. It is in this state that I, Don Thomas [*sic*] Catari again declare that I am a victim of the greediness of the *Corregidor* and that I am a poor, miserable Indian and a delinquent prisoner. But delinquent only because I offered to increase the Royal Interests [finances] of our great, wise and prudent Monarch Don Carlos the Third.

I assent to inform your Excellency of the general uprising of this Province, of the blood so many innocents have shed in the ravines provoked by the dark greediness of the *Corregidor* and his tyrannical *reparto*. But I can assure your Excellency that the *Corregidor's* hatred, resentment and cruelty are insurmountable, as my sufferings can attest. Without any other reason than my having obtained from your Excellency's grace a superior decree that protected my Government and Cacicasgo, he returned from the city of Buenos Ayres [*sic*] to my village and took away from me the authority that I rightly possess. Through depraved and malicious dealings he managed to bury your superior Commands so that he could oppress me. He punished me as much as his iniquitous desires demanded through whippings, jailings in several prisons—lately in the Court prison—where my sufferings increased daily without any recourse even for my daily food requirements. And I can assure your Excellency that I have not had any comfort other than my priest don Gregorio Josef de Merlos who, through wisdom and prudence, could have brought peace and calm throughout this Province and the pueblo of Macha; who as soon as he had arrived was able to secure the *Corregidor's* life from the Indians' furor, as our main Priest and our Redeemer, author of life itself. So many miserable [Indians] would have suffered while protecting themselves from the tyrannical *reparto* if Divine Providence did not send us this priest who otherwise would have controlled the violence. . . . [Merlos] would have defended our miserable lives, and he would have defended, with efficiency and care, the royal interests of our Catholic Monarch, persuading us and explaining to us the respect and veneration and blind obedience that our Royal Justice and the Higher Orders required. It is to this priest that we owe the abatement of the misfortunes of our people and of many other souls who would miserably have perished in a bloody war fueled by the greediness of the *Corregidor.* [W]hat awful and regrettable news would have reached your Excellency, what increased costs and losses would his Majesty have suffered, and how many worries to the Ministers and Judges! Ultimately [Your Majesty] would have been exposed to the total ruination of the Sovereign's entire Kingdom and Interests, as I will demonstrate with clear evidence. . . . The *Corregidor* left to meet the Indian *mitayos* at a site called Guañoma, where a considerable number of Indians gathered to denounce the tyranny of the *reparto* and demand the release of Catari. And the *Corregidor,* claiming that the Indians did not want to pay the Royal Tribute, armed 300 men to defend his clear and twisted designs. He never allowed us a hearing, dismissing the reasons of the poor Indian tributaries of the King [for their actions]. He maintained this situation until this past August 26th in the town of Pocoata when the unfortunate events and bloody war occurred in which 300 Indian tributaries of the king, and their main leaders, were killed. The cause [of all this] was, is, and will continue to be the tyrannical *reparto* of the *Corregidor.* It is possible Sir, that the dark greed of your Judge will suffice to shed the blood of so many innocent people, so that Your Majesty will experience a considerable loss in His income, so that the Royal *Mita* could be damaged, the sacred temples desecrated, and finally, that the entire Kingdom could be ruined due to the . . . disposition of the *Corregidor* and his ambition and greed. In this context it seems to me, My Lord, that this *Corregidor* is guilty of lack of respect and treason against our Catholic [faith], for having committed such crimes against the Crown.

It is true that in Pocoata some Spaniards died, and close to 300 Indians as already mentioned, but it is not for this that it can be said that the Indians staged an uprising. The Royal *Mita* already had been dispatched and the *Corregidor* Don Joachin Alos [*sic*] was informed that the Royal Tributes were ready. They would be handed to him, as customary, in the Town of Macha. And then an Indian from this *repartimiento* (Don Thomas Acho) came to ask the same *Corregidor* if he would free Don Thomas [*sic*] Catari, whom the Indian had been assured was being held in that Pueblo. He also offered to receive the prisoner himself in the workshops. The reply was to have Acho shot dead with a pistol in cold blood. And this painful death caused unrest among those poor Indians. . . . Being afraid of dying as poor Acho had, they defended themselves in every way possible and in a lot more humane ways than the Spaniards, who from the Church were shooting the miserable Indians who had taken refuge in the cemetery. The Indians carried away all the wounded so that they could be taken care of without their lives being ended. The Indians, out of respect for the King, did not kill the *Corregidor,* even though they could have done so out of anger. . . .

After the presidents and *oidores* [judges] of the Royal *Audiencia* who live in the area were able to recover from the uprisings they freed me from the prison in which the *Corregidor* had unjustly put me out of hatred, preventing me, along with my Priest, from freeing him from the prison in which he was being held, as well as finding a way to appease the spirits of those poor Indians who on that day were still totally subdued and were obedient to both Majesties (God and King). We put ourselves at the feet of your Majesty and beg for your protection of all Indians. . . . We ask that you allow Don Juan Bauptista Ormachea, Lawyer of the Royal *Audiencia* and judge named by such Tribunal, to deal with the cause of the increases that I have offered to make in the Royal Interests of your Excellency and the defense of the poor tributary Indians, so that we can live in peace attending to our obligations, women, children and crops serving God and the King. We also humbly ask you to name as our protector Don Isidro Serrano, a person who has our entire acceptance and who is capable and intelligent, and willing to serve your Excellency so that we will be able to live in peace, which is what our just wishes desire so that justice will not be delayed and the wrongs that I have been enumerating to your Majesty will be righted along with the delays, prejudices, and losses caused by the delays in the prosecution of this fair cause. I insist to your Majesty that there is no future restlessness foreseen, and that we all will live humbly and work to increase Your Majesty's treasury.

There have been many . . . reports that I, and other communities of this Province of the Royal *Audiencia,* have submitted begging for a general pardon and for Judges to govern us. But . . . to this day we have not even gotten a response. The reasons for all of us to ask for a general pardon have been many, but the main [one] has been to make it clear that the Indians did not rise up, that the Indians have always been prompt to serve God and the King; that the Indians did not, and do not, repeal the paying of the tributes, customs and *mita*. That the Indians did not rise up is evident because no one has denied owing blind obedience to the King. As it is, we suffer so much dereliction by the hands of the Ministers of this Royal *Audiencia* that they send soldiers to end our miserable lives and ignore the many recommendations and Royal Decrees of our pious and merciful King of the Spains and the wretched Indies. As proof of what we go through I will tell Your Excellency that your Royal *Audiencia* is busy trying to find out who were my friends in Chuquisaca, who wrote the briefs and petitions in my defense, who had influenced me in going to Buenos Aires, and who prepares my reports here. The result of all these inquiries is the imprisonment of very honorable subjects who have been forced to confess. . . . I, along with my whole community, confess to you, Your Excellency, that the Royal *Audiencia* is only bothering itself with these probes because I told them, when they made me confess in Chuquisaca, that I did not have any other motives than my own sufferings and those of my Indians and other communities of this province. What I have told you, Sir, is the truth, as it is true that their intention is to scare and frighten all the living and close or narrow the channels for defense, thus darkening the prospect for justice. Because it is quite clear that the intention of the King is to allow an audience to the most inhumane accused, attention should not be given to anything but finding the best way of successfully ousting the *Corregidor*.

I have to confess to your Excellency that it is impossible to doubt that the tyrannical *repartos* of the *Corregidores* are the main cause for the ruin of the whole Kingdom, as it is not only the *corregidor* who wants our skin but their lieutenants, tax collectors and [other] biased aids, as was seen with *Corregidor* Don Juachin Alos [*sic*]. He distributed more than 400,000 pesos to his Lieut. Luis Nuñes and to his wife an even bigger sum. To his Lieut. Lucas Billafan and his wife an equal sum, along with many other obscure dealings through which the *Corregidor* and his lieutenants come out laden with riches while the Indians are left without skin. As our most pious Father and true protector is so far away from this miserable land, we cannot find a way to let you know of all the miseries we encounter as your loyal children and subjects.

We hope [to receive] from your merciful Excellency a remedy for our miseries such as informing our master, the King, of our sufferings so that he could give us the grace of repealing the ever increasing burden of the tyrannical *repartos* that destroy us and kill us, and our children and women. At the same time we assure him that we will tolerate any other burden that his Royal Clemency deems necessary from his poor children, but that the *reparto* be cancelled as our miserable shoulders cannot bare more burden.

We await Your Excellency's response for our solace, for it is the only remedy for our conflicts. In the previous report that I submitted to Your Excellency we asked for Dr. Juan Bauptista Ormachea as magistrate. But so that your Excellency knows of our total obedience we would be happy with Dr. Manuel Balensuela, an impartial subject of Alos [*sic*], believing that he will treat us fairly. . . .

Many of the Priests from this province, forgetting their responsibilities as defenders of the Indians, have been busy accusing innocent people. One such is Don Isidoro Josef de Herrera, priest of San Pedro, who in his efforts to cover up for the *Corregidor* as his protector, defender, and advisor in his cruel dealings has falsely accused innocent Indians. Or Don Cortes, Priest of Aymia, who, feigning fear, has abandoned his Parish, leaving his poor flock in total abandonment. Or Don Viseten Birecochea, Priest of Chayanta, who in his zeal to follow the Court has done the same so that, Your Excellency, all the goals of the priests and ministers of the Royal *Audiencia* are to please the *Corregidor*, helping him to pillage and leaving us the poor Indians totally destitute. I can testify that the Priest Dr. Merlos has been the only one who has favored us and now I have been informed that he, having asked for permission from the Archbishop, will soon retire. Here at your Majesty's feet, I beseech you with the utmost respect to not allow this to happen because we would truly be miserably abandoned and lost.

Your Ministers, Your Excellency, only busy themselves in finding out who protects the Indians so that they have imprisoned several honorable subjects, among them a poor woman by the name of Doña Maria Esperansa Campusano who has been put in Public Jail only for being the servant of our Priest, Dr. Merlos. I beg your Majesty to order her release and that she be given all the recompense she is due for having unfairly suffered.

In previous documents, and in this report too, we have asked that Don Isidro Serrano be named as a Protector, but as the office of the clerk is vacant we respectfully ask you to allow him to fill it. Serrano possesses all the necessary requirements for the job, as well as the skills and abilities and love in serving Your Excellency.

At this date the job of administering justice is being filled by Don Juan Antonio Acuña, a deadly enemy of the Indians and partisan confidant and friend of Alós, and plainly the author of all his iniquities. This is the reason we are suspicious of him doing anything to end our unfair poverty. We beg Your Excellency that he be removed and that Dr. Manuel Balensuela, in virtue of his seniority and he being the first elected by your own Ministers, be put in his place.

We also beg for the clemency of Your Excellency [and] that the attached petition be presented to our great Father the King whose clemency and yours will hopefully alleviate our miseries.

May our Lord guide you through the years these kingdoms need for their greatest development. Macha, November 12th, 1780.

I remain at your feet as your rendered child and loyal tributary.

Thomas [*sic*] Catari. [*CDIP*, 63. 1780-XI-12]

103. The Viceroy Expresses Distrust of the *Corregidor* in His Dealings with Catari

Many royal officials, including the viceroy in this case, had grave doubts and a degree of cynicism about the actions and motives of certain corregidores. *They knew they were abusing their authority and not complying with orders; however, it was not easy to correct the situation on the ground. All power has its limits. In the following statement, Viceroy Vértiz makes clear his doubts about Alós, who has disregarded his orders and placed Catari in the position of* cacique.

. . . [I]t is clear that the *corregidor's* reports attributing the origin of the disturbance to Catari's distortion of my orders do not deserve credit because the *corregidor* does not prove it and the documents show otherwise . . . *nor is the reason the* Audiencia *alleged for arresting Catari—that he would seek a reduction of tributes—consistent with Catari's proceeding in Potosí to increase them;* thus, we should suspect that they try to disguise their own wrongdoing with the imputation of abuses to such a defenseless person. [*SCA*, 136. Translated by S. Serulnikov]

104. Uprising in the Province of Chayanta and What Happened in the Town of Pocoata

The following document relates many of the principal conflicts and actions that led to the Catari rebellion. It discusses the complaints of villagers in the province of Chayanta against certain caciques *and the* corregidor, *Joaquín Alós. The report makes it clear that Catari viewed himself as the rightful leader of the community and that he went to great lengths—even embarking on a trip to Buenos Aires—to garner legal support for his claim. The fallout of this con-*

flict led to Catari's detention. Eventually, his loyal supporters free him using the threat of force.

The report also discusses the mobilization of and increasing use of violence by the oppressed in the initial stages of the uprising, which developed into armed conflict and revenge killings. As the document points out, caciques—*and not just Spaniards—were sometimes targets of indigenous "justice," as villagers sought to restore a more just order to their world.*

The civil wars that have begun to develop throughout this Kingdom, which God decided to send us so that we could correct our debaucheries, have left us in a quite gloomy situation due to their sad consequences. For even though they are not worse than those already experienced, they are sufficient to be counted among the memorable and irreparable losses of our Spain.

The newly established Customs, State monopolies, and other consequences of the *Visita General* [Inspection] through which the legitimate contribution to Royal Taxes are fixed, are the touchstone for these peoples, and are given as the sole cause for all these rebellions. Trying to describe in detail what happened was too long and bothersome of an effort, and difficult to make fit the truth for many fables are being written about it, as everybody picks whatever suits their own way of thinking, ideas, or plans, as can be concluded from the inconsistency of the news. . . .

This past year, 1778, Don Nicolas de Urzainqui was the *Corregidor* of the Province of Chayanta in the jurisdiction of the Archdiocese of La Plata. Three Indians, *originarios* of the Cacique of Macha, Don Blas Bernal (and led by Tomás Catari, as representative of the Cacicazgo Aransaya in the *repartimiento* of Macha), traveled to the city of Potosí and appeared before Royal Officials. They complained of the damages caused them by the aforementioned *cacique*, Don Blas, who had taken their lands and harvests from them; and they denounced at the same time the usurpation of the 800 pesos of tribute that they paid annually. Having heard the case and the denunciation, the Royal Officials ordered that said *Corregidor* Urzainqui remove Bernal from the *cacicazgo*, and [that the *corregidor*] should investigate [the charges] and make amends with the plaintiffs. . . . But the *corregidor* did not pay any attention to this [order], even though the Royal *Audiencia* of La Plata also had expedited a corresponding Royal Provision.

In this state, the new *corregidor*, Don Joaquín de Aloz [*sic*], arrived in the aforementioned Province. Aware of the Royal Provision and informed of some movements caused by Catari that were disturbing the Province, he [Alós] had him arrested and dispatched as a prisoner to the mining center of Aullagas; but while passing through the town of Ocuri, the Indian miners confronted them and then took him [Catari] and sent him to the City of La Plata.

Catari appeared before the Royal *Audiencia* which issued a second order for the [fulfillment of the] Provision and he was sent back to the Province again with a letter from the judge. However, the Indian [Tomás Catari] did not want to obey and he went to the city of Buenos Aires at the beginning of the year 79, and presented to the Viceroy [the information concerning] his having been deposed from his *cacicazgo,* supposing it legitimately belonged to him. He asked to be given back his position and offered to considerably increase the . . . Royal Tributes. . . . [T]he case was not heard, but the Superior Government issued a writ [certifying] his . . . right to be reinstated [as *cacique*]. . . . He went back to Chuquisaca and presented the provisions to the Royal *Audiencia* and, without waiting for their resolution, he proceeded to the Town of Macha and persuaded the Indians of this *Parcialidad* that he had been in Spain and had kissed the feet of our Sovereign, who had treated him with the greatest demonstrations of love. And having been informed of the oppressions that the Indians were suffering, [the King] had released them from the *repartimientos* of the *corregidores,* and ordered that they only contribute one third of the tribute that they paid in the past, for which end he joined together with two other tribute collectors and together they went to deliver it [the tribute] to the Royal Treasury.

This news having spread, and been believed, all around the Province of Chayanta, *Corregidor* Aloz [*sic*] brought a complaint against Catari and issued an order for him to be detained in Potosí. He was taken prisoner by order of the Governor and put in jail for over nine months. That time being completed, one night he was released to twelve young men who had been dispatched by said *corregidor* at the request of the *cacique* of Macha. Burdened with shackles, he was taken on out of the way roads to near the town of Pocoata, where the Indians, and those of Macha as well, idolized Catari for all he had done. They freed him and took him to the city of La Plata where he brought his charges, making public his sufferings. The *corregidor* did not fail to send to the Royal *Audiencia* the charges that they had brought against him proving several crimes and mutinies. As soon as these were heard by the *Oydores* [*sic*] [judges], they ordered him [Catari] taken prisoner and put in the Royal Jail.

His brother, the one-eyed person named Dámaso Catari, took on the responsibility of his defense, stirring up the Indians about how his brother found himself in difficulties and in danger of being hanged for having represented them in a sympathetic manner and having tried to free them from the heavy yoke of *Repartos,* tributes, *Mitas* and other burdens under which they suffered. Meanwhile the *corregidor* was enriching himself with their blood and had persecuted him in order to prevent him from opposing such tyranny.

Moved by this situation, Indian men and women promised to contribute one *real* a person to help their Father Catari, for he was admired as one of their own. Not being able to free him, they organized for a general insurrection in the Pueblo of Macha on August 30th, the day when the List was made public of the 800 Indians who were to be dispatched as the *Mita* to Potosí, along with 51,000 pesos worth of tribute; however their impatience and a lack of leadership prevented them from achieving this hoped-for goal.

During the month of July some unequivocal movements were observed that made clear the Indians' intentions. Their gatherings, lack of obedience, and having told the *corregidor* that if he didn't bring them their Padre Catari, he would see what would happen to him, confirmed their designs. [The *corregidor*] informed the Royal *Audiencia* about all of this and he was ordered to treat the Indians in a gentle and wise manner, which he did as much as he was able to.

At the beginning of August, the Indians in the Pueblo of Macha apprehended the *Cacique* Governor of Alansaya, Dn. Blas Bernal, whose Governorship they say belonged to Catari. They placed him in prison, and after six days he was executed. The news reached *Corregidor* Alos [*sic*] who sent an order to the Captains of the Militias of the Province to gather on the 23rd of said month with their junior officers and soldiers in the Town of Pocoata. As expected, four companies composed of 200 men gathered on the set date and remained in their quarters on the 24th through the 25th when at four in the afternoon they took up their arms due to suspicions that the Indians of Pacanachi might do something while their *Mita* role was being called. It was . . . then that one of the Indians, a *cacique* of Macha, complained to the *corregidor* that an Indian who was present had assured them that the Viceroy of Buenos Aires had ordered that the Indians needed to pay only half of their tribute and that the authorization was in the hands of Tomás Catari. Upon hearing this the *corregidor* removed the Indian and put him in a *ramada* [in this case, it seems to be an enclosure of some sort—perhaps made out of branches, as the word suggests—not an arbor] so he could find out the truth later. From this it ensued that the Indians, being angry, entered the *ramada* and freed the Indian saying: that he was a *Cédula* (a *mitayo*) and could not be imprisoned. The *corregidor,* displaying great patience, told them that if he was *Cédula* they could take him, but jeering, laughing and making gestures the Indians desisted and left.

On the 26th at ten in the morning it was observed that masses of Indians covered the hills and countryside, and they were preparing themselves, with much yelling and sounds of horns, to take said Pueblo of Pocoata. At eleven Dámaso Catari, who was leading the crowd, put a petition in the *corregidor's* hands asking that his brother Tomás be freed, because he knew they were holding him prisoner. . . The *corregidor* gave the petition to Dr. Dn. Josef Benavides, a man who either by fate or destiny, and who was known for being a wealthy owner of mines, had accompanied him as his advisor. The Indian, observing this and feeling that [the demands] were not being dealt with fast enough said with resolute courage and without any fear of the soldiers that surrounded him while he was addressing the *corregidor: expedite my request because the Sun is setting* [it is getting late] *to give my orders, although for me and my people it is the same to die today as tomorrow.* He was given a decree so that he could go to the Royal *Audiencia* of Charcas where his brother was held prisoner. After leaving the *corregidor's* house, Dámaso went to the main square and lit fireworks as a signal for the Indians to approach the town with their slings and rocks in their hands.

Observing this movement the four companies situated themselves strategically to defend each entry into [the pueblos'] streets, and the *corregidor,* with his sword in his hand and riding his horse, sent for Don Pedro Caypa, the *cacique* and governor of said town, who until then had not done anything and remained indifferent. Having summoned him, he told him: *how could he allow the Macha Indians to defy his authority? and that he should gather his forces and go out and contain them.* This Indian got on his horse and together with two halberdiers (an honor conferred to the Governors of Pocoata thanks to Sr. Don Felipe Quinto) rode for about half a league, but instead of containing the tumultuous [Indians], he told them that it was time to attack, for the Spaniards were very scared and lacked the forces to control them; and that they were gathering their people within the Pueblo.

The *cacique,* having returned to Alos [*sic*], told him in a loud voice: *Corregidor, there is nothing you can do;* and turning around twice while spurring his horse, he held his hat in the air which was a signal to the Indians who were already nearby. They assaulted the pueblo screaming insults and making deafening noises with their horns through the four main streets and main plaza. They [the Spanish and soldiers] resisted from two to around four in the afternoon; but being forced to yield on account of the mob of charging Indians (based on conservative estimates, there were more than 10,000 without counting those from the countryside), they retreated to the Church while firing their arms. Finding it locked, and the keys in possession of the sexton who was with the rebellious Indians, they broke the locks with great shoving and were able to get inside it. The Indians saw this and determined to route them from the church in order to give each one of them a cruel and premeditated death. The Priest of Pocoata, seeing this horrific scene, wanted to try to invoke our Lord in an attempt to placate the tumult, but he was warned by the Indians to not get involved in anything and to go home before something very bad happened to him.

Thirty of our people died in this battle, and more than 200 from the Indians' side with a high number of wounded. The advisor, Benavides, was taken prisoner. His tongue was ripped out while he was still alive. He was finished off by being stoned and beaten to death. His body was then cut to pieces. Captain Dn. Joaquin Cueto was saved from danger by one of his soldiers who threw his lance, which was some two *varas* [approximately 66 inches] long so hard that he pinned three Indians together against a wall where part of the lance was stuck in the wall while he was surrounded by Indians. *A great move if what happened was truly accounted for by the one who told it or who did it.*

At four in the afternoon the priest of said pueblo advised the *corregidor* to flee before the Indians decided to invade and ruin the Church to get those who were hiding in it. The *corregidor* managed to escape but was thrown from his horse with a stone and taken captive. They took him unconscious to a hut where they took off his shirt and dressed him with an Indian garment and long trousers of coarse wool. Once he was conscious, they gave him poorly ground corn with chili pepper seeds while telling him that the poor Indians only had such clothes and food with which to pay tribute to the King, and to him, also, for his unjust *reparto*, for which they were disposed to kill him. And to this end they made him walk barefoot for four leagues through cold, rough mountains taking him to the Pueblo of Macha where they put him in shackles.

Those poor people who had taken refuge in the Church saw, through the cracks of the closed and locked door, the atrocities being done by the Indians to the cadavers that were lying in the Plaza and they were anxiously awaiting such horrors being done to them too. But after it became known in Pocoata that the *Corregidor* Alos [*sic*] had been jailed, the Indians calmed down. The Priest, without wasting the opportunity, went out wearing his sacred robes and with a Crucifix to courageously exhort them. The Indians offered to calm down as long as those who had taken refuge in the Church would surrender their arms, which they did to the Priest in the company of four Indian *principales* [Indian officials or men of consequence in the community]. But throughout the night the Indians went around making loud noises and shouting.

On the 27th at five in the morning the officers and soldiers came out of the Church one by one and were searched by the Indians who took everything they had and then forced them to walk to the mining center of Aullagas.

The bad treatment that *Corregidor* Alos [*sic*] had to suffer in prison can be deduced from the cruelty and barbarism of this people. And of course they would have ripped him apart if it were not for the proposal made by Dn. Miguel Arzadura, the priest of Challapata of the neighboring Province of Paria, offering to bring them the prisoner Tomás Catari if they would set the *corregidor* free. They agreed to it, and having gone to the Royal *Audiencia* of Chuquisaca and having negotiated the release of the Indian, the Priest from the Town of Macha himself, Dr. Merlos, brought Catari back, and the *corregidor* was released from prison. [The *corregidor*] immediately started back to Chiquisaca taking back roads and walking hastily, which worked well as he was not arrested again even though he was within the reach of over 500 Indians in the vicinity of La Plata, who could have killed him.

While Alos [*sic*] was imprisoned, Indians from Pocoata and Macha went to the pueblo of Moscari and apprehended the *cacique* and Governor Dn. Florencio Lupas. They conducted him thirty leagues by foot to Pocoata, where he was whipped with staffs covered with thorny branches at the four corners of the Plaza. Afterwards they brought him to Macha, where by order of Tomás Catari they beheaded him on the 7th of September, 1780.[1] The day of September 10th dawned with his head and heart nailed to the Cross of Quilpiñeraca. Horrified by this funereal spectacle, the *Audiencia* and neighborhood watches began to organize militias. On the 11th, twenty-two companies were ready, five being quartered at the Royal University.

The freedom given to Tomás Catari bred more insults for, going forward with his plans, he gathered more people and arms and mobilized the *caciques* of the neighboring provinces to kill all the Spaniards. Those who lived in the Pueblo of San Pedro de Buenavista were attacked by a mob of over 3,000 Indians and took refuge in the church. The priest Don Ysidro de Herrera succeeded in calming them down, but could not avoid the blow from a rock that broke his arm. The pueblos of Sacaca, Acacio, and Toracari were also invaded: and as the Rebels encountered no resistance, they ransacked the houses and haciendas that were left unprotected by the Spaniards, who fled for their lives, going to nearby cities where they still did not feel safe.

The Archbishop of Chuquisaca seems to have taken it into his hands to calm these rebels, to which end he directed his admonitions to said Catari. . . . But [Catari] wanted to impose Laws at his whim . . . making the most despicable proposals. There remains no other means than that of force to punish his daring; but there is no way to make amends for the innumerable harms he has caused. Plata and September 29 of 1780. [*CDIP,* 57. 1780-XI-29]

105. Alós as a Prisoner of Indians Tries to Lower Tensions

Corregidor Alós was taken prisoner by the people of Macha. While he was being held, he wrote the following message to the viceroy in which he claims that he has tried to soothe the fears of indigenous peoples while also sending a warning to Spanish officialdom about what could await them if and when troops were sent against the indigenous forces.   -

1. There are some discrepancies in the exact dates.

I have tried to erase their impression that Your Highness may wish to send a great number of soldiers, in which case, *these miserable Indians say that all the Kingdom will tremble [since] their number is overwhelmingly larger than that of the Spaniards; and everything could be avoided by not disturbing them.* [*SCA*, 152. Translated by S. Serulnikov, italics added]

106. Letter That Gives an Account of the Imprisonment and Death of the Main Rebel of Chayanta, Tomás Catari

The following document briefly relates the events that led up to the death of Tomás Catari at the hands of royalist forces as he was being taken from prison and moved to another spot. When those holding the rebel leader saw that they were going to be confronted by indigenous forces that wanted to free Catari, they killed him. The document also discusses the revenge killing by the rebel forces of the Spaniard who had Catari executed. The Spaniard apparently was lured out into the open by a person—seemingly an Indian—whom he had some reason to trust, even under these inflammatory circumstances, but he was wrong.

My Very Dear Sir: I see you are heavily burdened with all that has happened in the Province of Chayanta, jurisdiction of this Viceroyalty of Buenos Aires which is in the hands of the rebel Tomas [*sic*] Catari, whose exploits have been referred to in the Relation of the 29th of September of last year that I sent to you. Now I add that the imprisonment of the aforementioned principal rebel of the province, Catari, has been verified. He was captured by the well-known miner Alvares from the mine of Aullagas, and not because—and it has been said—he had abandoned his allies, but because he seemed to have quieted down due to the admonishing of His Excellency Monsignor the Archbishop, and having been admitted in the Province under the jurisdiction of *justicia mayor* [head magistratate], Señor Juan Antonio Acuña, who was sent by this *Audiencia,* Catari was moving about the above mentioned mine with complete liberty. But the reports given by the *justicia mayor* opposing Catari's activities, which were once again agitating the Indians, were the cause of orders being issued to the miner Alvares to capture the rebel, which in effect he did. And having put him [Catari] under the jurisdiction of the *justicia mayor,* the *justicia* was conducting him to this city along with fourteen other men. Seeing that the Indians from the Province of Yamparaes were coming to meet them, he ordered him killed before they could come and take him by force, and did the same to his scribe Serrano, whom they also held prisoner, leaving the dead bodies in the field.

The Indians were so inflamed by this act that they immediately killed the *justicia mayor* and five other soldiers. They would have killed all of them if the soldiers had not fled. From there they went in search of the miner Alvares who had been warned by some people to resist and defend himself from his enemies. After having courageously resisted three assaults, he left the fields and got to his mine from which, with deception, he was lured out by an Indian he knew well, and he was killed, along with forty other people. May God have them among his saints and your Excellency be protected for years to come. Plata, January 14th, 1781. [*CDIP,* 131. 1781-I-14]

107. Letter from the Officer of Carangas to the *Audiencia* of Charcas in Which He Informs about the Indians Having Killed Their *Corregidor,* Don Mateo Ibañez Arco

In the following document, a Crown official informs the Audiencia *of the violence that has transpired. The document details some of the beheadings and killings of Spaniards, including a* corregidor *and other officials, and the taking of monies from the royal treasury. The writer, drawing attention to the importance of religion, notes that people were killed without being allowed the sacraments. He also conveys his message by way of a priest, seemingly counting on the respect given to priests to provide him safe passage. The writer praises his own efforts to keep the situation under control by using his powers of persuasion to calm the rebels and save the royal monies. At the same time, he urges that prompt action be taken to try to calm the situation and save the region from further destruction, while making it clear that the excessive charges of the* corregidor *in the* reparto *was a primary cause of the violence.*

Very Powerful Lord:
On January 26th, at four in the morning, the Indians from the parishes and pueblos of Urinoeco, Guaillamarca, and Totora assaulted the *Corregidor* of this province of Carangas, Don Mato Ibañez Arco, who was in the pueblo of Corquemarca situated thirty leagues away from this settlement of Carangas. They cut off his head with great infamy; they did the same to three of his

Spanish relatives; and with two of the Governors of the town of Corque and one from Turco. Over 15,000 pesos that they found in the *Corregidor's* bedroom, as well as furniture and jewelry, were distributed among the commoners. Not content with this insolence, they named an Indian captain, somebody by the name of Miguel, who they say is from the town of Andamarca, with the order to come to this parish of Guachacalla and Carangas and behead their governors, and the one from the town of Saballa, which was verified.

From there he went to the settlement of Carangas on the second of this same month and at two in the afternoon, accompanied by more than 400 armed Indians from Sabaya, la Rivera, Todos Santos and Negrillos, and along with all the Spaniards and *mestizo* residents of those settlements who were at the time in the aforementioned town of Sabaya, where the Sanctuary of the Virgin of Purification is revered and where they were forced to swear obedience and loyalty to Tupac Amaro [*sic*] under oath, which they say they authorized and signed under great fear and to stay alive for better circumstances. This mob then went in search of Don Teodoro Ugalde, a relative of the aforementioned *Corregidor,* whom they beheaded. [They then] directed their infernal fury against the house of the Treasurer, Don Juan Manuel de Guemes y Huesles, and against the royal coffers: and having broken into [the house] they tied his feet and hands and took him to jail where they beheaded him in the stocks, forbidding anybody from taking care of the body which was partly eaten during the night by dogs. All these horrible and violent deaths were carried out without even giving those miserable peoples recourse to a sacred confession. Right after learning of the *Corregidor's* murder, and wanting, in part, to secure your royal treasury, I went by the Treasurer's house with witnesses, and from there to the *Corregidor's* house. These were duly sealed and duplicate keys distributed accordingly among us, so that we could perform an inventory which was not possible to do until the next day, as no Spanish witnesses were available as they had left for the fiestas.

Immediately after finishing with the two murders of Ugalde and the treasurer Guemes, the said Indian captain sent word to me, with two of the aforementioned Spaniards, Don José and Don Manzano, that I should come by the house of the *Corregidor,* that it was very important. Then I left my own [house], and I recognized the uprising and the peoples' *junta;* they requested that I open the *Corregidor's* house. With prudent reasons I opposed their nonsense: and convinced them to ask the treasurer's widow for the keys that she kept and that she should provide them, and that I would just keep those that I had, and that guards should be posted on those dwellings until the judge could come and that all those goods would be secured in that way. They made two keys for the lock on the deceased Don Teodoro Ugalde's bedroom, from which I took one and the other one was given to the *común.* From there I was taken to the treasurer's house, and after removing from it all the goods known to belong to his wife, the same procedural seizure of property was performed, duplicates of the keys were made, me keeping one and delivering the other to them.

The aforementioned Indian captain wanted to use force (and the *común* violence) to open the royal strongbox so they could see how much was in it. Risking my life, I opposed this with greatest ardor, because once the mob saw the money, they'd be bitten by the greed of pillage. I was successful through my persuasion, sometimes supported with reason and sometimes with threats, and it was decided that the treasurer's keys should be given to Don José Garcia Manzano. We agreed on those terms, and all the commoners and their captains acclaimed me *Corregidor,* Lawyer, and Defender: I condescended to that popular furor. The next day they left for Sabaya, taking with them all the Spaniards and *mestizos,* having perpetrated some robberies of lesser importance. I learned that they wanted to take them to the town of Corquemarca and I sent an order that they needed to come back to this settlement at once to guard your treasury, which they did today on this date. I am taking some actions in order to attain some tranquility in this province, which I think I will attain shortly if God favors my good intentions.

I have been unable to give Your Honor an account of these events before now, because these Indians have spies and guards on all roads so that no letters can travel either way, and this one I am risking in the hands of a priest from the province, whose zeal and loving desire to serve you I hope will deliver it into your hands so that you will promptly remedy these urgent needs, among which are: your royal treasury which is in danger, the total ruin of this province, and the lives of not only your loyal Minister (who truthfully gives you this account) but that of many of your vassals who have a knife at their throats, so that you can give serious attention to the coincidence of so many provinces in rebellion. First and foremost, and as fast as possible, you should designate a worthy subject to govern this province, and an interim treasurer who would attend to the businesses of your treasury. . . . [You should also] have as a primary concern a resolution which would work the desired remedy of all, for they are unanimous in conspiring for the abolition of *repartimiento,* something that the laws prohibit. You should oblige them to pay the *Corregidores* respectively, according to the work and latitude of the provinces, also charging each Indian, in addition to the legal tribute, four, six or eight pesos to pay for the salaries; raise the customs duties, which I understand is very common, as I have been told by them. You should keep in mind that these *Corregidores,* with their excessive *repartimientos,* required seventy or even one hundred pesos a year from each Indian on goods that they did not need; forced to buy them, the Indians lose more than half of their principal. The love and dedication that I profess to you has forced me to produce this judgment which Your Honor will surely correct. . . .

May Our Lord keep Your Honor's important life for many years. Royal Treasury of Carangas, February 7th, 1781. [*CDIP,* 148. 1781-II-7]

108. Indigenous Women Challenge Church Authority

Women were often very active in upheavals, particularly those that took place in their own community and that were smaller in scale. The people involved in these upheavals often knew one another. In the following account, an indigenous woman named Tomasina Silvestre from the community of Macha spurs her people to action. The community members had chased a cacique *whom they disliked—named Pascual Chura—until he took refuge in the church. The priest's assistant tried to pacify the situation. It was then that Silvestre took action.*

[She] said aloud that only the women should enter the church to capture the refugees because the men would be excommunicated, and so she headed the invasion with a sling in her hands, shaking it as if she were in the countryside; and she uttered these formal words: 'why are you worshiping this piece of tortilla when the sacristan makes it with flour of the valley; if it were God it would not have allowed our God and King Catari [Katari] to have been killed, Come on priest, ask me now the prayer as you used to do!' [*SCA,* 202. Translated by S. Serulnikov]

109. Nicolás Catari Frees People of Taxes and Warns Spaniards Not to Try to Collect Them

To gain support for the rebellion and to erode colonial authority, the Chayanta rebels took actions to liberate indigenous people from the colonial exactions and burdens placed on them. In the following document, another brother of Tomás Catari, Nicolás, issues a proclamation in Santa Lucía de Pitantora telling people they no longer owe taxes on livestock and food items.

In the town of Santa Lucía de Pitantora, today, February 4, 1781, I leave this in favor of all the tributary Indians. I, their governor don Nicolás Catari, [declare] that the said tributary Indians who paid *veintenas* and *primicias* will be freed and none of them will have to pay *veintenas* or *primicias* of livestock, such as calves, lambs (*Carneros de Castilla*), donkeys, colts, nor those of wheat, potatoes, onions, and maize. Neither single men and women nor households have to pay as it used to be . . . and all [the Spaniards] must be notified, because it is clearly established by law that there are not *veintenas* and *primicias* for the tribute payers. . . .

Governador Principal Nicolás Catari.
[*SCA*, 191. Translated by S. Serulnikov]

110. Nicolás Catari Warns Indians to Resist Spanish Troops or Face Further Exploitation

The following document deals with the increasing tensions between the Spanish authorities and the communities and their indigenous leaders in early 1781. In this selection, Nicolás Catari warns communities such as Yocalla and Tarapaya that the Spanish are sending soldiers against them. Nicolás states that the soldiers are coming to crush their efforts to exert control over their own destiny. He warns the communities to resist the passage of these troops because a defeat would mean continued subjection to, and exploitation by, the Spanish colonial system.

. . . [S]oldiers are being dispatched from all the big towns such as Chuquisaca, Potosí, and other places, and for this reason I write to you because we the Indios *Originarios* from all the *corregimientos* are subjected to the works first for God and our Lord the King and the other governors, and considering this you must put all your effort into not allowing the soldiers to pass because if the soldiers pass they will attack us and do whatever they want with us. And we in all the provinces of communities on this side are holding on so as not to be defeated . . . and I warn you that if you do not strive to resist, you will see the works that will be imposed on us in the future; and thus my brothers I ask you to be watchful of the soldiers that will be sent from Potosí, and I hope you warn the same to the people of Puna and Timabi who are part of the tributary people. Let God preserve you many years, [signed] Macha, January 28, 1781. Your servants who want to serve you, I Nicolás Catari and the Communities. [*SCA*, 192–3. Translated by S. Serulnikov]

111. The People of San Pedro de Buena Vista Defend Themselves against the Spanish and Invoke the Leadership of Tupac Amaru

In the following letter, an Indian named Simón Castillo warns the people of San Pedro de Buena Vista to defend themselves, to attack the Spanish who have sought refuge in the church, and not to let another group of Spaniards arrive. Meanwhile, the indigenous people hoped for the arrival of Tupac Amaru. During the attack on the church, the people of Moscari joined those of San Pedro. The priest, a cacique, *and other important people—including Apolonia Hinojosa, the wife of Florencio Lupa—were killed. One Indian personally killed his master. Thus, the larger project of rebellion sometimes manifested itself in personal ways.*

Be this note dispatch[ed] to Moscari and all the towns and parishes of this province. This is, by orders of Señor don Grabriel Tupacmaro [*sic*], to help the people of the community for the war and defense of the community of this town of San Pedro de Buena Vista. Don Francisco de Arsiniega has been appointed captain of the Spaniards and it has been published that Our King has deserted us and we will be finished off, and that only God protects us and has mercy upon us, and his Holy Mother with her piety does not leave us, we hapless sinners. And thus all the governors and *Alcaldes Mayores* or *ordinarios* dispatch all the people without exception [blank space] all, but Caracara, are sheltered inside the church, more than 200 soldiers and so would it not be the case that they finish us off, we must unite among us as they do. . . . The big column of soldiers is also coming, and thus you try to get this done as soon as possible, and God bring good to all of you.

Your servant, Simón Castillo. [*SCA*, 207. Translated by S. Serulnikov]

112. Viceroy Vértiz to José de Gálvez on the Causes of the Rebellion, April 30, 1781

In the wake of the rebellion, authorities looked for the causes of such a traumatic disturbance that had threatened the social order and Spanish imperial control. In this letter from the viceroy of Río de la Plata, Juan José de Vértiz, to the former visitador *(visitor or inspector) and then minister of the Indies, José de Gálvez, the viceroy indicates that he saw many different abuses from various segments of society that led to the rebellion, including trying to register, for taxation purposes, those who had been exempt from the head tax or tribute imposed on indigenous people. He also saw the potential for foreign influence. Not surprisingly, in this letter he does not draw attention to his own role in enforcing new measures or not fully addressing abuses.*

I note (and with reason) that the origins [of the insurrections] cannot be explained by any single cause; it is certain that religion, vassalage, and how many of our sacred principles; all have been trampled with a brazen inhumanity that perhaps has no previous example. Therefore I have repeated in my strict Orders that there be inquiries into the cause of each particular action, and of all the rest in common, and with special care if they have root in some foreign influence that caused such disorder.

The innovation of registering *Cholos* and *Zambos* also had its influence: this subject has always caused serious revolutions in the Kingdom. . . . [*RTA*, 719–20]

113. Dámaso Catari Expresses His Loyalty to Tupac Amaru

Although the movement of Tomás Catari and his brothers in Chayanta preceded that of Tupac Amaru, the Catari brothers nonetheless expressed an affinity for the Cuzco-centered movement. In the following reading, Dámaso Catari, the brother of Tomás, expresses his reasons for following Tupac Amaru.

. . . [A]s Tupac Amaru was native of this country, he was of the same nature as they are; and as they inhabited these lands from the beginning all have served for [Dámaso] and his partners as an incentive and driving force. They believed that by offering their alliance and by seeing by himself their misery, [Tupac Amaru] would redress their hardships, being also thankful for all their effort in advancing his cause. [*SCA*, 187. Translated by S. Serulnikov]

114. Dámaso Catari's Goals
in Laying Siege to La Plata

In the following excerpt, Dámaso Catari discusses the goals of the rebel movement in laying siege to La Plata. The rebels anticipated the arrival of Tupac Amaru and his forces to help establish the new order. By this time, Tomás Catari had already been killed by the Spanish. As often happened in the Andes, the indigenous people chose an important ritual moment—in this case, carnival —for the assault.

[They expected] a thorough change in the government . . . [which] should be equitable, benign, free of pensions; and in retribution for a good they expected as well as for having a native King, they wanted to wait for him by conquering a city and putting it under his feet with the obedience of all the Indians that should inhabit it; and with his arrival they expected to be free from tributes, taxes, *repartos,* tithes, and *primicias,* and to live without the worry that these contributions bring, making themselves lords of their lands and the fruits that these produce, with peace and quiet. [*SCA,* 196. Translated by S. Serulnikov]

115. Spanish Attack and Slaughter
Those Besieging La Plata

A Spanish witness to the siege of La Plata—and the attack of the Spaniards against the rebels to break the siege—gives us this account that attests to the brutality of the Spanish, who were enraged that indigenous peoples had taken similar actions toward them. They referred to the rebels as "beasts." It is interesting how those who feel they are in the right justify committing the same brutal acts as those whom they oppose; somehow, when the "right" side commits the acts, it does not detract from their moral position. In this account of the Spanish victory, rebels are beheaded and women killed.

. . . [A]fter they realized that their deluge of rocks was impotent to stop the advance . . . they tried to save their lives by running away; so that as a herd of sheep they scattered all over the hill looking for hidden places in caves and ravines, where our [people] beheaded all those who failed to flee, even staining their weapons with the blood of the hapless women. More than 300 Indians lay dead besides the many wounded who passed away in the surroundings afterward. . . . [*SCA,* 198–99. Translated by S. Serulnikov]

116. Sentencing of Eleven Convicted to Die in the Gallows on March 17, 1781, in the City of La Plata

In a battle on the outskirts of La Plata (Sucre), in a place known as Punilla, rebel troops gathered to attack or siege La Plata. However, forces from La Plata attacked them first, killing many and capturing others. Some were leaders, some were followers, and some were just caught up in the situation. The following sentences reflect the different degrees of involvement in the rebellion as perceived by the Spanish. The leaders were to be hanged and beheaded. Others were to have two ears cut off, be whipped, and then put to forced labor. Some were to lose just one ear, and others were only whipped and forced to work. To serve as an additional warning to indigenous peoples, homes in the villages of the rebels were to be torched. Executions, mutilations, and destruction of property were used not simply as punishments, but also to make others think twice before supporting any movement against Spanish authority.

Plata, March 9th, 1781
JUDICIAL DECREES AND CONSIDERATIONS: based on the indictments and . . . trial of the felons caught on February 20th in the field of La Punilla; to wit: Nicolás and Dámaso Catari, rebels and conspirators against the state and public peace, who pursued the goal of assaulting and taking this city by surprise, as they had planned to do on the Tuesday prior to Ash Wednesday; being the facts obvious and satisfactory as evidence so that we can proceed with the process . . . and having gone through the legal procedures, your Majesty should bring the decrees to the fore and give definitive sentences to the aforementioned parties, keeping in mind that all corresponding procedures have been cleared for these ordinary decrees.

It is what I witness and he submitted, ordered, and signed.

Sebastian De Velasco
Estevan de Loza, Scribe of his Majesty

SENTENCE: Based on the criminal case brought by Royal Justice . . . against the rebels and insurgents in the place called La Punilla, which lies two leagues from this city, and having been made prisoners on the afternoon of February 20th of this year through an assault . . . to prevent them from rebelling . . . sixty convicted subjects were caught and accused according to the terms required by extraordinary cases calling for swift redress. . . . SENTENCE: being mindful of the judicial decrees and merits of the informative process to which I refer . . . and based on their guilt and the charges against them that have been levied based on their own confessions . . . I have to declare, and I declare that four types of crimes have been committed among the rebels in the site of La Punilla, where Nicolás and Dámaso Catari had gathered with the goal of assaulting the city. These four types of crimes are as follows: first, the one committed by the heads of the rebellion. Second, those who, due to their own restless spirit and relaxed customs have not needed to be seduced and have voluntarily joined the rebellion with the aim of stealing. Third, those who not wanting to pay tribute, *repartos* and other taxes joined the Cataris, and fourth, those cowards, who not having the liberty to resist the threats nor flee, found themselves trapped in the field. Based on this information, I have to condemn, and I condemn, in the first category, Alejo and Isidro Itucana, Diego Chiri, Pedro and Marcelo Gualpa to be hanged publicly in the gallows until dead. After their natural death, they should be beheaded and their heads taken to their communities of origin or residence, or wherever it is more convenient, to serve as a warning and horror to those rebels who have followed and continue to follow the rebels Nicolás and Dámaso Catari, and also to satisfy public vindication. Moreover, I condemn them to lose all their property . . . as well as having their houses and farms set on fire, for horror and to frighten their neighbors.

Those who fall in the second category I condemn to the loss of two ears, half of their belongings, and they are to be given 200 lashes and be forced to work in the royal mines of the city of Potosí for two years; and they are Mateo Roque, seducer and author of the two letters included at the beginning of the file sixty-six, Alejo Cardoso, Lázaro Achala, Remigio Crespo, Miguel Gualpa and Cipriano Cardoso.

Those of the third category are: Juan Colque, Cruz Challgua, Ramon Mendez, Agustin Chaves, Diego Quespi, Marco Flores, Juan Gaigua, Felipe Lobera, Mateo Ticona, José Mamani, Constancio and Manuel Paita, Javier José, Ildefonso Araca, Miguel Saigua, Ambrosio Crespo and I sentence them to lose one ear, one-third of their goods and their bread rations for one year, along with a whipping.

To those of the fourth, Juan Aguilar, Ildefonso Romero, Lucas Vilca, Simon Toribiano, Ramon Gutierrez, Pascual Sino, Vicente Herrero, Carlos Mamani, Manuel Chaves, Ambrosio Flores, Pedro Mendez, Antonio Sirari, Lorenzo Mamani, Gregorio Condori, Carlos Aguilar, Juan Araca, Silvestre Quespi, Felipe Gonzalez, Nicolas Araca, Francisco Petrona, Diego Barrios, Estevan

Barrios, Andrés Garnica, Pedro Crespo, Lorenzo Cruz, Eugenio Yayo and Diego Calli, shall not be mutilated or given a monetary sentence. They are sentenced to be whipped and to a loss of bread rations for lesser time than those of the third category, and to be publicly shamed through having their heads shaved. . . .

Sebastian De Velasco. [*CDIP,* 159. 1781-III-9, 17]

117. Two Views of Dámaso Catari Being Brought into La Plata As a Prisoner

On the first day of April 1781, Dámaso Catari and other prisoners, including his wife, were brought into the city of La Plata. The impression that Dámaso made on the local population that watched the procession varied greatly, depending on who the observer was. He had on his head a crown made of feathers and was made to carry a horn that served as his scepter or staff. All of this was meant to make him seem ridiculous—a bit of psychological warfare and public degradation by those who held him prisoner. For those who both feared and hated him, this spectacle created a distinct impression. For those who had sympathy for him and the cause, an entirely different impression was formed. Following are two images of this procession, the first by those who opposed Catari and the second by those who sympathized with him.

Document 1: Oppose Catari

. . . [N]either his person nor his attire conveyed any authority whatsoever to warrant obedience, and on the contrary it provoked derision and mockery for being a disgusting and ragged Indian who did not stand out from even the most ridiculous *pongo* [domestic servant].

Document 2: Sympathize with Catari

. . . [I]t provoked admiration to observe [Dámaso Katari's (*sic*)] impassive demeanor and his great dignity looking at the balconies without showing any sign of fear, so that once he was inside the jail he asked [*oidor*] Cernadas for something good to eat and something to drink because he was thirsty. [*SCA,* 212. Translated by S. Serulnikov]

118. The Execution of Dámaso Catari and Other Rebels

Dámaso Catari was one of more than fifty insurgents executed in La Plata, a group that included Tomasina Silvestre, who was involved in the attack on the church in Macha, and Dámaso's brother Nicolás. Many more were punished in other ways, including flogging and mutilation. This was just the beginning of the retributions; the victorious Spanish also carried their campaign of "justice" and "revenge" to the countryside. The first of the two brief selections that follow is the sentence to be carried out on Dámaso Catari, which included beheading and quartering. The second discusses the calm and defiant manner in which the rebels faced their deaths, including chastising the priest who railed against their sins. They, as most other rebels who faced execution, remained true to their cause.

Document 1: Sentence of Dámaso

[The condemned Dámaso was] to be taken out from the public jail to let people see him dragged by a big animal to the gallows that will be placed in the Plaza. He will be hung until he is dead and then his head will be cut off and his body split into four parts in order to exhibit them in public places. His head can be dispatched, if necessary, to the place where he resided to be shown there.

Document 2: Rebels Face Death

It was very noticeable . . . the cool demeanor with which these hapless people stepped up to the gallows, more worried about earthly than heavenly things. It is motive of much pity and confusion for us who profess the Catholic religion to see these miserable people walking to their death chewing *coca*, others refusing to take off their hats [*monteras*] or put down their *coca* sacks [*chuspas*], and others getting upset at the priests' exhortations, telling them to go scold someone else. [They faced their execution with] no sign of regret for their faults. [*SCA*, 214. Translated by S. Serulnikov]

119. Two Officials' Views on the Role of Bad Government Officials in Provoking the Insurrection

Although some high officials had been aware of problems before the rebellion, several of them were more reflective on the situation that had led to the uprising once it was over. The following two selections fall into the latter category. In the

first, written in 1783, the president of the La Plata Audiencia, Ignacio Flores,
condemns some judges of the Audiencia for their poor education and corruption.
In the second selection, the minister of the Indies, José de Gálvez, comments on
corruption, tyranny, and greed, as well as the lack of guidance provided to in-
digenous peoples, as a source of the rebellion.

Document 1: I. Flores

. . . [T]he ministers of this court will always be a bad example for America
because being ordinarily devoid of moral virtues and a liberal education they
do not resist the precious bounties of Peru . . . the interest unites them, and
then separates them, and each day they represent a ridiculous force . . . so that
the King does not possess a more hollow and despicable kingdom.

Document 2: José de Gálvez

. . . [I]n Peru, the sole occupation was drawing from the hapless Indians as
much material benefits as possible, without inculcating in them religion, customs, utility, knowledge, nor obedience and love to the King. As they had
not seen [anyone] but tyrannical *corregidores* and priests, and the same for all
those who had dealings with them, they became mean to an extent impossible to fathom. [*SCA*, 227. Translated by S. Serulnikov]

PART THREE

TUPAC CATARI, THE SIEGE OF LA PAZ, AND THE STRUGGLE FOR THE *ALTIPLANO*

X. Tupac Catari, the Growth of Discontent, and Rebellion

120. Spanish Description of Tupac Catari

The Spanish put great emphasis on social status and on factors that figured into their concept of honor. This normally involved having been born into the higher socioeconomic ranks of society, not doing physical labor, and having a physical presence that included good attire. The fact that Julián Apaza, more commonly known as Tupac Catari, was not of the indigenous high-born and did physical labor helped explain, in part, his unpredictable, frequently violent behavior to the Spanish. The following physical description of him after his capture reflects these attitudes as well as a physical reality. An Augustinian friar who had been in Catari's camp described the rebel leader "as looking 'quite ridiculous' as a political and military chief."

The said Julián Apaza was a native of Ayoayo, an Indian of very low condition, who had labored in the lowest occupations, being one of the poorest of people during his life. He was of middling stature, with an ugly face, somewhat deformed in his legs and hands, but his eyes, though small and sunken, along with his movements demonstrated the greatest astuteness [*viveza*] and resolution; of slightly whiter color than most of the Indians from this region. [*WAWR*, 184. Translated by Sinclair Thomson]

121. Tupac Catari and Religion

Tupac Catari, like Tupac Amaru, saw himself as being sent by God. His words and actions carried the divine spirit, or at least that is what he told others. In fact, he believed that God and other spiritual forces communicated to him. According to the following readings, this communication was carried out by means of a small box he seemed to consult. These abilities no doubt enhanced his stature and power in the eyes of his followers while increasing the ridicule of his enemies. He took religious issues and powers seriously. These values were syncretic in that they were a blend of Andean and Christian spiritual traditions. The following passages give a sense of his immersion in, and use of,

*religion in the movement. The second document is a view of Catari's religious
actions by someone—probably Spanish—who sees Tupac Catari as a charlatan.*

Document 1: Tupac Catari

Tupac Catari declared "I am sent from God, so that no one has the power to
do anything to me, and thus it seems to me that all I say is the work of the
Holy Spirit." He also had a small silver box that "he opened slightly, looked
inside, and then closed. Once in a while, he put it up to his ear, demonstrat-
ing to others that because of what was communicated to him by means of the
box, he knew everything and was incapable of making a mistake in the pur-
suit of his aims. He even went so far as to profess that God Himself spoke
into his ear."

Document 2: Opposing View

This idolater begins looking at himself in the mirror and then he declares
"Now I am seeing. I know everything that happens everywhere in the
world." He continually takes his box (robbed from some church) out of his
pocket, he looks at it and puts it to his ear and to his eyes. Then he repeats
the same thing, that he knows and understands everything. With this trick,
the Indians are left in full admiration and very satisfied with his knowledge
and power.

Document 3: Tupac Catari's Letter to the Bishop of La Paz

In the end, God above all else. We are following this judgment: what is God's
to God and what is Caesar's to Caesar.

Document 4: Letter to Sebastián Segurola, General Commander
and Intendant

Our aim is to die killing because this whole time we have been subordinates,
or better yet like slaves; and in this assumption the Sovereign Legislator has
awarded us this relief, because they were exceeding the law of God, and that
is why now what is God's returns to God and what is Caesar's to Caesar.
[*WAWR*, 201, 203, 205. Translated by Sinclair Thomson]

122. Early Displeasure of People of Calacoto with *Kuraka*, 1720

The rebellion that erupted in the region of Alto Peru (now in Bolivia) where Tupac Catari emerged as leader had roots that even preceded the Bourbon reforms. One of the major factors in the destabilization of colonial rule was the breakdown in the reciprocal relationship that traditionally guided a community's relationship with its kuraka. *The Canqui (Cisicanqui) family had served as* kurakas *in the community of Calacoto since the sixteenth century and apparently had met communal expectations. In the early eighteenth century, Juan Eusebio Canqui took over this position, and a brother of his, Francisco, served in another important community post. Unlike their ancestors, however, these two members of the Canqui family caused great commotion in the community because of their exploitation of community members. They were among a growing number of older ruling families who, by the eighteenth century, had started to pursue their own interests at a high cost to the community.*

This practice, apparently much more common in Alto Peru than in the regions nearer to Cuzco, was an important factor in the growing discord of indigenous peoples in the region as the century progressed. The following brief readings make it clear that problems emerged as early as 1720. Juan Eusebio Canqui had community members perform a variety of unpaid personal services for him, and he also appropriated communal lands, animals, and rents. He did not defend the community's lands and rights, and he and his brother were abusive of community members. The Canqui brothers had quite a different interpretation of events; the quotes that follow provide their point of view of the situation. In the first quote, Juan Eusebio Canqui places the blame on the community by stating that the people resisted his attempts to instill a proper Christian and political ethic. In the second quote, Francisco Canqui tries to portray his behavior as normal.

Document 1: Juan Eusebio Canqui

[The *cacique* (Canqui) expressed that] "the Indians of the community have grown to hate him only because he has entreated them to lives as Christians, attending the holy sacrifice of mass and Christian sermon. In this he has taken special care, as he has also done in increasing the royal treasury [by raising the number of tributaries and exposing Indian efforts to dodge tribute]."

Document 2: Francisco Canqui
[Francisco Canqui explains why Indians hire themselves out to his brother Juan Eusebio]: "Like anyone else who can afford to pay the Indians in exchange for pasturing his mules and livestock and guarding his fields, he normally pays fifty-two pesos a year to those Indians selected and drafted for the Potosí *mita*. . . . In order to avoid going to the *mita*, they accept his offer and pay money to their *mita* captains." [*WAWR*, 86, 89. Translated by Sinclair Thomson]

123. *Kurakas* Abuse Their Positions

As the previous document demonstrated, one of the problems that came to the fore in the region of what is now Bolivia was the decline in the relationship between kurakas, *or ethnic leaders, and their communities. Many of the* kurakas *appointed by Spanish officials were* mestizos. *In addition to not being Indian, some even came from other communities or* ayllus. *Tupac Amaru was himself a* mestizo, *and there were other* kurakas *like him who did their job well. However, all too many of those who were neither Indian nor from the community were not as conscientious as people like Tupac Amaru. They served their own interests and those of the* corregidor *more than the interests of the villagers they governed. This began to erode their legitimacy in the eyes of community members. One such* mestizo kuraka *was Atanasio Villacorta (document 1). Those who opposed him derided him for being a* mestizo *with no heritage. As document 1 shows, they attacked his character partly for this very reason. Another* mestizo *who became* kuraka *was Francisco Sensano (document 2), who had been appointed to the position in Zepita, Chuquito. The Indians of the community complained that this poor* mestizo *became rich off of them and bribed the* corregidor.

Document 1: Attack on Atanasio Villacorta
[He was] a poor vagabond whose origin is unknown. . . . [His problems were said to stem from] the unfortunate character of this interloper and his very nature since *mestizos* despise Indians. . . . This is surely why the laws of the kingdom strictly prohibit this bastard caste of people from becoming *caciques* in towns of Indians.

Document 2: Attack on Francisco Sensano
Before becoming *cacique,* the *mestizo* lived in utter indigence. Everyone knows how he used to dress in nothing but a cut of rough yellow cloth and supported himself by busting wild mules. Today, at our expense, he sports silks and brocades, fine cloth from Castille and frill. He spends his money on perpetual drinking and bribes for *corregidores.* [*WAWR,* 78, 79. Translated by Sinclair Thomson]

124. Indigenous People Kill Their *Corregidor* and Force Other Spaniards to Dress as Indians

In the period before 1780, tensions in many of the communities often came to a boiling point and led to violence. This is what happened on Saturday and Sunday, November 1 and 2, 1771, in the region of Pacajes. The Spanish corregidor *and some of his aids were killed by people in the community of Jesús de Machaca. When supporters of the* corregidor *who lived in the community of Caquiaviri sought to aid the* corregidor, *thinking he might still be alive, they and the townspeople they recruited were confronted by the people of Jesús de Machaca and forced to retreat to Caquiavari. In Caquiaviri, the Indians took the soldiers prisoner and castigated the townspeople for showing solidarity with the deceased* corregidor *instead of the Indians. The indigenous people had to decide what to do with the soldiers and others over whom they had taken control.*

Their actions reflected a high degree of coordination as they went to local communities and haciendas to talk to other Indians about what should be done. In the end, they settled on a rather novel and nonviolent solution that raised their status by putting everyone on equal footing under the rule of the king. They forced non-Indians to demonstrate equality by dressing as Indians. The first of the following two quotes demonstrates their coordination, and the second quote describes the imposed equality. This forced equality or identity symbolically brought the outsiders in line with the community and apparently was meant to cleanse them of their betrayal. One wonders what those people who were made to become symbolic Indians through the change of clothes understood of this action.

Document 1: The *Mayordomo* of *Estancia,* Comanchi
Tuesday night, three Indians came to the estate in order to persuade the Indians there to join with those from other areas in the town of Caquiaviri to see what was to be done with the prisoners. . . . Wednesday morning an Indian *alcalde* from Caquiaviri arrived at the *estancia* to convene the Indians. They brought nine *peons* [*yanaconas*] before this witness who delivered them over because nothing could be done to prevent it.

Document 2: Francisco Rivera (?)
They later returned saying that they would not kill them after all, because the secretary had told them that all were vassals of the king, but that they must dress like Indians, with woven mantles and tunics, to unite with them [*mancomunarse*], and that they had to go to Jesús de Machaca for the same purpose. [*WAWR,* 155, 157. Translated by Sinclair Thomson]

125. Gregoria Apaza, Sister of Tupac Catari, on the Growing Rebellion in the Name of the King

In the region of La Paz, where Tupac Catari emerged as a major figure in the uprising, the influence of both Tupac Amaru and Tomás Catari was felt by the local population. In February 1781, the sister of Tupac Catari, Gregoria Apaza, commented on the influence the rebellion and governmental reaction were having, and on the indigenous uprisings that were already spreading into Oruro and other regions of what is now the central and more northerly parts of Bolivia. Like Tupac Amaru, Gregoria Apaza declared that the rebels were really doing the work of the king of Spain as they fought against the reparto, customs duties, bad corregidores, *and other abuses. She also claimed that the leader of the insurrection in the region of Charcas, Tomás Catari, had been granted powers by the king to do his work, and that indigenous people in the region of her brother's natal pueblo were already carrying out the work needed to move the rebellion forward. Rumors even circulated in the countryside of Tomás Catari journeying all the way to Spain and holding a private interview with the king. Thus, just as in Cuzco and Chayanta, rebels following Tupac Catari were led, at least initially, to believe that their rebellion was in support of the king.*

The motive for rising up was the *repartos* of the *corregidores,* the customhouses, the commercial monopolies, and other exactions that were charged them. They intended to abolish them, taking the lives of *corregidores,* Europeans, and other employees who collected these taxes. The Indians declared that there was a decree from His Majesty to this effect, and its executor was one Tomás Catari who came from up there and from Spain. . . .

With this news [of Tomás Catari's commission from the king of Spain], the Indians of Calamarca and Ayoayo were stirred up and resolved to prepare for him with the atrocities and destruction that they wrought in Sicasica, Sapahaqui, Ayoayo and Calamarca. [*WAWR,* 188–89. Translated by Sinclair Thomson]

126. Lampoons (*Pasquines*) Threatening Don Bernardo Gallo, Head of La Paz Customs

The new customhouse and the increased duties were some of the Bourbon "reforms" that fostered a great deal of anger. They raised the ire of criollos, mestizos, and Indians against the colonial government and led to strident protests. The lampoon, or pasquín, was a favorite method of expressing urban colonial dissent, particularly by the literate criollos. Following the tumults against the aduana (customs) in Arequipa, another round of threats developed against the La Paz aduana and its head, Bernardo Gallo, in March 1780. In the following lampoons, Don Bernardo Gallo, the head of customs in La Paz, is threatened with death, and his actions are denounced as surely leading to bloodshed. The author(s) also have fun with the name Gallo, which means rooster or cock. Gallo was eventually hanged by the rebel leader Andrés Tupac Amaru for his role as the head of the aduana.

The lampoons selected here give a sense of the nature of the threats and displeasure of those opposed to the new customs duties. The first lampoon notes that, because of bad officials, harm may come to the king and his empire, and there would certainly be fighting and blood in the streets. The second threatens Gallo, plays with his name, and again stresses the suffering that will occur.

Document 1

Long live God's law and the purity of Mary! Death to the king of Spain and may Peru come to an end! For he is the cause of such iniquity. If the monarch knows not the insolence of his ministers, the public larceny, and how they prey upon the poor, long live the king and death to all these public thieves since they will not rectify that which is asked of them. . . . We will weep with grief since because of two or three miserable thieves among us many innocent lives will be lost and blood will run through streets and squares. [*WAWR*, 135. Translated by Sinclair Thomson]

Document 2
This is the third and final announcement, and we will cry with sorrow, because as a result of two or three unworthy thieves, many innocent people will die. And blood will flow in the streets and square on the 13th of March; it will run like water, if the creoles are not defended. And this thieving old cock [Gallo] will be skinned alive, cut into pieces and thrown into the river. He is perfectly aware of what is happening here, and cannot claim that his misfortune is due to unforeseen circumstances, since this is the third announcement. It is only regrettable, that because of this villainous thief, many will pay with their lives. [*RR*, 188. Translated by Scarlett O'Phelan Godoy. This document is also included with the Tupac Amaru materials, document 33.]

127. Spanish Lack Legitimacy in the Eyes of the Rebels

From early in the colonial period, many indigenous people claimed that Spanish control of the Andes was not truly legitimate. The indigenous chronicler Guamán Poma made this clear in his writings of the late sixteenth and early seventeenth century, even though this work never made it to Spanish officials. During the rebellion, some of the insurgents claimed to act in the name of the king, whereas others stated that Spanish rule was illegitimate. The following letter, written by Father Matías Borda, comments on the letters that Chuquima-mani, an advisor to Tupac Catari, wrote denouncing Spanish rule.

He wrote letters to La Paz full of a thousand follies, proposing in them that our king and lord had obtained this kingdom unjustly, that it was time for the fulfillment of the prophecies to give to everyone what is his, and what is Caesar's to Caesar. He also explained this to the Indians in their language, so that they would not falter in their campaign to take the city, and so forth, exaggerating the advantages they would enjoy in the future when they ruled. [*WAWR*, 206. Translated by Sinclair Thomson]

128. Order to Kill Officials and Spaniards, Including Women and Children

As the level of conflict increased, so did the tensions. Some people became more radical, whereas others reconsidered their actions or commitment to the rebellion. After a massacre in Tiquina (Lake Titicaca), Tupac Catari had one of his men, Tomás Callisaya, deliver the following message to the people gathered in Tiquina in the name of Tupac Amaru. This message was designed to radicalize the movement and heighten racial tensions. It ordered the killing of not only Spaniards, including women and children, but those who dressed like Spaniards or helped them, including priests. Tupac Catari also threatened to burn the churches and suspend Catholic sacraments if people sought sanctuary or if priests gave them sanctuary, as was the custom, in the church. According to Sinclair Thomson, the messenger who pronounced the edict of Tupac Catari even "stood at the cabildo *with a noose around his neck (indicating he should be hung if he did not tell the truth)." We have included a second translation of the same document, by Lillian E. Fisher, to show how translations can differ even though they carry the same meaning.*

Document 1

The sovereign Inka [*sic*] king orders the execution of all *corregidores,* their ministers, *caciques,* tribute collectors, and other dependents, women and children without exception for sex or age, and anyone who is or appears to be a Spaniard, or who at least is dressed in imitation of Spaniards. And if they are favored in any sanctuary and any priest or anyone else impedes the primary aim of executing them, they will be completely overcome, the priests being executed and the churches burned down. Neither should there be mass, confession, or adoration of the Holy Sacrament. [*WAWR,* 212. Translated by Sinclair Thomson]

Document 2

The sovereign Inca king orders me to put to the knife all *corregidores,* their ministers, *caciques,* collectors, and other dependents; likewise all *chapetones,* Creoles, women, and children without regard for sex or age, and every person who may be or seem to be Spanish, or at least is dressed in imitation of such Spaniards. And if this kind of people is favored in any place or places of refuge and, if any priest or other person hinders the beheading of them, he also shall be trampled under foot by all. The priests shall be put to the knife and the churches burned. Mass shall not be said, or confession made, or the least adoration given to the most holy sacrament. [*LIR,* 246. Translated by L. E. Fisher]

129. Rebels Desire to Rid Themselves of *Mestizos*

During the insurgency, a great deal of uncertainty existed as to what was actually going on and what the leadership said, as a result of communication difficulties and differences between leaders over policy. The underlying racial tensions in the movement were stronger, or more pervasive, in some regions than they were in others. In the following document, communities nominally under the leadership of Tupac Catari express their concerns about Tupac Amaru's real desires not being known because of their having been suppressed. At the same time, they express their desire to rid themselves of all mestizos. *For these people, the war had moved beyond the need to eliminate just Spaniards and* criollos *and took on broader racial dimensions, in which many indigenous people increasingly saw themselves as the only legitimate inhabitants of the Andes.*

The edicts issued by Sr. Gabriel Tupac Amaru have not been declared; they have all been covered up. This is why we are now motivated to see . . . that there be absolutely no more *mestizos*. For us the issue is to die killing, since all this time we have been subordinate, or better put, like slaves. . . . Though our viceroy proposed to us that we be humble, this is impossible. Inevitably we will finish you off because we have determined to do so. [*WAWR,* 210. Translated by Sinclair Thomson]

130. Spanish Exploitation Leads to a Call for Their Death in Oruro

The rebellion also extended to Oruro, a mining center with a large Spanish population. Many indigenous people in the region had been exploited and oppressed by the Spaniards in an effort to enrich themselves. In the following selection, the head of the rebellion in Oruro, Santos Mamani, addresses the issue of exploitation. Mamani uses the Aymara term q'ara *to describe the nonindigenous population in Oruro. Sinclair Thomson argues that this term was used in Oruro to refer to "an unproductive class of people that did not maintain itself but lived parasitically off the labor and resources of Indians. The term encompassed creoles, Europeans, and* mestizos *and it was used throughout the Aymara territory during the war."*

. . . [T]he time had come for the relief of Indians and the annihilation of Spaniards and creoles whom they call "*q'aras*," which in their language meant "naked," because without paying taxes or laboring they were the owners of what they [the Indians] worked on, under the yoke and burdened with many obligations. They obtained the benefits, while the Indians spent their lives oppressed, knocked about, and in utter misfortune. [*WAWR*, 216. Translated by Sinclair Thomson]

131. Indigenous Peoples of Oruro Want Land and Mines

Oruro and the surrounding region was a very significant target of rebel insurgents. In this important mining and economic center, many indigenous people not only worked in the mines but had been squeezed off their land. Originally, Oruro rebels had criollo *support; however, as indigenous actions became more radical—they wanted the land and mines redistributed to them, and they planned to end tribute—*criollo *support lessened dramatically. The destruction of official buildings, such as the royal treasury, was another important goal. Following is the testimony of an elderly Indian, Antonio Ramos Chaparro, who participated in the assault on the city. He makes it clear that he and his fellow Indians took the actions they did to restore their usurped lands and free themselves from colonial burdens.*

To obtain possession of the lands that intruders usurped many years ago, because long before they had belonged to the community of his town. They took them under the pretext that they were surplus and sold off by the king [a reference to the colonial *composición de tierras,* by which purportedly excess community lands were sold by the state to private buyers], and they have been divided up among so many owners that they harm his people. This motivated him to be free of them [the intruders], and hence he advised the members of his *ayllu* how to achieve his desire, and because it is in the interest of all of them to take advantage of what is theirs. . . . This is my only crime, and having believed that once this city was destroyed we would pay no more tribute or other taxes, and that my community would be the owner of everything. . . . Unfortunately, it has all come to naught. [*WAWR,* 176. Translated by Sinclair Thomson]

XI. The Siege of La Paz and the Death of Tupac Catari

132. Tupac Catari Demands Creoles to Turn Spaniards Over to Him During the Siege of La Paz

As a center of Spanish power and settlement, La Paz was one of the main battlegrounds of the insurgency. The rebels laid siege to La Paz for over three months. In the following document, Tupac Catari tells the criollos *of La Paz to turn the Spaniards over to him. The insurgents frequently distinguished between creoles and Spaniards. They did this to help gain support from the creoles, recognizing that many of them had legitimate reasons to be upset with Spanish rule. Bourbon reforms had cut into their businesses and limited their access to higher offices. The rebels also did this to try to divide the opposition by making creoles wonder if it might be possible to save themselves by turning the Spaniards over to the insurgents. Tupac Catari's plea encourages the creoles to save themselves from his army by turning the Spaniards over to him or killing them themselves. If not, he makes it clear that they too will face the wrath of his army.*

Now if you Christians wish evil, tomorrow you shall see it with the favor of God. Already I consider it necessary to attack, as I have no other remedy. If you persist in your obstinacy, there is not more than three hours' work, with the help of God, for I tell you my soldiers will finish you without doubt. Notwithstanding the arms you have, you must know that, with the help of God, I will reduce you to clay and dust. You will see that God will aid us, that we are right vigorous fellows, and that it is decreed from above. It is my will, Don Julian Puma Catari, that you Creoles shall bring well secured to me those thieves, and you shall be pardoned. You must deliver up the other European

Spaniards, which will insure pardon to all. . . . If you Creoles do not unite and put to death all European Spaniards . . . take heed unto this my present warning . . . for everything will be turned into ashes and you shall not live eight days. In the meantime I hope for a speedy conclusion of this affair.

I, the Señor Viceroy Tupac Catari. [*LIR,* 291.
Translated by L. E. Fisher]

133. Tupac Catari Informs the Bishop of La Paz That Charles III Has Resigned in Favor of the Inca (Tupac Amaru)

Disinformation was an important tool, used by both rebels and loyalists, to try to win people over to their side or maintain their support. It also served to create doubt among the enemy. In the following brief statement, Tupac Catari responds to a letter from the Bishop of La Paz by telling him that Charles III has resigned, and therefore they cannot expect help from Spain.

I will now thank your Grace to let me know how your Grace has learned that a number of ships are coming from Buenos Aires with troops to destroy us, when your Grace knows that Charles III has resigned in favor of the Inca king, on account of the wrongs and robberies committed. . . . May God preserve your Grace many years!

I, the Señor Viceroy Tupac Catari. [*LIR,* 290.
Translated by L. E. Fisher]

134. Letter from Sr. Juan Bautista de Zavala, Resident of the City of La Paz Which Relates in Detail the Ravages That the Rebel Indian Julián Apaza Perpetrated against Said City

Following is the first of two letters written by Juan Bautista Zavala about what he observed and experienced during the siege of La Paz by indigenous forces under Julián Apaza (Tupac Catari). He took special note of the suffering from

*hunger, as well as the deaths incurred in the fighting. The population of La
Paz was reduced from 30,000 to 18,000, and much of the city was destroyed.
Zavala was impressed by the fearlessness of the rebels in their attacks and upset
by the inept action and lack of discipline displayed by the troops from
Chuquisaca who come to their rescue. There is a tone of irony in his discussion
of the relief column. One can only imagine the suffering and fear experienced
by the loyalists and their families as La Paz was largely destroyed, "bullets fell
like hail," and thousands starved to death.*

Compatriot and friend of mine, worthy of my highest esteem—In the month
of January of the current year, Don Sebastian de Segurola, Lieutenant
Colonel of the Royal Armies and *Corregidor* of Soroata started to take important measures aimed at going out on a military campaign to catch the
Rebel Tupac Amaru; but realizing that the Indians of the surrounding areas
were starting to rebel, he decided to fortify himself in this city. . . . There was
no lack of critics who said he was uselessly wasting the King's money, and
they did not support him in doing this, and if they could have effectively hindered him they would have. But, as this gentleman had been appointed as
leader of this city by His Excellency the Viceroy of Buenos Aires, he could
rule them in whatever manner, although not always as he wished; his great
desire was to take 10,000 pesos from the Royal Treasury and have the where-
withal to survive for the next, come what may. He warned those living outside the city that they needed to bring their belongings inside, and they paid
no attention at that time. But after suffering the consequences of this inac-
tion, they could not but recognize how poorly they had acted by not listen-
ing to what the Commander had forewarned, as the multitude of Indians who
descended on them all at once was so large that only with great difficulty were
they able to escape with their persons, leaving behind their worked silver. Not
only did they suffer this damage, but the enemies did not leave a door, lintel,
or ranch unburned.

The rigorous siege of this unfortunate city started the 14th of March, when
it was surrounded on all sides by more than 20,000 Indians according to some
accounts, and from 16,000 to 18,000 from others. These were led by a certain Julián Apaza, who in those days was titled Tupac Catari. Despite this Indian's lowly birth, he knows how to fool these Indians to such a degree that
they willingly died having been persuaded that they will be resurrected after
five days by their King Tupac Amaru. These roguish peoples have carried out
as many atrocities and cruelties as one could imagine. Of the four areas that
composed this city, only one of them remains barely standing while the other
three have been reduced to ashes; and if we had not built trenches around the
main city square we all would be forgotten, because the sole determination

of the Indians has been, and continues to be, the idea of burning us all to ashes, to which end they have made many bloody attacks both during the day and at night.

A lot of good was done by the fact that Cdr. Segurola kept disciplined troops ready for any nocturnal attack by the enemy, as was shown by two false alarms during the night before the siege that were responded to so swiftly that at the first cannon shot the forts were occupied by the troops and neighbors. And this was done with such good will that nobody was missing. With the same will they participated with gracious donations to cover the needs of the current war.

The *Audiencia* of Chuquisaca [also known as Charcas and later as Sucre, the royal administrative center of the region], having observed that they had received no news from this city since the beginning of March, determined by the first of June to send aid in the form of 500 men who were carrying 300 muskets and four stone-firing cannons. They reached the town of Sicasica, which is twenty-five leagues from here, extremely tired from having stayed awake the previous nights. Then seeing that no rebel Indians had appeared, some of them went to sleep and others went to rob, forgetting to leave a sentry to guard their arms. At that point, the Viceroy Julián Apaza, alias Tupac Catari, descended on them with 11,000 Indians and beheaded them; he seized all their arms and came to [La Paz] with the Indians shouting and with all the heads of the dead. Even with your aid [in our defense], that devil has taken everything! Some consolation for those who have been besieged for the last three months without having the means to resist. To this it should be added that the citizens lost, in one sortie, four cannons and many of their rifles. With these munitions the enemy attacked the city with such force that a person could not walk on the streets, because bullets fell like hail.

The damages perpetrated by these rascals in this city comes to more than 4 million pesos. Up to this date, I personally have lost more than 30,000, and based on this you can estimate in what condition this city has been left. During the mentioned siege we arrived at the extreme of eating dogs, cats, mules, and hides and in consequence more than 11,000 persons died and a thousand more died in . . . the fighting. The population has been reduced from 30,000 to 18,000. The siege lasted 109 days during which we were attacked many times during the day and night so that it is more than a miracle that this part of the city has been saved.

After all these delays and losses the Commandant General, Don Ignacio Flores, resolved to come in person with the dragoons of the Saboya [Savoy] Regiment and some *Cochabambinos* who together numbered 1,800 men. This gentleman had several encounters with the enemy. . . . He finally reached the *altiplano* above this hapless city on June 30th for which reason the siege was lifted opening the roads to Cuzco and Oruro. Some provisions were brought in, like cows, sheep, and some lambs; but as they were devoured we are in the same situation as before as we cannot find them at any price and because of this we are very worried. Added to this is the fact that . . . [Flores'] troops want to return to Cochabamba and leave us without protection and the necessary provisions.

I send you this letter via Oruro as it seems that some troops are leaving through that city with the goal of recruiting up to 6,000 men in the province of Cotabambas as nothing can be done without them. For the uprising is general and I can assure you that there is not one Indian who is on our side as they are all rebels. During the day they use their slings and firearms with as much dexterity as the Spaniards and deliver themselves to death as lions would do, for it is their aim to keep this Kingdom and finish with the Spanish nation. May God look at us with eyes of piety and give Your Majesty peace. July 30th, 1781. Your most beloved compatriot and true servant.

—Juan Bautista Zavala.
Sr. Don Manuel Ignacio de Arazun.
[*CDIP* 215. 1781-VII-30]

135. Letter from Don Juan Bautista de Zavala That Summarizes the Calamities of La Paz During the Second Siege

The siege of La Paz and the surrounding region by the forces of Tupac Catari and troops remaining from the forces of Tupac Amaru seriously threatened not only the Spanish hold on the region but the very lives of the Spaniards and their loyalist supporters. The following document, like the previous one, was written by Juan Bautista de Zavala. He may well have been as competent as he saw himself, but he certainly did not shy away from self-adulation. He does share his glory with a couple of others, but he notes that many people of high status stayed in their houses out of fear, and he castigates others with more than a little irony and sarcasm.

The author takes pains to mention the wholesale killings that were perpetrated by both sides. He also notes that, in certain areas, every Spaniard was put to the knife and the rebels willingly died for their Inca king. He seems to lament that 12 rebels who were about to be executed did not accept Jesus, but then, with what must be a touch of irony, he adds that the other 600 they executed had not accepted Jesus either. In the end, he draws attention to the seriousness of the situation and calls for some 8,000 to 10,000 more troops to be sent and to begin cutting off heads. The document reveals the fears and character of many of the people caught up in the siege and the chaos that reigns as order breaks down and the loyalists are forced to confront the imminent possibility of a brutal death. It also expresses the satisfaction that Zavala felt at the capture and execution of Tupac Catari.

My very esteemed friend. [I write to you] In the midst of all the travails I have suffered during these two sieges, the first lasting 109 days and the second 15. In both of them, more than 14,000 will have perished in this unhappy city, the great majority through starvation; others were shot, and still others were beheaded by the rebels in the fields that many attempted to cross even though they knew that the rebels would not show them any mercy if they looked Spanish in any way. And I, in the middle of all this misfortune and despite having as many bullets pass over me as passed over Carlos Federico of Prussia, I am still alive up to this date and after having satisfactorily carried out all the enterprises entrusted to me by my friend Commander Segurola, and having shown myself on all occasion to be very competent, and with a selfless love of service towards both Majesties, risking my life and everything I own to defend this hapless city. And everybody has celebrated, but especially said Commander, my activity and boldness at night as well as during the day, as I could always be found in the most dangerous areas of this wretched city, supervising and reprimanding those officers who were slack in their duties. Whatever happens from now on, God was served.

The issues brought up by the current rebellion would already be forgotten if they had been handled from the beginning with love to God, to the King, and the State. But unfortunately this issue was seen with the coldness that I expected, and thus it continues to destroy the entire Sierra (as, without exaggeration, in this Episcopate alone over 10 million pesos have been lost) as I have said in my previous statements, and few Spaniards remain.

With the arrival of Sr. Medina at the encampment of the auxiliary army, which was twelve leagues from here in the area called Las Piñas, at a blow things have taken a favorable turn, and the Indians have asked to be pardoned for their errors. Things looking as good as they looked, it seemed to Cdr. Reseguin that the rebellion was over and, with this Mallorcan mindset, he decided, all of the sudden and without having fired a single shot, to retreat to the city of Oruro, as he indeed did, claiming it was due to the high numbers of desertions from his forces, the lack of provisions, and the poor state of his health. Our Cdr. Segurola and Mr. Medina thought about these things seriously and shared the opinion that his strange retreat could be fatal. They also shared their opinions with Mr. Flores, current President of La Plata, who, once informed of all that had happened decided that command should be turned over to Mr. Segurola and that Reseguin should retire in search of a better climate to recover from the afflictions of his all-important health. But when this order arrived, Reseguin had raised his camp and had already marched away some four leagues distant. As soon as this news spread, some of the *cholos* already pardoned returned to take up their arms and entered the Province of Larecaxa and the towns of Chuma and Agata and put to the knife as many Spaniards as they encountered. . . . The Indians did not spare anything that day, I believe not leaving one Spaniard alive in the Sierra, and God needs to favor us with his mercy for these perverse ones do not fear any consequences. As soon as the troops turn their faces, they are whispering treason. During the day, Spaniards only think of themselves, their own matters, and the iniquity of their own hypocrisy. The honor so glorified by our army officers here is not observed, and thus I believe that with these examples of "aid" the entire Sierra will be depopulated, as we are already seeing; for the few Spaniards that were able to save their own lives during both sieges are moving to other areas where finding something to eat is easier than in La Paz. Among them all, there are only two individuals who deserve to be commended. They are Mr. Segurola and Mr. Medina, both of whom, for their obvious generosity and love for the service of both Majesties, should be rewarded.

There is no Indian who is not a rebel; all die willingly for their Inca King, without coming to terms with God or his sacred law. On October 26th twelve rebels were beheaded and none of them were convinced to accept Jesus; and the same has happened with another 600 that have died in executions during both sieges.

All of our haciendas have been devastated and are still in the hands of the rebels. I have lost over 30,000 pesos so far.

In these nine months we have survived eating biscuits and to do this we have been taking the tiles from the roofs of our houses. I, who find myself taking care of the gunpowder during the day, have estranged almost all the city. Nobody wants to fight willingly; most of them are unworthy Tupac Amarus, Tupac Cataris and Tupac Onofres, (and if we four Europeans and some noblemen hadn't defended them, these Tupac Amarus would have died in the middle of the rebels' frenzy from which no one has been forgiven). I have threatened them with military execution and have promised to spare their heads as long as they obey me.

As I have at least sixty men under my command, I have dedicated myself to cleaning the streets as the members of the City Council and the Corregidor, to whom these duties pertain, are locked in their houses and convents dying of fear. I also have the responsibility to chase the thieves and vagabonds, who run away from me as they do from the devil. On November 8th Tupac Catari was taken prisoner as a result of the decisions taken by our Medina and many of his colonels, and on the 9th this traitor was brought to our camp which is twelve leagues from here and he was executed and quartered on the 16th or 18th of the same month.

Also due to the actions of our Medina, a Miguel Bastidas, a *mestizo* or *cholo,* was taken prisoner along with some of his officers. It is said that this one has not committed so many inequities as Catari and that perhaps his life might be spared. It is said that he is a nephew of the impious traitor José Gabriel Tupac Amaru. The aforementioned Bastidas made his public entrance in this city on November 13th accompanied by twenty-six officers, some of them under his leadership and some of them commanded by the traitor, Tupac Catari. Three women were also part of the rebel force, two were the women of this *cholo* and the last of one of these unworthy rebel officers, all of whom should be taken care of with the exception of the one who says he is Tupac Amaru's nephew, whose life, based on various considerations, should be spared for the moment. Among the leaders who have turned themselves in between the 16th and 20th of November at the encampment of pardoned Indians, is one who says he is the nephew of the traitor Tupac Amaru. Here he will be given the punishment he deserves for atrocious acts, the head of the infamous Tupac Catari still hangs from one of the gallows of this square, and on the 20th of last month they began to form the cases against twenty-four of the principal rebel officers who served under his perverse and iniquitous command. Equal diligence is being practiced against five women who are being held in the command post of this square. Among them is Catari's sister and one of his women with the same inclinations as that iniquitous Indian, who must have come from the depths of hell.

More troops are needed from both Viceroyalties or from Spain, some 8,000 to 10,000 men to make Our Sovereign's name respected throughout the entire Sierra and to finally, once and for all, cut off some heads and be finished with all these cursed relics. We need, I repeat, seasoned troops and these as soon as possible. Friend, to speak of these matters is to never end, so thus I conclude by praying that God keep Your Mercy for many years. La Paz, November 3rd, 1781. Your very affectionate friend.

—Juan Bautista de Zavala. [*CDIP,* 234. 1781-XI-3]

136. Letter That Exposes the Calamities of the City of La Paz with More Detail

The following letter provides further evidence of the suffering of the peoples of La Paz during the siege, including people being starved down to mere skeletons while others died in the streets as they looked for food. All this happened under the constant attacks and cries of the rebels, who continued to menace them with death. The author is especially bitter about the actions of the forces from Cochabamba who, while bringing some food, charged outrageous prices and entered people's homes and stole from them because the people were too weak and defenseless to resist. The Cochabambinos even mutinied when the commanding officer tried to exert some discipline. They returned to Cochabamba to continue their commercial activities while La Paz remained under the threat of indigenous attack, even though the siege had been disrupted—if not completely broken—by the same forces who then proceeded to "rob" them. The relationship between desperation and greed or avarice speaks volumes about this society and what human beings, even those on the same side, will do to one another for personal gain when order breaks down.

Dear Sir: I did not wish to take up my pen in order to write of such mournful tragedies, but there are occasions in which it is necessary, in order to alleviate the feelings, to communicate all the evils. He who through God's will finds himself (as I do) in these unhappy lands has not only heard, but has seen and experienced the horrors of death that constantly threatened at the hands of those barbaric and inhumane Indians. With what words, with what illustrations, can he make his fear perceptible? In such circumstance, it may be better to just remain silent . . . without presenting the facts in black ink when they should be exposed with the reddest blood. More than enough of that has been spilled by innumerable people who have died in the fields, hills, towns, provinces, and cities. La Paz still does not find itself free of the possibility of total devastation. In the long siege that lasted 109 days it has suffered the anguish of a continuing death, without leaving its inhabitants any feeling save that of being martyred at the hands of the unhappy enemies, who without pause day and night pester the inhabitants with their lethal weapons of war. And at the same time fathers watch their children, and mothers watch their husbands, become walking skeletons or consumed by consumption and these, taking their first steps in the street to find something to eat, fall unexpectedly dead from hunger without the breath to even moan, a spectacle so horrid and pitiful that it would have horrified even the hardest and most barbaric heart. One's hearing was the most taxed [of the senses] by the incessant shouting and angry alarms from the Indians and the sad whining of children asking for something to eat, without any human chance of being given something. The olfactory sense, though not accustomed in the beginning to the stench and fetidness, was able, with some industry, to tolerate them. But the sense that suffered the most was that of taste due to the ravages caused by the bitterness of weeds and roots that were foraged, and hunger itself made things more repugnant and abominable. And finally the [sense of] touch, which one would presume would have suffered less, was not without torment. This sense, needed to keep an individual alive, forced us to touch the bones of cadavers which had turned to dust, forced us to leave nothing untouched, even the most despicable hide or anything else regardless of how disgusting it looked.

All that has been referred to in some detail has been the reason that this city, so opulent and rich, is today reduced to a small plot with a few entrenched blocks if only to maintain its name, and if it weren't for this, it would already have been reduced to ashes, along with all its residents, ending up like one of the other four city sections, entirely destroyed down to its foundations. . . .

Commander Segurola (to whose military skills this city owes its existence) made some attempts and sorties to see if he could repel the enemy forces, but this was not possible due to the excessive multitude of the rebel masses; nevertheless, a friend has written to me, saying that some prisoners have declared that their number does not exceed 10,000. But if this were so, how could it be possible that the rebels were able to circle the city without leaving any place where the circle could be broken and destroyed? The prisoners undoubtedly gave this information, but who knows whether they minimized the number so that we would not send sufficient troops to defeat them and force them to flee. This bad idea of believing that the number of enemies was small led many an expedition to failure, so that the rebels have become too defiant and they've seized our arms to wage war against us, and no one knows when it will end.

In these very unhappy circumstances, God wished to alleviate us in some manner from our calamities and misery with the assistance which appeared on June 30th. Veteran troops, protecting provisions, arrived along with many Cochabambinos who have taken advantage of these unhappy times to sell their produce for its weight in gold and silver. . . . [F]or a handful of flour, they were asking a handful of fine pearls, and for a piece of jerky a pair of diamond earrings mounted in gold that a woman who was weakened by hunger was wearing.—It is like this that they carried away much of the gold and silver that was available, because these rich metals serve for nothing in the greatest necessity. They not only committed these excesses, but they would enter peoples houses under the pretext of selling people goods and then steal everything they could right under the eyes of their owners. As they were loaded down with so much money, gold, and silver jewelry, all that they wanted to do was to return to Cochabamba so they could once again engage in their infamous commerce. Cdr. General Ignacio Flores was assessing the whole situation, but he could do nothing as a mutiny was staged against him, and placed him in such state that after leaving us with some cloth and provisions which would only suffice to feed the city for sixty days, he was forced to retreat to Cochabamba promising that he would come back with more troops and more provisions. He could not be convinced to change his plans by the many envoys sent by that city [La Paz] due to the uprising of the Cochabambinos, whose decision was guided by their greediness, something for which they should all be punished with death. . . . May God allow Sr. Flores to deliver what he promised in good time, and that we may not have to go through the same travails and penuriousness described here, as I fear. The Indian siege continues in some areas as we can see them. And as soon as they learn that the troops have left, they will come back to surround us and attack us without respite. Enough of lamentations even though I could mention that my wounds are cancerous and my flesh eaten down to my bones, but even if only a skeleton, I offer my services to Your Majesty, for this love will go with me to my tomb. May God protect Your Majesty for many years. [La] Paz, August 19th, 1781. [*CDIP,* 218. 1781-VIII-19]

137. Letter from Commander Don Ramon de Arias Written in La Paz Relating the Good Deeds of His Troops

Mobility, supply, and transportation were very important for both the rebels and the loyalists, and these were achieved largely on the backs of mules. In the following letter, written as the Spanish were in the final phases of consolidating their hard-fought victory over the rebels, a loyalist officer discusses a recent battle in which his forces were engaged. The battle proved to be a victory for the loyalists in terms of dead and wounded. However, the rebels escaped and, in the process, took with them a very large number of mules as a result of negligence on the part of the muleteers. Knowing the use that could be made of the mules by the rebels, and without the mules for their own needs, the officer notes that the triumph on the battlefield was not worth the loss of the mules.

Here I am, impatiently waiting to march down the river as was planned. In my previous letters I have already shared with Your Majesty two of the actions that took place on the 2nd and 4th of the current month and that were executed so brilliantly by our *Arequipeños* against the Indians in the ravine downriver. But the one on the 10th of the current month was even more glorious although we lost, as you will see, many mules due to the roguishness of the muleteers. Among those who were killed by the Indians was one who had gone to sleep, whom they called the "Englishman." We did not have any other casualties in this action.

On the 10th the main leader of the rebels, Blas Choque (one of the ones from the ravine down the river), brought together all those [enemy forces] who had been in three different camps as indicated by the declarations of three female Indians and one Indian who were captured alive and then killed. Based on what those three said, and what we have been able to calculate, there were around 3,500 Indians. All of them slept hiding and divided into many groups around Potopoto. Our scouts had gone out to check the surrounding region to see where the cattle could graze, and not finding anything to report, they allowed the muleteers to go there with their animals. . . . Some of them, without paying attention to the orders to not separate the livestock, exceeded what they should have done. And at ten A.M. the Indians attacked from all sides so that the muleteers didn't know where to turn, and the confusion being so great, the Rebels were able to capture a great number of mules, I believe more than 400 in total. While the battle was still going on, I was informed of this event and left with the necessary infantry and cavalry and, after dividing them into three groups, we attacked the rebels with so much ardor and effort that despite the resistance that they mounted from a hill named Pampajasi, from which they were throwing rocks and boulders, they were forced to flee up to the Pampa. There the other two groups [of our forces] attacked from the right and left at the same time, throwing the enemy to the other side of the Pampajasi river, and on the banks of that river were some Ranches, which were burned along with some Indian women who were inside them.

The Indians witnessed this from the other side of the river and, seeing some of my soldiers attacking them and having already suffered in past encounters, they started to run towards the hills and they reached the peaks. Not knowing what else to do, our forces which had been divided into groups went out . . . to retake the mules that were being brought by the Indians from the left; but, as soon as they saw the troops coming . . . [the Indians] started to divide the mules into three groups and took them up to the hills. The troops realized they could not follow the Indians through those snow-covered peaks due to the heavy rain and hail, and since it was already past five in the afternoon, they retreated. They regretted that they had lost the mules, even though they caught some of those that were ridden by the rebels. These [the rebels] left many dead throughout the areas where they had been chased and the number of wounded must have been very high if one considers the amount of blood that could be found along their path. All this does not balance out the loss of the mules which we need so much. [La] Paz, March 14 1782.

—Ramon de Arias. [*CDIP,* 253. 1782-III-14]

138. Certification by Major General Don Joaquin Valcárcel of the Death of Carlos (Puma) Catari at the Hands of a Grenadier Soldier by the Name of Antonio Supanta

Sometimes chance, as well as skill and daring, played an important role in the outcome of events. As the Spanish tried to subdue rebels on the northern and eastern side of Lake Titicaca in the provinces of Larecaxa, Azangaro, and Carabaya, one of the important rebel leaders, Carlos Puma Catari, continued to lead his forces into battle against the Spanish. The following account describes how a soldier searching for rebels who were in hiding after being defeated in battle captured an enemy whom he then threatened to kill if he did not get the desired information from him. The soldier used this captured rebel to lead him to another rebel. The second prisoner, whose life was also threatened, took the soldier to the place where their leader, Carlos Puma Catari, was hiding. The soldier, upon seeing the rebel leader, took no chances and immediately shot him; he then ordered one of his prisoners to behead the rebel leader so he would have proof of the rebel's death. Thus, through diligence, luck, and threat, the Spanish eliminated another rebel leader.

On May 16th, 1782, in the camp of Cachupampa, I Joaquin Valcarcel Major General of the column led by the Inspector and Commander General of the Arms and the Field Marshal of the Royal Armies, Don Josef [*sic*] del Valle, hereby comply with verbal orders . . . to take sworn testimony from the grenadier from the Regiment of Parinacochas named Antonio Supanta. This was to be done in order to verify the means and circumstances in which the feat of killing the rebel Carlos [Puma] Catari was accomplished during the attack by the troops . . . [after the] Rebel had taken up a position in the high and rugged hills of Quillina, jurisdiction of Combaya [Carabaya?]. I made him [the grenadier] appear before me and, learning the reason for his being called, he made the sign of the cross and swore in the name of God our Lord that all that he was about to tell us was what had truly happened in the actions of the attack, such as having killed the renowned traitor by his own hand. And he declared so in the following manner: The Señor *Comandante General*, on his authority, had destined four columns of 200 men who were ordered into battle with the enemies who were occupying the mountain. The witness, with his company of grenadiers led by Crl. Don Josef Menaut, went to the peak of the mountain despite the resistance and opposition of the enemy, who were totally defeated in the fighting. He decided to separate himself from his comrades with the goal of searching the thickets to make sure that there were no living enemies of the King. At sunset, after following a ravine, he found one whom he threatened with . . . his musket and told him: *if you tell me where Catari is hiding, I will spare your life.* The rebel promised to tell him, so the witness tied his hands and ordered him to lead him to Catari, which the Indian did, and soon they arrived at a place very near the Rebel commander's camp. But first it occurred to Supanta to order the Indian to call out to Catari in his own voice so that Catari wouldn't flee if he first heard the voice of the witness. He did so and an Indian Colonel, by the name of Andres Gutierrez, appeared and the witness told him: *come closer, if you don't I will fire this musket and kill you.* [The Indian] came closer to him and the witness searched him to make sure he did not have any weapons . . . and he then tied him up very securely. . . . Upon finishing this he told him: *guide me to where Catari is hiding and if you don't both of you will die.* He was taken to the desired place and he found [Catari] next to a fire with his saber in his hand. Not wanting to give him any chance to move, the witness shot him with such precision that the bullet went through his throat, but seeing that [Catari] was not dying and was trying to get up, he went towards him and took his saber away and finished him off. He then commanded Colonel Gutierrez to cut off [Catari's] head and after being untied he punctually carried out the order. . . . [The] witness, finding himself on his own amidst these two enemy Indians along with the wife of said colonel and a young boy who had been accompanying Catari, was forced to call a soldier from Cotabambas named Josef Gonzalez who happened to be walking by with his spear and told him: *comrade, come with me to take these four prisoners as it is already night and I am on my own.* They walked through a very narrow pass . . . where they came across another rebel Indian and when he was about to kill him, the witness pardoned him instead, due to the supplications of the other prisoners.

As it was already very late and they could not continue their journey to the camp, which was over a league away, [the witness] decided to stop until daybreak. Both soldiers kept guard with the precaution of loading their muskets and aiming them at the prisoners who, terrified, never stopped begging for his clemency. As soon as dawn broke, the witness and his comrade started the journey again until they reached the Commander General and all his columns. He then presented him the five mentioned prisoners, along with the head of the rebel Catari and his saber, asking him to take care of the soldier from Cotabambas as he had helped him very much. All this he declares under oath, all which he affirms and ratifies adding that there is nothing he would add or subtract; that he is thirty-two years of age, married and from the town of Lampa in the province of Parinacochas and that even though he had not been drafted for the war, he had presented himself to Major Don Josef Ignacio Briceño, so that he would assign him to the grenadier company led by Captain Don Juan Ignacio Porto y Morales who named him first grenadier, all of which can be affirmed if his Sergeant Major is asked for the required certifications. As he did not know how to sign [his name], he asked his captain, Don Tomas Casal, Captain of light cavalry and who was also a witness in this deposition, to do so in his name. Both signed, as did I, due to the lack of a scribe, for which I certify.

Joaquin Valcárcel.
—At the request of the grenadier Antonio Supanta
and as witness to this deposition.
—Juan Ignacio Porto y Morales.
—Witness of this declaration, Tomas de Casal.
[*CDIP,* 268. 1782-V-16, 21, 25]

139. Death Sentence of Tupac Catari

Tupac Catari had the reputation of being one of the more volatile and violent of the rebel leaders. There was no doubt about what would happen to him if he was captured. In November 1781, he was betrayed by one of his men, Tomás Inca Lipe, who entertained Tupac Catari and then made it easy for him to be captured. Tupac Catari's wife, Bartolina Sisa, and his sister, Gregoria Apaza, were also captured and sentenced to death and dismemberment for their role in the insurrection. Gregoria was especially derided for her service as "queen" and her role in the sentencing to death of Spaniards and whites in the pueblo of Soroata at the hands of the "butchers and bloody tyrants." The executions of the rebel women were ordered in September 1782 by Judge Francisco T(h)adeo Diez de Medina of the Audiencia of Chile. Almost a year earlier, on November 13, 1781, the same judge had ordered the execution of Tupac Catari at the Sanctuary of Nuestra Señora de las Peñas. The following is the sentence that was rendered and then carried out on the leader of the insurrection that had controlled much of the altiplano *and laid siege to La Paz.*

I ought to condemn, and I condemn, said Julian Apasa [*sic*] (alias) Tupac Catari . . . to death. . . . I order that he be taken from prison with an *esparto* grass rope around his neck and that he be dragged from a horse's tail to the Plaza of this Sanctuary, where the town crier will publicly make known his crimes. Indians from the nearby provinces should be brought [to the Sanctuary] so that before the execution it is explained to them how pleasing . . . [the execution] will be to God and King, and worthy of justice, beneficence and the sustenance of [the Indians] themselves. And tied by strong ropes he should be quartered [pulled apart] by four horses . . . until he dies a natural death . . . and this being done his head should be taken to the City of La Paz in order that it be placed on the gallows of the central Plaza . . . and that after some time it should be burned and the ashes thrown in the air. His right hand shall go first to his natal pueblo of Ayoaio and afterward to Sicasica where the same shall be done [burned]. The left hand to the pueblo . . . of Abachuchi. . . . The right leg to the Yungas and the provincial capital of Chulumani and the other to Caquiabiri in Pacajes. . . . Any of his goods which have been or can be found are to be confiscated. In conformity with his infamous crimes of treachery, sedition, murder, and being a cruel man or monster of humanity in his inclinations and abominable, horrible customs, I do pronounce and sign this definitive sentence.

Francisco Thadeo Diez de [Medina]. [RTA, 545–48]

140. *Caciques* and Community Rule in the Wake of the Rebellion: A Desire to Return to the Past

Following the end of the rebellion, the Spanish wanted to make sure that there would be no more rebellions, especially any led by former nobility who could still claim legitimate authority. In rural Cuzco, many such people were removed from their positions as kurakas, *and many others close to the royal family who had not been executed were taken to Lima or even to Spain. This policy perpetuated a practice that led to the rebellion in the first place, mainly exploitation by* kurakas *who were from the community or who were not doing a good job of representing their community. As time passed, some of this reform zeal waned, and Spanish officials began to wonder if* kurakas *were even necessary—*

especially those from the outside or different racial groups. The following selection is from the daughter of a former cacique *who the community requested be appointed to the position of* kuraka. *This* kuraka (cacica), *Felipa Campos Alucca, wrote the following to the viceroy in 1796 to explain her position and that of her people as they desired to return to an older ruling structure. Though they had been defeated on the battlefield, little more than a decade after the rebellion indigenous communities re-exerted their desire for an older system of governance that was legitimated by the traditions and cultural understandings the Spanish had sought to undermine, and that had helped create the solidarity that made the rebellions of 1780 possible.*

The height of my misfortune was to have my *cacicazgo* usurped because of the new dispositions and mutations in government at the time of the new intendancy administration. My loss lasted for sixteen years until your highness in his pity emitted a royal provision ordering that *caciques* of legitimate descent be restored to their *cacicazgos* and where there be none, that three Indian *principales* be put forward so that one be confirmed from among them. The subdelegates are to retain only a faculty to name tribute collectors who should in no way intervene in the proper functions of the Indians due to their repeated complaints and petitions. Impoverished and fed up with the mistreatment of the Spanish *caciques* who have governed them provisionally, they motivated your highness, after consultation with the attorney general for Indians, to order the restoration of the usurped *caciques*. [*WAWR*, 264–65. Translated by Sinclair Thomson]

GLOSSARY

aduana: Customhouse

aguardiente: Distilled spirit, usually of sugar cane

alcabala: Sales tax

alcalde: Mayor

alguacil: Constable

altiplano: High, broad plane between ridges of the Andean sierra

arancel: List of fees

arroba: Weight of about twenty-five pounds

audiencia: High court of appeal and its jurisdiction

ayllu: Primary living or identity unit of Indian peoples based on kinship or access to land; usually there were several *ayllus* in a community

cabildo: Town council

cacique: Community or *ayllu* leader, often hereditary and of noble birth; see also **kuraka**

catarista: Follower of Tomás Catari and his brothers or Tupac Catari (Julián Apaza)

cédula: Term applied to those who served in the Potosí *mita* by royal decree

cerro rico: The silver-bearing mountain in Potosí

chacra: Small farm

cholo: Indigenous person who dressed as a European or who did not live under community guidance

chorillo: Small textile mill

cobrador: Person who collected tribute and other colonial exactions

coca: Plant whose leaves were chewed to help provide endurance and cut appetite; also chewed socially and during rituals

compadre: Godfather to one's child

corregidor de indios: Magistrate of a province who also received tribute payment and distributed the *reparto*

criollo (indio criollo): White person born in the New World (indigenous persons born and living in Potosí were known as *criollos*)

cura: Parish priest

doctrina: Parish

Don: Honorary form of address for males; traditional gift or offering

enterador: Community member who delivered *mita* contingent to Potosí

estancia: A property dedicated primarily, although not necessarily exclusively, to livestock raising or grazing

forastero: Indigenous person who left his community of origin and no longer possessed the rights, especially access to land, and obligations of a community member; subject to tribute in Cuzco region beginning in the 1720s

ganado mayor: Large livestock such as cattle and horses

ganado menor: Smaller livestock such as pigs, sheep, and goats

kuraka (curaca): Andean term for *cacique*

leguaje: Travel compensation for the Potosí *mitayos*

mayordomo: Overseer

mestizo: Person of mixed Indian and European ancestry

mita: System of forced labor for Indians; a turn

mitayo: Person serving his *mita;* the terms *cédula* and *septima* were also used for such workers

natural: Colonial term for indigenous person

obraje: Textile mill

oidor: *Audiencia* judge

originario: Person who lived in a community and had access to land and other rights and was required to meet colonial obligations in exchange for these rights

parcialidad: Moiety of indigenous community; most communities were divided into two sections or *parcialidades—(h)anansaya* and *(h)urinsava—* which in turn were composed of *ayllus*

peso: A coin of account or circulation; the common *peso* consisted of eight *reales,* and the *peso ensayado* was twelve and a half *reales*

principal: Person of standing in the Indian community; often hereditary

protector de los naturales: The person entrusted to bring and argue cases before the court or appropriate legal authority on behalf of the Indians.

pucacunca: Derisive Quechua term for Spaniards; literally, "redneck"

puna: High, cold region suited mainly for grazing, although at lower levels some bitter potatoes are also cultivated

remuda: Relay of workers

repartimiento: Allocation of indigenous labor by the state; also a district. See **reparto** or **repartimiento de mercancias**

reparto or **repartimiento de mercancias:** Compulsory distribution of goods to indigenous tributaries by the *corregidor*

sacristan: Sexton

septima: One-seventh; term used for *mita* or forced labor because only one-seventh of tributaries were to be forced to provide service at one time

topo or **tupu:** Agrarian measure used in the Andes since the time of the Inca; equivalent to one-third of a hectare (2,705 sq. meters) but usually dependent on the productivity of the soil

vara: Approximately thirty-three inches

vara de justicia: Staff of office carried by authorities such as *kurakas*

visita: Tour of inspection; one who conducts such an inspection is a *visitador*

yanacona: Indigenous person in service to an individual or the crown; sometimes defined as a serf or servant

zambo (sambo): Person of mixed black and Indian ancestry